Books *by* CLIFFORD DOWDEY

Death of a Nation (1958)

The Great Plantation (1957)

The Land They Fought For (1956)

Experiment in Rebellion (1946)

Bugles Blow No More (1937)

Death of a Nation

THE STORY OF LEE AND HIS MEN
AT GETTYSBURG

DEATH
OF A NATION

*The Story of Lee and His Men
at Gettysburg*

By CLIFFORD DOWDEY

NEW YORK

Alfred · A · Knopf

1958

Above the bayonets, mixed and crossed,
Men saw a gray, gigantic ghost,
Receding through the battle-cloud,
And heard across the tempest loud
The death-cry of a nation lost!

—WILL THOMPSON

Contents

MAPS

(by Guy Fleming)

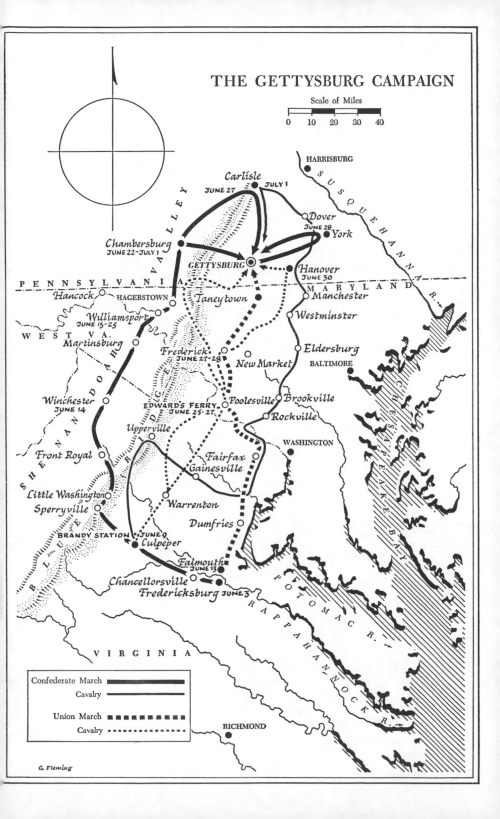

THE GETTYSBURG CAMPAIGN

Scale of Miles

0   10   20   30   40

HARRISBURG

Carlisle
JUNE 27   JULY 1

Dover
JUNE 28   York

Chambersburg
JUNE 22–JULY 1

GETTYSBURG

Hanover
JUNE 30

P E N N S Y L V A N I A

Hancock   HAGERSTOWN   Taneytown   M A R Y L A N D   Manchester

Williamsport
JUNE 15–25   Westminster

W E S T   V A.
Martinsburg   Frederick
JUNE 27–28   Eldersburg

New Market   BALTIMORE

Winchester
JUNE 14   Poolesville   Brookville

EDWARD'S FERRY
JUNE 25–27   Rockville

Upperville

Front Royal   Fairfax   WASHINGTON
Gainesville

Little Washington
Sperryville   Warrenton

Dumfries

BRANDY STATION   JUNE 9
Culpeper

Falmouth
JUNE 13

Chancellorsville
Fredericksburg   JUNE 3

V I R G I N I A

S U S Q U E H A N N A   R.

S H E N A N D O A H

B L U E

D. C.   R.

C H E S A P E A K E   B A Y

P O T O M A C   R.

R A P P A H A N N O C K   R.

RICHMOND

Confederate March	━━━━━
Cavalry	─────
Union March	▰▰▰▰▰
Cavalry	▪▪▪▪▪

G. Fleming

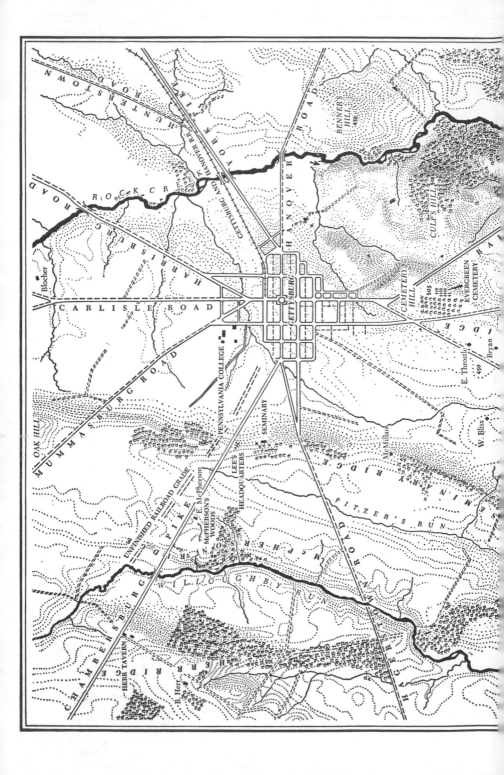

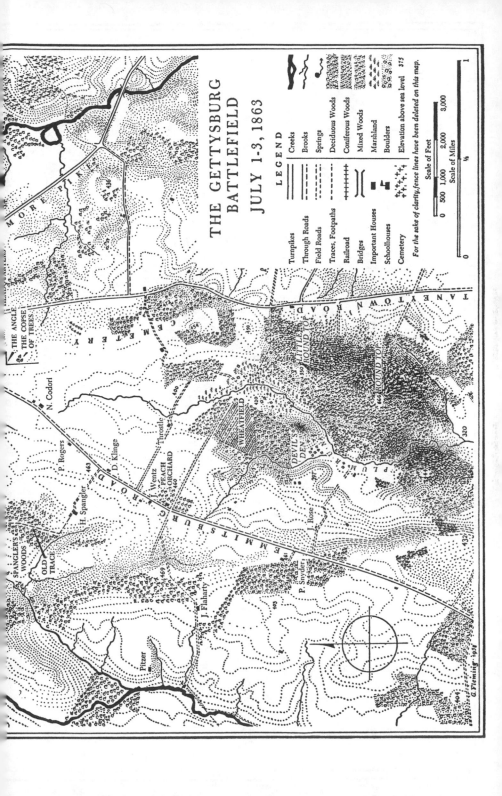

THE GETTYSBURG
BATTLEFIELD

JULY 1-3, 1863

LEGEND

Turnpikes — Creeks
Through Roads — Brooks
Field Roads — Springs
Traces, Footpaths — Deciduous Woods
Railroad — Coniferous Woods
Bridges — Mixed Woods
Important Houses — Marshland
Schoolhouses — Boulders
Cemetery — Elevation above sea level   375

For the sake of clarity, fence lines have been deleted on this map.

Scale of Feet
0   500   1,000   2,000   3,000

Scale of Miles
0   ¼   ½   1

G. Fleming 1961

THE ANGLE
THE COPSE
OF TREES

CEMETERY

TANEYTOWN ROAD

LITTLE ROUND TOP

ROUND TOP

WHEATFIELD

DEVIL'S DEN

PLUM RUN

EMMITSBURG ROAD

N. Codori

P. Rogers

D. Klinge

H. Spangler

SPANGLER'S WOODS

OLD TRACE

Pitzer

J. Flaharty

P. Snyder

J. Rose

Wentz

PEACH ORCHARD

Trostle

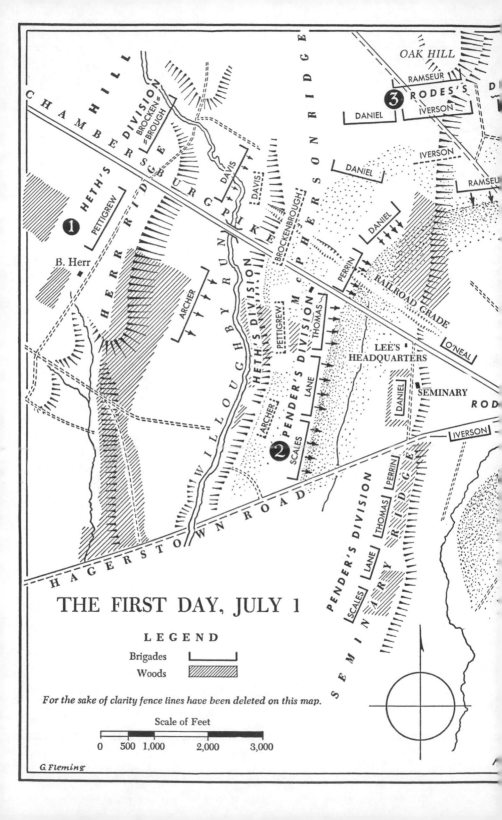

THE FIRST DAY, JULY 1

LEGEND

Brigades

Woods

For the sake of clarity fence lines have been deleted on this map.

Scale of Feet

0   500   1,000   2,000   3,000

G. Fleming

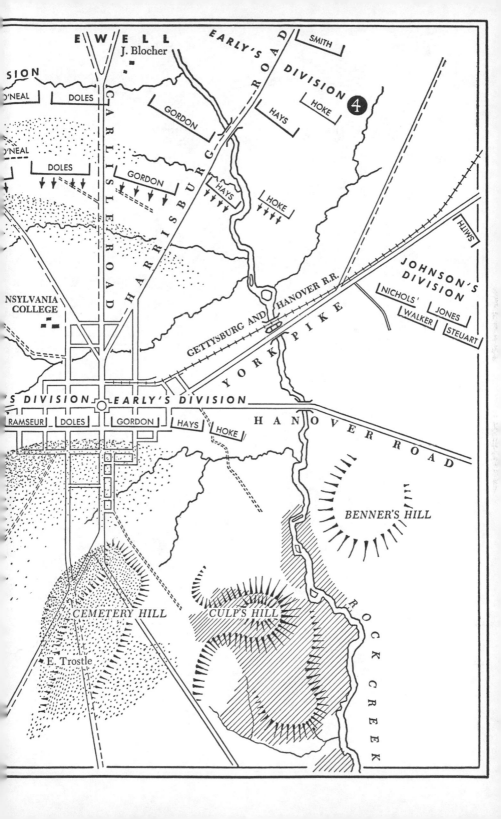

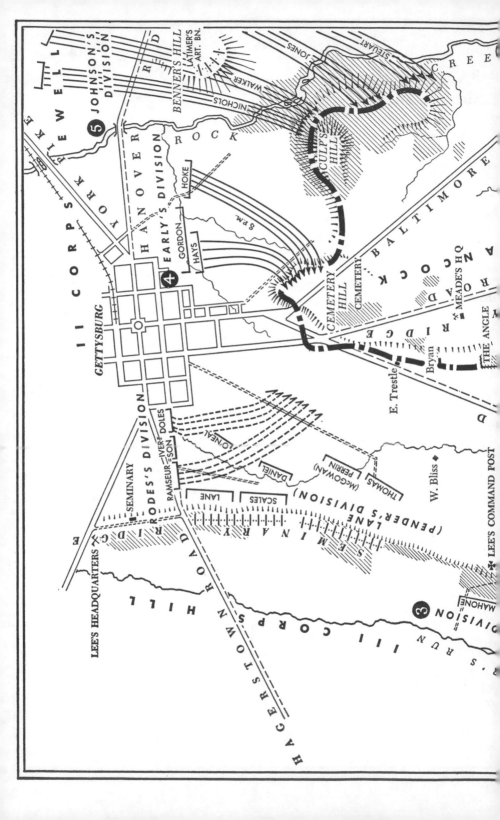

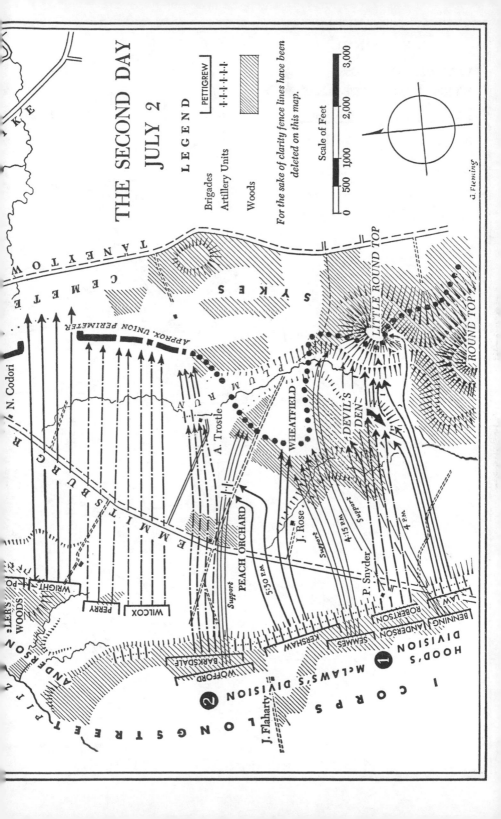

THE SECOND DAY
JULY 2

LEGEND

Brigades		PETTIGREW
Artillery Units		-|-|-|-|-|-
Woods		▨

For the sake of clarity fence lines have been
deleted on this map.

Scale of Feet

0   500   1000   2,000   3,000

J. Fleming

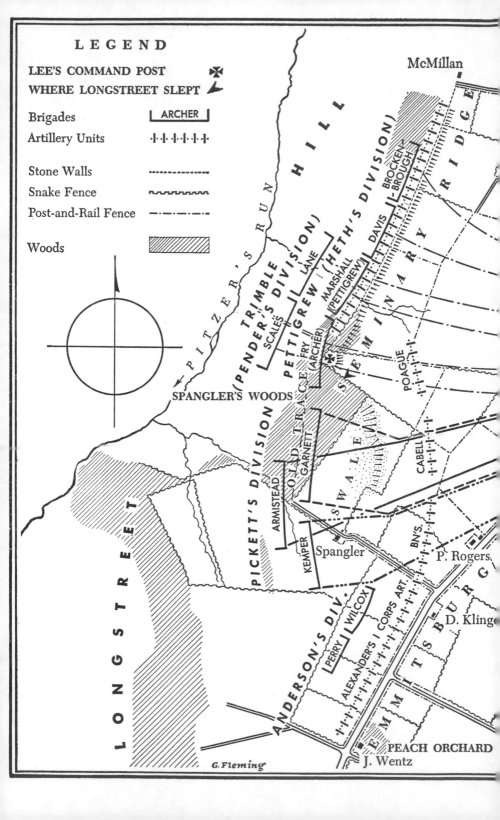

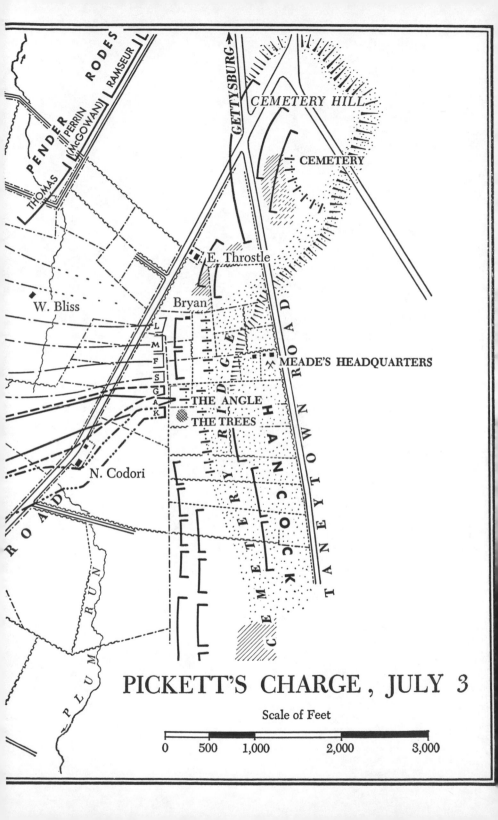

PICKETT'S CHARGE, JULY 3

Scale of Feet

0   500   1,000   2,000   3,000

Death of a Nation

THE STORY OF LEE AND HIS MEN
AT GETTYSBURG

Rendezvous with Disaster

THE SUBSTANTIAL market town of Chambersburg, Pennsylvania, seemed unusually quiet, even for a Sunday, after the noisy passage of troops of the Army of Northern Virginia during the week. The houses and stores were shuttered, and the front doors of the Franklin Hotel were locked. Citizens dressed for the Sabbath moved with wary curiosity about the streets.

They were hostile but not apprehensive, as the Confederate soldiers had not committed acts of vandalism or abused the inhabitants. On the contrary, the troops had been highly good-humored in the face of taunts and insults.

Despite the good-humor of the soldiers and the strict discipline maintained by their officers, Lee's army had levied heavily on the storekeepers and the citizens of the bountiful Pennsylvania countryside. They had been orderly about it, all very businesslike, giving scrip in their own money for everything they confiscated. These items included boots, suits, shoe leather, horseshoes, bacon, flour, coffee, sugar, sauerkraut, and neat's-foot oil. The list was endless.

3

The enemy troops seemed in need of every necessity for living, and the enlisted men displayed a passion for stealing hats which defied the most rigid supervision. The soldiers would put up with anything—patches, ill-matching clothes, broken shoes or none—except the absence of a hat. Marching through the Northern towns, the men became very adept at snatching hats from the heads of civilians standing on the sidewalk. They would quickly ball the hats up and tuck them under their arms. Even if an officer tried to recover the property of an outraged civilian, he could not well stop several miles of soldiers to search under each arm.

The Chambersburg citizens had also seen hundreds of cattle and horses that, by their silkiness in comparison to the Confederates' animals, they recognized as having belonged to their own people.

Yet in Chambersburg all had not been taken. As the requisitioning officers had been courteous, the citizens surrendered only what was visible, and stores still remained in locked cellars. The natives knew from rumors that the last of the enemy troops had passed through the town.

Six divisions of infantry were now camped outside of Chambersburg on farms along the roads to the north and northeast. There the hard-bitten troops were taking their own Sunday ease—bathing their sore feet in the creek, mending their poor clothes, and eating more heartily than they had in months. They carried very little equipment, far less than the civilians had seen on any of their own soldiers. Some carried only a canteen and knapsack stenciled with the faded letters of VERMONT, MASS., or N.J.—relics of old battlefields. Filling their knapsacks from the quartermaster wagons, the lean men looked very unwarlike, and no stranger coming upon their cheerful camps would have suspected them of being an invading army in the enemy's country.

Closer to town, their headquarters camp was pitched informally in the roadside grove called Shetter's Woods, where picnics and Fourth-of-July celebrations were held in the shade. Canvas-topped wagons marked "U.S." were parked without order beside a group of tents. The picketed horses of the staff officers, better mounts and in better condition than those in the cavalry that had come through town, foraged for grass. To and from one of the tents, indistinguishable from the others, officers and couriers came and went all through that warm Sunday of June 28, 1863.

There was no air of urgency about their visits. Inside the tent, the gray-bearded general received the messengers calmly and talked with apparent good cheer. He was a powerfully built man in his mid-fifties, dressed neatly in a long gray jacket that had seen its best day, dark trousers in high black boots, and a medium-brimmed light-gray hat. There was no ornamentation on the simple uniform, and only the three stars of gold braid embossed on his collar suggested anything military. He wore neither sword nor revolver. His handsome, classically carved face was characterized by dignity and a vast composure, and there was in his presence an unmistakable bearing of leadership. Any stranger would have recognized Robert E. Lee on sight.

Captain James Power Smith, a staff officer who visited Lee's headquarters, said: "He was a kingly man whom all men who came into his presence expected to obey." Lee's young son Robert added to that: "I always knew it was impossible to disobey my father."

Shortly after noon the sound of axes on hardwood dimly reached the general's camp. Under orders of his chief commissary officer, soldiers were breaking down the locked doors to the Chambersburg cellars, to levy on the secreted caches of supplies. Lee did not like to do things this way. But his people needed the food, especially for the sick, and Federal troops had ravaged his country until their own cupboard was bare. The enemy's people would have to suffer some, too. General Lee stepped outside the stuffy tent, as if attracted by the crashing noises from town.

Colonel Charles Marshall, his bespectacled aide, watched him intently. He knew the signs of worry beneath the general's air of calm. For two days Lee had been concealing his anxiety over the absence of any news from his cavalry. Lee's army was farther north than any Confederate army had ever come, farther from any base, and for the first time since he assumed command General Lee had lost contact with his cavalry—the "eyes" of his army.

Thirty-year-old J. E. B. Stuart, a cadet at West Point when Lee was superintendent there, had served the Army of Northern Virginia as no other cavalry leader had served an army during the war. Skillful, meticulous, and aggressive in reconnaissance, Stuart, Lee said, had never brought him a piece of wrong information, and his screening of the army was flawless. Perhaps Stuart liked fighting for its own sake a little too much, and a tendency to vainglory led him occasionally into rather gaudy exploits, but he was a dedicated Confederate and an instinctive soldier, and he knew his role in this desperate invasion.

Lee had marched his three corps of thirty-seven brigades, with over 250 guns and miles of wagons, widely strung out, west of the mountains that ran from Virginia across Maryland into Pennsylvania. As cavalry chief, it was Stuart's job to learn what the enemy was doing east of the obscuring mountains, and to prevent Federal troops from popping through any of the passes to surprise Lee. Stuart's orders had been clear. Although some discretion had been allowed him, as was natural in operating with a trained and zealous cavalryman, there was nothing to explain Stuart's disappearance, leaving Lee to grope blindfolded through a hostile country.

All other units were accounted for. Part of Ewell's corps

was at Carlisle, thirty-odd miles north, preparing to take Harrisburg. Jenkins's cavalry, a group of raiders borrowed for the invasion, were already at the capital of Pennsylvania. Early's division of Ewell's corps, paralleling his line of march thirty miles to the east, were entering York. A. P. Hill's corps, having passed through Chambersburg, were camped on the road to Cashtown, and Longstreet's veteran corps were camped on the farms outside Chambersburg.

Lee could feel that all his lieutenants were accounted for —except the one from whom he most longed to hear. His own army was under his watchful eye, but only Stuart could tell him where the enemy was.

General Joseph Hooker, commanding the Union army that Lee had defeated at Chancellorsville two months earlier, was an aggressive leader not likely to sit idly in middle Virginia while Lee's army moved North. In the soaring confidence that victory had given Lee's subordinates, the younger officers regarded General Hooker very lightly, and some of them assumed that the Union Army of the Potomac had indeed remained inactive far behind them. With the sole responsibility of the invasion burdening him, the rapidly aging Lee could assume nothing. He did not know whether he was the hunter or the hunted.

2

The sound of axes in Chambersburg ceased, to be replaced by the thinner sounds of barrels rolling onto wagons. The commissary officers had got a poor yield from the cellars—chiefly molasses and whisky for their sick.

In his tent, Lee was asked by an aide if he would receive a Chambersburg lady who had come on an urgent mission about bread. She wanted to see the commanding general personally. Although Lee had been in command of the Army of Northern Virginia little more than a year, the one successful

Confederate force had become known to the world as "Lee's army." Having grown up in Virginia's patriarchal, aristocratic tradition, he understood the impulse of individuals who wanted to see only the chief, and his innate courtesy demanded that the lady be admitted to his tent, where she was seated on a campstool.

Mrs. Ellen McLellan had come because the prominent men of the town were in hiding, fearful that Lee's soldiers might make reprisals in Pennsylvania for the desolation brought to Southern homes. She told the general simply that a number of families faced starvation because of the levying on provisions by his troops. The general appeared astounded that anyone could suffer in such a fertile countryside. She reminded him that the grain was some weeks from harvest and that General Ewell—the first of the Confederates to pass through—had done a thorough job in his polite requisitioning.

Lee said: "We requisitioned to provide food for our troops, so that the men could be kept from coming into your houses themselves. God help you if I permitted them to enter your houses." He did not add: "as your people entered ours," but each knew what the general meant. Then he suggested that a miller come and tell his commissary officers the amount of flour required for the emergency, and he promised to have it provided.

Thanking him, Mrs. McLellan arose and then paused, studying, as she said, "the strength and sadness" in his face. Impulsively she asked for his autograph.

"Do you want the autograph of a Rebel?" he asked.

"General Lee," she replied, "I am a true Union woman, and yet I ask for bread and your autograph."

Murmuring that it might be dangerous for her to have his autograph, he wrote "R. E. Lee" on a scrap of paper and passed it to her. Then, mentioning the cruel thing that the war was, he said: "My only desire is that they will let me go home and eat my own bread in peace."

Late in the Sunday afternoon all sounds ceased in Chambersburg. Long shadows fell across the diamond-shaped public square. Confederate sentries shifted restlessly at their posts, protecting the houses against soldiers who might slip the cordon and steal into town to forage on their own. On the farms outside the town, colored cooks began to prepare mess fires, grumbling at the forbearance of Lee in refusing to allow his soldiers to bring retaliation on the enemy for the ravages in the South. The Negroes had looked forward to a continual feast, but Lee's published order had read: "It must be remembered that we make war only upon armed man, and we can not take vengeance for the wrongs our people have suffered without . . . offending against Him to whom vengeance belongeth. . . ."

At Lee's camp, his personal servant prepared his skimpy supper—the cornbread flavored by the confiscated molasses —and served it with a certain flair on the pewter dishes from the camp chest. When supper was over, dusk was deepening. Officers began to visit back and forth. In some of the camps, bands began to play "Nellie Gray" and "Lorena" and "Home, Sweet Home."

Perhaps the songs reminded the silently worrying Lee of Sweeney, the banjo-player who used to ride with Jeb Stuart, when Stuart's golden voice would join with those of young Pelham and Lee's own son Rooney and nephew Fitzhugh in singing "Kathleen Mavourneen." Now young Pelham was dead; Lee's son Rooney, wounded at Brandy Station just before they started north, had been left behind; and nephew Fitz and his brigade were off somewhere with the missing cavalry.

With the coming of night, the camp sounds faded. For a while candles stuck into bayonet loops flickered over scraps

9

of paper as soldiers cramped all the words possible on the limited space in letters home. In A. P. Hill's corps a newly promoted division commander, twenty-nine-year-old Dorsey Pender, was writing his wife in North Carolina. A reflective and religious man, Pender wrote: "I am tired of invasion, for although they have made us suffer all that people can suffer, I cannot get my resentment to that point to make me indifferent to what goes on here."

Then the candles began to be snuffed out, and lanterns went out in the tents. In the commanding general's tent the lantern burned on. Uneasy, Lee could not go to bed in this alien land.

His apprehension over Stuart's absence had not yet been generally perceived. In one of the tents in his headquarters group, Walter Taylor, his good-looking young assistant adjutant general, was writing: "With God's help, we expect to take a step or two toward an honorable peace."

At ten o'clock that night a worn and dirty civilian appeared out of the shadows and approached the Confederate camp. Challenged by a sentry, the bearded man said wearily that he brought an important message for General Longstreet, commander of Lee's First Corps. The sentry summoned the provost marshal, who immediately arrested the stranger. Under the man's urgent protestations, the provost sent an orderly to the tent of Colonel Moxley Sorrel, Longstreet's chief of staff, who was already asleep. Rousing himself, Sorrel recalled a civilian scout named Harrison whom Longstreet had sent out from middle Virginia just as the invasion was starting, and he left his tent to interview the civilian.

The travel-stained man was of middle height, muscular and well-formed except for a stoop in his shoulders, and beneath the signs of hard wear his clothing indicated an unpretentious respectability. His beard and hair were brown,

10

and his hazel eyes belonged to a man of action. He had come, Harrison told Sorrel in his tired voice, all the way from Frederick, Maryland, more than fifty miles distant beyond the mountains. He had hurried because the Union army, rapidly following Lee from Virginia, was at Frederick and headed for the mountain passes.

Not waiting to hear more, Sorrel hurried the man to Longstreet's tent. At once Longstreet decided that the news should go directly to the commanding general. Curiously, he sent the information to Lee's headquarters by an aide, Major Fairfax.

Lee, fully dressed, answered the tap on his tent pole, and Fairfax blurted out the spy's information.

Lee listened skeptically. "I have no confidence in any scout," he said.

Yet, troubled, the general asked Fairfax what he thought of this Harrison. The major did not presume to offer an opinion, and Lee dismissed him.

Lee brooded over the irregular report. In his anxiety about the lack of information through regular channels, he decided to question Harrison personally. Twenty-five-year-old Colonel Sorrel escorted the weary spy into Lee's tent. Harrison, originally recommended to Longstreet by War Secretary Seddon, told his story again.

With the gold provided him by Longstreet, Harrison said, he had frequented the Washington saloons, striking up casual intimacies with Union officers, from whom he had learned that Hooker's army had crossed the Potomac. Although most spies were suspect because the gold of both sides looked the same to them, this doughty Harrison proved that his loyalty had been bought at least for the duration of the current campaign. From Washington he had walked the roads at night in order to mingle by day with the Union troops converging on Frederick. It was in Frederick that he, a supposed innocent, had quite casually learned that Lee's army was at Chambersburg. That part of his story had to be accurate.

On his way to Chambersburg, Harrison added, he had learned that two Union corps were close to the mountains. Then, as an afterthought, Harrison mentioned that General Meade had replaced Hooker in command of the Union army.

This was more ominous news to Lee than the proximity of the enemy. Lee never minded pugnacious blusterers such as Hooker. They could be counted on to defeat themselves. But General George Gordon Meade, an old friend from the regular army and husband of a girl with Virginia connections, was of a different breed.

"General Meade will make no blunder in my front," Lee said and prophetically added: "and if I make one he will make haste to take advantage of it."

To Harrison and Sorrel the middle-aged gentleman showed only his usual composure, though he had questioned and listened with the most concentrated attention. Convinced that Harrison was telling the truth, Lee did not reveal even this conviction. However, as soon as Colonel Sorrel had left with the spy of good faith, the general summoned his staff officers.

His scattered northward movement into the fertile Cumberland Valley was placed in jeopardy by the movement of the Union army toward the other side of those mountains which, as they protected him, also concealed the enemy. The separated corps of the army must contract. In the baffling absence of Stuart's cavalry, the infantry must cross the mountains and discover the intention of "those people," as Lee invariably referred to the Federals.

Couriers were dispatched northward to Ewell at Carlisle, instructing him to abandon his attack on Harrisburg and return southward. The same orders went to Early's division at

12

York. Riders started south to bring up two cavalry brigades that had been left to guard the mountain passes in Virginia. Others went west to summon the semi-independent command of Imboden's raiders, who had been pillaging farms while supposedly guarding the left flank a day's march away. As no order could be sent to Stuart because his whereabouts were unknown, the last order went to the newly formed corps of A. P. Hill. General Hill, in the absence of cavalry, would move east of the mountains on a reconnaissance in force. The next morning Hill was to start eastward through a sinuous mountain pass that opened on the other side at Cashtown, and, eight miles farther on, at Gettysburg.

Having done all he could to meet the emergency, Lee went to bed late. He had confided to no one any sense of apprehension. But from its inception the invasion had been a desperate gamble, undertaken half reluctantly, and the portents had been unfavorable from the first.

The Opening Phase

THE GETTYSBURG campaign opened on May 15–16, 1863, in Richmond, Virginia. There President Davis began the course that determined the nature of the invasion, restricted its scope, and was to make his part in the battle as decisive as that of any man who fought on the field.

On May 14, Jefferson Davis had called General Lee away from his army at the Rappahannock River defense line, fifty miles north of Richmond, to attend a cabinet meeting in the White House. The South's greatest general and the seven civilians gathered in the small oblong room on the second floor to decide on emergency measures to meet a crisis in the military fortunes of the two-year-old nation. The crisis was caused largely by the defense policies of the president, though Davis would never have admitted it.

Among the limitations of this self-aware gentleman was an inability to acknowledge himself in the wrong, and in military affairs his need to be right was aggravated by delusions of genius. His military experience was really very limited. It consisted of a mediocre career at West Point,

14

routine garrison duty for a couple of years before he resigned from the army, and a moment of minor heroics in the Mexican War as colonel of Mississippi volunteers. But Davis came under the influence of the South's image of itself. In a land where the age of chivalry was perpetuated, the military leader embodied the gallantry, the glamour, and the privilege of the aristocrat in a feudal society. His shrewd older brother had earned his way into the aristocracy that emerged from the frontier in the Mississippi delta country, and Davis took his status with the seriousness of one not born into the ruling class. He confused his susceptibility to the officer symbol with talents in the honored profession of arms.

Jefferson Davis was supported in his delusion by an excellent record as war secretary for President Pierce (1853–7), when he had been one of the most powerful figures in Washington. Apparently the ambitious man regarded his efficiency in this paper work relating to peacetime garrisons as qualifying him to command armies in the field. He went further than that: he regarded himself as the one person in the South fitted to command the generals of armies, to plan the war policy and design its execution in detail. In his one-man show Davis brought to war the same bureaucratic cast of mind and methods which had made him so successful as peacetime war secretary, and he guarded his authority as jealously as a Caesar.

From the beginning of the war, both presidents had taken quite literally their title of commander in chief. In this capacity, however, less was demanded of Lincoln than of Davis. As leader of an established nation, Lincoln had at his disposal unlimited wealth, the organized machinery of government, a navy, the war potential of heavy industry, and a four-to-one manpower superiority. Davis led a disorganized movement in self-determinism composed of proud and fiercely individualistic provincials who had scarcely declared independence before their borders were pierced by invading armies.

Moreover, unlike Lincoln, Davis lacked the capacity for growth, for changing as events changed. The more the war went against the Confederacy, the more he exhausted his mind and his associates' patience by a concentration on bureaucratic details. There was something compulsive especially about his passion for interfering with troop dispositions. He endlessly shifted units from one post to another, frequently over the protests and sometimes to the outrage of generals in the field. His clerical work, which properly belonged in the war office or adjutant general's office, seemed to afford the harassed man a sense of adequacy in the press of events beyond his capacity to direct. The consequences of this mania, and the policy behind it, caused the White House conference in which was born the desperate plan that ended at Gettysburg.

From the first, Davis's policy was based on his fear that the states comprising the Confederacy could not win their independence from the Union, and his purpose always was to defend territory until the enemy lost the will to subjugate or until, as in the Revolution, help came from Europe. In his tenacity to hold ground, the president scattered his available troops in what might be called a strategy of defense by dispersal. Wherever the enemy posed a threat, there he hurried troops. As the enemy had more troops and superior lines of communication, by common arithmetic the Federal forces outnumbered the Confederates at any given point, and the results were inevitable. By May of 1863 the Confederate territory was being chewed up in detail.

West of the Mississippi, except for causing the dispersal of some Federal troops, the Confederate forces had virtually ceased to be a military factor. The buffer state of Tennessee was largely lost, including the river port of Memphis, at the Confederacy's northern end of the Mississippi River. At the southern end, New Orleans, the South's largest port, had long been a base for Federal operations. The only Confederate port still open was Vicksburg, approximately midway between Memphis and New Orleans, and this city was undergoing a siege from the river and the land. The river country to the north and south of Vicksburg was either occupied or had been ravaged in invasion; the defending Confederate forces were divided and ineffective; and unless the Confederate government could change the situation, its big river and the entire Confederate west would be lost.

In considering a change in this critical situation, Commander in Chief Davis had at his disposal two other major armies—the Army of Tennessee in the Confederate center and the Army of Northern Virginia protecting Richmond—along with assorted garrisons of various sizes awaiting any threatening movements the enemy thought of to disperse the Confederate strength further. In meeting similar crises Davis's habit had been to hurry troops from one army to another, risking the less-exposed force to add some strength to the more-threatened. At the time of the threat to Vicksburg, however, no other Confederate army or even garrison force was safe from immediate danger.

Jefferson Davis had never before been confronted with a military dilemma that could not be solved, at least theoretically on his charts, by the shifting of troops. In his present consternation, he even asked the advice of his current secretary of war.

James Seddon was the fourth man, and by all odds the best, to try to serve in the post which contemporaries said the president reduced to the status of a clerk. A scholarly Virginia planter and avocational politician, Seddon was intelligent, a devoted patriot, and knew his limitations in mili-

17

tary affairs. He personally favored sending reinforcements from Lee's army to Vicksburg, but he did not feel qualified to make such a momentous decision. The result was the high-level conference that the South's only successful command-ing general was summoned to attend.

2

When General Lee left his army camped outside the sacked old city of Fredericksburg to come to Richmond, his thoughts were heavy, but none of his broodings touched upon a town in Pennsylvania of which he had never heard.

Although Davis exercised the prerogatives of his supreme authority with everyone, he had respect for Lee as a soldier, and, due to Lee's patience and limitless tact, the president and the general enjoyed cordial relations. Neither was a revo-lutionary type, and Lee, having been trained from birth to respect constituted authority, gave the president the defer-ence that Davis demanded. Beyond these surface relations, no two men could be more dissimilar.

Davis, at fifty-five, was a lean, attenuated man above mid-dle height who gave the impression of being tall because of his erect military carriage. His features were well defined, and, when younger and at his best, he had made a handsome appearance. Under the stress of responsibilities beyond his capacities his features had sharpened, his cheeks hollowed, and his mouth tightened. Except when he was relaxed with intimates, a cold rigidity of expression gave him the look of an unapproachable autocrat, which he was becoming in-creasingly by the spring that ushered in the third year of the war.

A glaucoma had blinded one eye twelve years before, and the eyestrain of his paper work, along with the nerve-strain of his tensions, caused excruciating pain in his good eye and neuralgic spasms in his facial muscles. When he was suffering his organism's protest at the unnatural burdens his will placed upon it, he became irritable and more highhanded than usual. When the attacks had passed, the effects showed in his expression and manner. At the conference of May 15–16 he looked an overtaxed man concealing his worries behind a mask of taut, proud reserve. Although as unaware of others' dignity as he was sensitive about his own, when not affronted Davis was punctilious in manner.

While everything about Davis had been made, Robert E. Lee was a complete natural. Of a family that in all its interlocking branches had been powerful and distinguished in Virginia's ruling class since 1641, he was the most perfectly proportioned product that plantation culture could produce, and he looked it. Massively built, he moved with the quiet assurance of a man born to rule, and his heroically molded face reflected his habit of authority. Lord Wolsey said that, of all the great figures he had met, "Lee alone impressed me with the feeling that I was in the presence of a man who was cast in grander mould and made of different and finer metal than all other men."

One year older than Davis, General Lee was aging more rapidly, and probably was suffering already the early stages of the hypertension that was, with a cardiac condition, to cause his death in his sixty-third year. Lee was normally a sweet-natured man, gentle of manner, and his graciousness derived from that true courtesy which, the antithesis of Davis's formal manners, was founded upon consideration for all others. This was the *noblesse oblige* of his class, which he inherited along with its privileges, and it should not imply any softness or false modesty about his gifts as a leader. He knew what he was and what he had; he never had to impress his status on anybody. He had a quiet humor, loved family society, was a devout Episcopalian, and, outside his sphere of war, was not a reflective man.

A career soldier, he was, except for his wife's entangled estate at Arlington (which the Federals had confiscated), dependent on his army pay for support of his large family. In the army, after a brilliant career at West Point, his promise as general-officer material had been recognized by Winfield Scott during the Mexican War. By April 1861, when he resigned his commission as colonel of the 1st U.S. Cavalry, Lee was the most highly regarded soldier in the army and had been unofficially offered command of the Federal army destined to invade his native state.

The painful decision to end his thirty-two-year association with the old army, which had begun in his eighteenth year, was motivated entirely by his instinctive allegiance to his native land. As Washington and Jefferson meant Virginia when they said "my country," Lee was a Virginian before he was anything else, American or Confederate. He would have gone with Virginia, whichever side his state had chosen. A disbeliever in slavery and not politically minded, he said it all in the simple words: "Save in defense of my native state, I never again desire to draw my sword."

In surrendering his life's career in defense of his state, Lee's concept of a successful defense was based upon inflicting defeat on the enemy. His purpose was to *win* independence. While Davis clung to every foot of Confederate soil in order to impress on the world the success of the young nation's defense of its right to exist, Lee believed that military victories would impress the world more than the amount of territory possessed, and cared nothing about holding ground. Always he strove for the large maneuver that would inflict on the enemy the decisive defeat; but always Davis restrained him. In Lee's two years of Confederate service— barely one as the commander of the force that he molded into the Army of Northern Virginia—his military relations with Davis had represented a continuous compromise be-

20

tween the president's undeclared policy of outlasting the enemy and the general's purpose of winning by breaking the enemy's will to continue their effort at subjugation.

When Robert E. Lee came to Richmond that May, he had grown depressed by the fruitlessness of victories won on the barren defensive line of the Rappahannock River, across the east-central section of the state. Although this plantation country had been fought over and occupied by the enemy until its fertility was destroyed for the foreseeable future, and although the terrain made a successful counteroffensive impossible, President Davis kept Lee's army chained there to avoid even the temporary abandonment of a few miles. To Lee, this containment of the enemy in middle Virginia was at best a stalemate, and, by the logic of arithmetic, stalemates doomed the Confederacy to slow defeat.

From the beginning Lee had feared a long war that would exhaust the Confederacy's resources. By the opening of the spring campaign of 1863 the tolls of attrition were evident in every branch of the service. The men could barely subsist on their rude rations; their clothes were ragged makeshifts of worn-out uniforms and civilian garments, with shoes gleaned from the dead; and their horses, from hard use and poor forage, looked to a Northern observer like the animals of immigrants' wagons on the way to Chicago. More serious even than the failure of the supply system was the loss of irreplaceable manpower. Most serious of all was the steady draining from the shallow pool of general-officer material.

Only a few days before Lee took the train to Richmond, the Confederacy's armed forces had suffered their most grievous blow in the death of Stonewall Jackson. Wounded by his own men in the dark at the Battle of Chancellorsville, General Jackson had contracted pneumonia following the amputation of his left arm and died on the afternoon of May 11.

Lee's grief at the loss of his personal friend and most

trusted associate sharpened his awareness of the futility of defensive victories whose cost the South could not afford. At Chancellorsville (May 2–3), against double his own numbers, Lee defied all military maxims by dividing his army in the presence of a superior force and, in a movement of incredible audacity, carved the battle masterpiece of the age. Yet, with one fourth of his army dispersed in other areas, Lee lacked the concentration of forces to make his victory decisive. The greatly acclaimed defeat of "the finest army on the planet" was, to Lee, only a checkmate to the powerful force of Major General Joseph Hooker. Already pugnacious "Fighting Joe" was plotting new maneuvers for coming at Lee again.

When General Lee joined the president and the gentlemen of the cabinet in the room at the top of the high, winding staircase, his forming plan for meeting the Confederacy's crisis was in unspoken opposition to the president's existing policy. Lee's purpose was to break the stalemate that Davis sought means of continuing. In resolving the undeclared conflict between their views, Lee and Davis reached an ultimate in compromise, which determined the nature of the campaign that ended at Gettysburg.

3

Lee was grave during the conference. War clerk Jones noted in his diary that the general looked "a little pale." The six cabinet members, none of whom had had any military experience, said little. They did not need special training to recognize that Davis's policy of passive defense was losing their independence. But these worried men were not accustomed to the president's seeking their advice in military affairs, and doubtless they were confused by all the details of their emergency as presented by Davis.

The problem was fundamentally this: how to send reinforcements to Vicksburg without exposing other major objectives of the enemy? These were the arms-producing center of Richmond—the Ruhr of the Confederacy—and Chattanooga at the gateway to Atlanta, the railroad and supply center in the heart of the lower South. The fundamental problem was beclouded by the variety of the enemy's minor threats that unsettled Davis's system of fixed dispersal. He had already scattered available forces so widely, reducing Lee's army to do so, that not even a brigade was left to be moved to newly threatened areas.

The enemy was threatening the interior of North Carolina from the inland waterways of the coast, threatening southeastern Virginia from occupied bases in the Norfolk area, and perennially threatening the port of Charleston. Davis had managed to spread detached units in all those sectors, but now the multiplying forces of the enemy were threatening Richmond from the Union-held Fortress Monroe to the east, and "armies" were converging on the fertile Shenandoah Valley from the north and west. Cavalry raiders had recently ranged through Virginia, between Richmond and Lee's army, stealing horses and tearing up railroad tracks, and more of the same could be expected. Davis's usual methods of meeting such threats offered no solution to the situation.

Not a man or a gun could be spared from the Army of Tennessee. Bragg, its inept and unpopular commander, was waiting apprehensively for the enemy's move, and there had been speculation in the war department about the advisability of sending troops to prop him up.

That left only Lee's army, already depleted by the absence of two of Longstreet's veteran divisions and Longstreet personally, and two fine brigades under experienced leaders detached in North Carolina. Cleared of all the confusing details, the problem as presented to Lee was reduced to a choice between sending his temporarily detached veterans to the relief of Vicksburg and recalling them to his army as replacements for the Chancellorsville losses. On the surface, removed from the context of the total military situation, the decision could appear to be merely a choice between Vicksburg and Richmond; many observers then and critics since have regarded the decision as that simple.

General Lee, however, went to the inwardness of the crisis. On no other occasion as commander of the Army of Northern Virginia did he conceive so largely the totality of the South's armed struggle for independence.

The apparent choice was, in his concept, no choice at all. Additional men sent to Vicksburg, where a poor command situation divided troops and authority, were by no means certain to lift the siege. But it was certain that Lee, with the reduced numbers left him, could do no more than retreat to the works around Richmond and subject his mobile army to a static defense. At best, the Confederacy would have two key cities under siege instead of one. At worst, Vicksburg would be lost anyway, while Lee's skillful veterans would lose that maneuverability without which no hope of striking a decisive counterblow existed.

Lee's actual choice, then, lay between striking for a decision while his army still retained the physical potential for an offensive and assuming a passive defense that doomed all Confederate forces by time and attrition. By the logic of arithmetic, to which Davis seemed blinded, the ratio of strength and losses at Chancellorsville afforded a warning illustration.

Hooker's army of 130,000 had lost nearly 17,000 in casualties; Lee's army of 62,500 had lost more than 13,000. At the ratio of three Confederate losses to four Federal, where the opposing strengths were one to two, four more such battles would obliterate Lee's army while Hooker would have the number with which Lee had begun. As the opposing armies then faced each other across the Rappahannock River, Lee, after a brilliant victory, could muster something under 50,000 —a serious reduction of his army by one fifth—but Hooker's remaining 113,000 would not have been affected by a loss of little more than ten per cent.

An element complicating this somber appraisal was the increasingly critical scarcity of food for men and animals. This was another problem to which Davis appeared blind, but Lee said: "The question of food for this army gives me more trouble and uneasiness than everything else combined." The supply situation was grave under existing conditions, but if the Army of Northern Virginia became immobilized in works, the Shenandoah Valley harvest would be gleaned by the enemy and Lee's men would be confronted with starvation.

A final consideration was that none of the defeatist makeshifts would meet the scattered threats by which the enemy goaded the president into further dispersals of his main armies.

It is known that General Lee pondered these factors before he went to Richmond. It is reasonably certain that, in his own mind, he had reached a simple solution to the complex problems. When he was asked, in effect, to decide between Vicksburg and Richmond, his answer was to recommend a counterinvasion of the North.

Lee's reasons in support of his suggestion were developed in detail after the conference, in letters to Davis and the war office, but their essentials were already in his mind when he presented his drastic measure to the meeting.

The general offered two fundamental reasons of equal importance, one strategic and one of immediate practicality. It can never be sufficiently stressed that Lee's practical reason for the invasion was to victual his army. He said that an invasion "relieves our country of his [the enemy's] presence, and we subsist . . . on his resources" while "the absence of the army from Virginia gives our people an opportunity to collect supplies ahead." From this viewpoint, the Gettysburg campaign can be called the largest commissary raid in the history of modern warfare, and the desperate necessity was symptomatic of the collapse of Confederate resources.

Lee's strategic reason illustrated more than any other single campaign the essence and the scope of his cause-and-effects concept of war—and more than any other instance its evisceration by Davis.

Lee's own words left no doubt about his repudiation of Davis's policy and the presentation of his own to supplant it: "An invasion of the enemy's country breaks up all his preconceived plans of invasion."

Concerning the enemy's scattered thrusts in the area of southern Virginia and coastal North Carolina, he said: "It should never be forgotten that our concentration compels that of the enemy and . . . tends to relieve all other threatened localities."

In a final affirmative summary, he said: "It seems to me that we cannot afford to keep our troops awaiting possible movements of the enemy, but our true policy is . . . so to employ our own forces as to give occupation to his at points *of our selection.*" (Not his italics.)

It is doubtful if the worried cabinet members appreciated this epitome of Lee's strategy: by removing the initiative from the enemy, he would force the Federals to contract their dispersed threats in order to defend themselves. However, they did recognize that the general offered the only concrete, aggressive plan to replace the defensiveness that was permitting their country to be destroyed in detail. Probably because the plan was presented by Lee, five of the six members voted for it. Only Texas's John Reagan, postmaster general and personally the most loyal liege of Jefferson Davis, voted against it.

The president went with the majority, but only to the limited extent that he accepted Lee's decision to invade as the alternative to sending troops from Lee's army to the support of Vicksburg. His rigidified mind could not conceive of the projected invasion as a change in the existing policy, a shift from the defense to the offense. To Davis, Lee's invasion was merely a necessary expedient in the policy of static, scattered defensiveness.

For more than a month after the conference Lee repeated his arguments for a concentration to force the enemy's constriction, but his urgencies made no impression on the commander in chief. Davis had not the slightest intention of reducing a single garrison to support Lee's offensive.

This was not revealed at the conference. Lee never expressed in words the change in over-all strategy which was implicit in his plan, but he expected Davis to perceive the necessity of giving less consideration to the scattered points in order to concentrate all possible strength in the invasion force.

Following the conference, as his plans matured, Lee's letters did make explicit the scope of his intention as it related to the total military situation. Writing that "the enemy contemplates nothing important" in all his menacing gestures, Lee suggested that "the best use that can be made of the troops in Carolina, and those . . . guarding Richmond" would be to assemble them, with other idle troops in South Carolina, in a single force in middle Virginia under Beauregard, commander at Charleston. Old Bory still had a name, and Lee said that even "an effigy of an army" under Beauregard, threatening Washington while the main army moved northward, would be worth more than small detachments rushed anxiously to all points of the enemy's selection.

Along with this, he suggested a similar concentration of the scattered forces in the middle Confederacy. These could swell the projected army under Beauregard to a size with which he could make a limited thrust through northwestern Virginia toward the Ohio; or these forces could join Bragg and build his strength sufficiently for him to undertake an offensive instead of waiting on the enemy's initiative.

These proposals were clearly designed to turn the enemy's strategy on him. Lee had proved before that seizure of the initiative caused the enemy to contract and, even under the extreme restrictions imposed on him, he was to prove it again. But he never really reached his commander in chief.

At the Richmond conference Lee did not suspect that he and Davis were talking about quite different things. Of all the "ifs" that have been raised about Gettysburg, the one never asked was this: would Lee have launched the invasion if he had known on May 16 that the president would restrict its scope and go so far in retaining his own policy that Lee would be denied even the full strength of the army he had built?

Lee discovered it slowly, as he became increasingly committed to the invasion. But the opening phase of the Battle of Gettysburg had been fought and lost in a house on Eleventh and Clay streets in Richmond before one soldier moved northward from the Rappahannock River.

What has been called "the high tide of the Confederacy," and what Lee designed as a total stroke from a concentration of its armed strength, was reduced to a desperate, unsupported gamble of one man with one army—and not all of that.

3

"We Must All Do More Than Formerly"

ONE other man who was not at Gettysburg contributed even more to the nature of the campaign than the Confederate president. This was Lieutenant General Thomas J. Jackson. As his death hung like a pall over the South, so his absence hung like a shadow over the army that he had done more than any other person except Lee to build into its mobility and striking power. These qualities, along with the men's ability to endure long on short rations, were the fundamental characteristics of Lee's army at its peak. It is probable that the Army of Northern Virginia would not have been formed in that precise character without Stonewall Jackson.

Between Lee, the Tidewater aristocrat, and Jackson, of mountaineer yeoman people, there existed a personal affection and a curious affinity in the making of war. Like collaborators, they were perfectly met. Their concepts of warfare were identical, and each was wholly committed to the conviction that independence would be won only by taking the war to the enemy. To be withheld passively on the defense, allowing the enemy the initiative, was maddening to

29

Jackson, and in audacity Lee could suggest nothing too bold for Old Jack to attempt. Because of their intuitive argeement on war policy and battle strategy, in tactics Jackson operated like an army of Lee's brain.

Of him Lee said: "I had such implicit confidence in Jackson's skill and energy that I never troubled myself to give him detailed instructions. The most general suggestions were all that he needed." Lee could have added that the most general suggestions were all that he wanted. In Jackson's two greatest offensive achievements, Second Manassas and Chancellorsville, he acted in semi-independent command, where he was out of contact with general headquarters and completely responsible for his own part of the battle.

These characteristics of the man who was not at Gettysburg exerted a profound effect on General Lee through habits Lee had formed during his operations with Stonewall Jackson.

From the moment Lee learned of his loss, he recognized that the army could not function in the organization that had evolved out of the collaboration. When Lee had inherited a year earlier the hodgepodge of forces which he built into the Army of Northern Virginia, he had followed no regular charts of organization. Adapting to his material, he had formed two very large corps of four divisions each. To slow-moving and tenacious Longstreet was allotted the orthodox work, largely under Lee's eye, while Jackson's Second Corps took the risks and did the marching. "Jackson's Foot Cavalry," the men called themselves. Without Old Jack, this arrangement was no longer possible.

Saying that "I know not how to replace him," Lee did not try. He reorganized the army into three corps, hoping that two men would prove adequate where Jackson had excelled. He said: "We must all do more than formerly."

Mechanically his reorganization to compensate for Jackson's loss was sound in design. However, it was untried in battle, and, because of Davis's exercise of his prerogatives as supreme commander, details in the new army were not as Lee designed them.

2

Lee's purpose in reshaping the army was to maintain what he called a "proper concert of action" between his proved units. As his infantry contained roughly 60,000 troops, he formed three corps of approximately 20,000 each. Longstreet retained the First Corps, minus the division of Richard H. Anderson. Richard S. Ewell, formerly Jackson's dependable division commander and recently returned to the army after having a leg amputated, was promoted to lieutenant general and given the old Second Corps, minus the six-brigade division of A. P. Hill. Powell Hill, the most highly regarded division commander in the army, was promoted to lieutenant general and given command of a newly created Third Corps. This was to be composed of Anderson's division, a division of four brigades from Hill's famous "Light Division," and a new division to be formed of two brigades from Hill's old division plus two other brigades. To fill the complement of Hill's new division, Lee expected the return of his two veteran brigades, under proved leaders, then detached in North Carolina.

In this new organization, which was to be tested in an invasion, Lee counted on an all-veteran personnel accustomed to his habits of command and adapted to the peculiar demands of the Army of Northern Virginia. Rightly though not officially called "Lee's army," this most personal of all armies was a reflection of Lee's character, particularly in its relation to the Southern character.

The region from which the soldiers came was a limited, restricted world that demanded conformity to its concept of gallantry. Although real enough, the life resembled a drama in its preconceived pattern, its conscious design, and its ritualized forms for the actors. And, just as the stage imposes physical limitations, this environment imposed limitations on the range of thought, of decisions, and of action.

As a part of its self-concept as a region of the aristocratic republic, the South naturally produced a concept of its individual model, a prototype of its perfected citizen. This ideal embodied not only the best traits that the society had produced according to its nature, but a distillation of the best that it aspired to, that it fancied itself as possessing, and that it attributed to itself from its past legends.

At bottom, there was an inviolability of personal dignity. As in religions, many subscribers to the Southern ideal were more perfect in the forms than in the substance. It was a sorry kind of man who, however far short he fell of the model, would not stand on his personal rights and frequently assert them violently.

Because of this element, discipline in the army was a fantastic problem, especially complicated where officers, in exercising their duties as soldiers, must conform to the mores of the society. Frequently privates were socially superior to their officers, and the consequences in a caste society were awkward. Privates who were social equals of their military superiors thought nothing of challenging them to duels, and the Confederacy was probably the only country in the world where generals would meet enlisted men at grand affairs— and call them "Mister" too. Only the officers of the rank of colonel or below had been elected, but the men had the feeling that they had chosen all their officers.

Where the relationship of officers to their men was that of members of a club who had been elected to office, and no effective machinery of an established nation controlled the individuals, the good officers commanded by moral force and the confidence they inspired through demonstrated capacities for leadership. The reason the Army of Northern Virginia became the best fighting force in the South was that its leader personified the ideal individual concept of the Southern people. As in the concept of the region's exemplar there was inherent the image of the Hero, Lee embodied the image of the patriarchal planter who, as military leader, assumed benevolent responsibility for his domain.

He really ruled rather than led, and his often-mentioned gentleness was that of a strong father who raises his children by kindness instead of sternness. The men's affectionate reverence for him was shown by their referring to him as "Uncle Robert" or "Marse Robert." The "Marse" today smacks of the treacly myths of the plantation era, but in their time it was only a slurring of Mister or Master as a prefix of respect for one sufficiently intimate to be addressed by his first name. "Mister" and "Uncle," as well as "Miss," have customarily been used before first names in the South for older intimates of one's family or respected elders in the community.

Lee's understanding of the nature of his force and of his relationship to it produced the nature of the command situation in the Army of Northern Virginia. As with the head of a large family, the general as patriarch encouraged the diffident, restrained the overconfident, settled quarrels, averted duels, soothed injured feelings, separated antagonistic personalities by placing them in different corps. When officers failed to adjust to the character of his army, he tried to transfer them to areas where their usefulness would not be lost to the country. When officers simply failed, he did not care where they went; he got them out of his army. Some officers were forced on him by Davis's political considerations, and sometimes a man was promoted on grounds of his patriotism and his troops' devotion to him. But Lee, when given a choice, judged on performance as coldly as Lincoln and Napoleon.

33

The problem after the Chancellorsville losses was that he no longer possessed a choice. In the new organization, Lee's general-officer personnel would contain two newly promoted lieutenant generals, neither of whom had commanded a corps even temporarily. New major generals commanded four of his twelve divisions. Twelve of his thirty-seven brigades were commanded by men new to their posts, several of such doubtful quality that they were placed in temporary command and not promoted above the rank of colonel. None of the general officers had commanded more than a company before the war. One new major general, a V.M.I. graduate, had had no army experience prior to the war, and many of the brigadiers had come directly from civilian life.

When Lee said: "We must all do more than formerly," he expected the men promoted to new responsibilities to demonstrate initiative within the framework of team unity. Lee's type of command presupposed proved units with experienced leaders who were accustomed to working together and were acquainted with one another's methods and potentials. But even while Lee was changing the structure of his successful command across the river from Hooker's masses, he received the first intimations of the interference with his own army which was to result from Davis's fixity of purpose in maintaining his defensive system.

With every garrison force in the eastern Confederacy from Charleston to Richmond held unchanged where it was, veteran units on which Lee had counted in his reorganization plans were kept away from his army on detached duty, guarding railroads and supply depots. Instead of the two highly regarded brigades that Lee had designated for the new division in A. P. Hill's new corps, Davis arbitrarily sent him two brigades unknown to the Army of Northern Virginia. One of these, itself newly formed, contained green troops and was led by a general innocent of combat service

—the president's own nephew. This consequence of Davis's compulsion to manipulate troop dispositions was a fateful factor in the Battle of Gettysburg.

Lee was profoundly disturbed by the lack of support for his bold stroke which was evidenced by this immobilizing of two brigades trained in maneuver and as familiar with him as was he with them. In writing Lee of the continuing threats of the enemy which he must guard against, the president revealed how completely he had missed Lee's point of a concentration to force a contraction of the enemy's forces. In substituting second-line strangers for an equal number of known veterans, he revealed his total misunderstanding of Lee's needs in rebuilding an army for an invasion. More depressing proof was to follow.

One of the two divisions of Longstreet's corps which had been detached at Chancellorsville, Pickett's, was the largest in the army, numbering nearly 8,000. The division most rested and the least fought in the past six months, it was one of the two in the army whose all-veteran command, from colonels to major general, had been unchanged in the reshuffling. To Lee's dismay, its largest brigade was detained on guard duty in North Carolina and the other four brigades were assigned to guard Hanover Junction, twenty-odd miles north of Richmond. Even the usually equable Pickett wrote exacerbated letters about the waste of sending four of his crack brigades off on fruitless marches in response to the alarums that goaded Davis into sending orders unrelated to any military plan at all.

By the time Lee finally received the promise of the release of three of Pickett's brigades from Hanover Junction, Davis's course had shaken the general's resolution about the invasion. Still hoping for the fourth brigade, on May 30 he wrote: "I fear the time has passed when I could have taken the offensive with advantage."

In deep pessimism, he warned Davis that if the enemy moved against him, "there may be nothing left for me to do but fall back."

Then, apparently trying an oblique approach through the secretary of war, he wrote Seddon that he had "greatly relied" on the brigades withheld from him, and, as it was, "if the Department thinks it is better to remain on the defensive, guard as far as possible all avenues of approach, and await the time of the enemy, I am ready to adopt that course."

Seddon responded to this feeler by a warm assurance of his support for Lee's invasion. Three of Pickett's brigades would be sent on, and he promised to try to release the fourth from its desuetude. Although no war secretary could speak for the commander in chief, Lee appeared to be heartened by Seddon's moral support and the expectation of four of Pickett's brigades.

As it happened, Davis overruled Seddon. Only three of Pickett's five brigades joined Lee. The division, formerly the largest, became the smallest in the army. Lee did not learn until he had crossed the Potomac that four of his best brigades, the equivalent of a division, were to be uselessly employed away from the army. But, even while still expecting troops that never came, the burdened general was unsettled by the limitations imposed on his planned offensive. It was not at all the way he wanted to make an invasion, and he showed an unusual indecisiveness.

Yet there was nothing else to do. Hooker, with all his huffing and puffing, would not commit his army to attacking, and, as Lee wrote to Richmond, there was no military profit in attacking the Federals on the Rappahannock River line. Also, his troops were daily growing hungrier and his animals leaner.

Writing more importunities to Davis, Lee, with a divided

mind and a sense of desperation, gave the marching orders to his new and incomplete army on June 2.

3

The Wednesday morning of June 3, 1863, was pleasantly warm, and the commanding general on his familiar gray horse gave every outward appearance of calm confidence. The troops, after a month's rest, were pleased to be leaving the desolate, ravaged countryside, and cheerful at the prospects of getting to the enemy's wagons. Although the men were beginning another risky operation of dividing their forces in the presence of an enormous enemy, they were not students of the military maxims of what should not be done and they felt confidence in any movement ordered by Uncle Robert. The very fact of repeating earlier successful maneuvers gave the troops a sense of reassurance.

Leaving the three divisions of A. P. Hill's new corps across the river from Fredericksburg to guard against sudden thrusts at lightly protected Richmond, Lee marched his other five divisions in an arc around Hooker's flank to Culpeper, in the rolling blue country of central Piedmont. From there, midway between Fredericksburg and the passes into the Shenandoah Valley, Lee could either march westward over the Blue Ridge or, if Hooker moved, recontract at the Rappahannock River. His caution reflecting his irresolution, Lee halted at Culpeper, writing more appeals to the war office while he waited for Pickett's brigades.

The land was great horse country, and the day before Lee decided to move on westward he permitted General Stuart to indulge his vanity with a cavalry review. Jeb Stuart had built his mounted force to the highest strength it was ever to know, 9,500 troopers, and on a vast grassy plain the young cavalryman enjoyed a re-enactment of a time when knighthood was in flower, preceded and followed by dances in the red-hot Rebel neighborhood. The trouble with this "military foppery and display," as a tough-bitten captain called the grand review, was that the cavalry regarded their assignment of screening Lee's infantry as mere routine.

The result was that, on the day Ewell's corps started for the Blue Ridge, Stuart's cavalry was caught in a surprise attack by an even larger Federal force, led by capable young Pleasonton. At Brandy Station (June 9) Jeb Stuart experienced the hardest fight of his life in the largest mounted action that had ever taken place on the continent. He emerged from the close call badly shaken and was very sensitive to the jibes of newspapers and rivals about his humiliation following the pageantry.

As one of the proved dependables, Stuart had not given much assurance in this engagement that he would "do more than formerly," but Lee did not seem especially disturbed. To offset Stuart's bad day, General Richard S. Ewell, the new Second Corps commander and one of the doubtfuls in Lee's mind, acted like a reasonable facsimile of Jackson in his first contact with the enemy.

Despite the cavalry's difficulties on June 9, Lee had permitted Dick Ewell to start for the Blue Ridge as planned. The commanding general remained with Longstreet's two divisions at Culpeper, still waiting for Pickett, and A. P. Hill held alertly at Fredericksburg. On June 14, one month after the day Lee had gone to Richmond for the conference, Ewell's corps fell on a Union force at Winchester and disposed of it, with the usual welcome acquisition of stores and guns.

The consequences of this action bore out Lee's belief in forcing the enemy to constrict instead of dispersing to meet his numerically superior dispersals. The Union's Milroy had been waiting at Winchester to join another Union force from the western mountains and threaten the fertile Valley, in the expectation that Lee would detach forces to save his "bread-basket." Instead, with Milroy gobbled up in passing and Lee headed north, the western force abandoned the Valley project. Also, because of Lee's counterthreat, a hostile force approaching Richmond from the east was withdrawn and turned to defense. Finally, Hooker acted as Lee had anticipated: he broke camp to move northward, shifting to place his army between Lee and the city of Washington.

Having seized the initiative from the enemy, Lee sent Longstreet after Ewell into the Valley and northward, and directed A. P. Hill to follow Longstreet. By mid-June, Virginia was left exposed save for Davis's scattered garrisons.

Riding with Longstreet's corps along the Shenandoah Valley northward out of Virginia, Lee was still depressed about those scattered garrisons and continued to importune Davis and the war office with pleas for support of his total plan. In his anxiety, he wrote Davis instructive essays on the rudiments of military strategy. The letters were not answered.

Then, as his widely separated forces stretched out in Pennsylvania, General Lee became preoccupied with a more immediate and acute problem—the continued and unexplained absence of Stuart's cavalry.

Stuart had guarded the Blue Ridge passes against the probing enemy until Lee's infantry marched northward. In the cavalry's movement, Stuart was given the choice of moving north on the east side of the mountains or of following the infantry to the Potomac crossings and then pushing eastward through the passes. In either case, his orders were to guard the passes and the army's flank, and to provide information about the enemy's movement. As it was evident that Stuart had not followed the infantry west of the mountains, Lee expected daily that the cavalry would appear through one of the passes to the east. But each night when the commanding general went to his tent there had been no sign of his troopers and no word from Stuart.

Nothing like this had ever happened before. It was incredible that a commanding general, burdened with the responsibility of directing an invasion of the enemy's country, should have his attention distracted and his energies diverted by wondering where his own cavalry was. While his men marched confidently northward, an apprehension settled on Robert E. Lee which conditioned all of his actions on the campaign. His concern over the loss of Jackson, over the size of his force, over the halfhearted support from the government, and over the strange disappearance of one of his most trusted subordinates unsettled Lee inwardly as he had never been unsettled on any previous campaign.

4

The commanding general's forebodings were not communicated to the army. The men walked the strange roads under their red battle flags in the highest spirits. Indeed, such was their faith in Lee that the soldiers marched northward away from their own land, with their army divided into three parts, in the mood of tourists.

Shielded by the ramparts of the Blue Ridge, the men walked a steady fifteen or twenty miles a day in good order through the Virginia counties (now West Virginia) north of the Shenandoah Valley. "This country enchants me more and more," artillerist Ham Chamberlayne wrote his mother. After a year among the war-made barrens of middle Virginia, the twenty-five-year-old lawyer stared in admiration at the untouched land "covered with the richest green; clover and timothy knee high and thick as the best wheat. . . ."

His battery, with Ewell's corps, crossed the Potomac into Maryland at Shepherdstown. Henry Kyd Douglas, another young lawyer, had grown up in that region. A former staff officer with Stonewall Jackson, Douglas now served on the staff of division commander Edward Johnson in the old corps.

When Ewell's advance forces reached John Bloom's toll-gate, the old gatekeeper recognized the neighborhood boy and said to Douglas: "Who is going to pay for all the horses and wagons I see coming?"

"I am, Mr. Bloom," the staff officer answered. "I'll give you an order on President Davis. Take it to Richmond and get the money."

"Jeff Davis! I'll see him in hell!" the old man spluttered. Then he resignedly told Douglas to take "this crowd" on through and said: "I'll charge the toll to profit and loss."

Longstreet's First Corps, accompanied by General Lee on his gray horse, crossed the Potomac farther north, at Williamsport. The men took off their shoes, socks, and patched pants, made them into bundles on their rifle barrels, and waded across the river in a steady rain. They were leaving Confederate territory, but there were still many friends about, and the citizens were as curious about the Confederates as the soldiers were about the country. Especially, the people wanted to see General Lee.

Beyond Hagerstown the troops soon marched into Pennsylvania. Lieutenant Caldwell, of the 1st South Carolina, said: "This was, we felt, our really first invasion of Federal soil." Maryland they did not regard truly as enemy country. At the beginning of the war the Southern states had hoped that Maryland would join the Confederacy, and, though the state remained with the Union, many of its citizens joined Lee's army. "But," wrote Lieutenant Caldwell, "Pennsylvania was quite another thing."

The men became acutely aware of being on foreign soil. Jacob Hoke, the observant merchant in Chambersburg, believed that the Confederates were awed "at the rich and beautiful country," and commented that "the evident superiority of the country north of the Potomac to that south of it . . . exercised a discouraging effect upon the soldiers. . . ."

This was a hopeful assumption. From Mr. Hoke's city, Captain Blackford, of Lynchburg, Virginia, recently transferred from cavalry to Longstreet's staff, wrote his wife: "We are now in the Cumberland Valley, and a fine country it is, that is as yankees count fineness—small farms divided into fields no larger than our garden, and barns much larger than the houses in which live their owners, their families and laborers. The land is rich and highly cultivated, much more highly than the men who own it. . . ."

Among the people, Blackford wrote, "while I note physical comfort, I see no signs of social refinement. All seem to be on a dead level, like a lot of fat cattle in a clover field. . . . You never saw a country so densely populated. . . ." And: "Never in my life have I seen as many ugly women since coming to this place. . . . The men are not remarkable either way. They have an awkward, Dutch look. . . ." The Dutch appearance of the stolid men who observed the Confederates caused the soldiers to yell: "Och, mine contree."

Impressed they were by the richly cultivated land, but, like Captain Blackford, the men were more oppressed than awed by the smallness of the farms. They commented on the closeness of the farms to one another, the lack of timber and of shade, and the cramped atmosphere in comparison to the breadth of their land-holdings. In a North Carolina regiment there was a preacher's son, twenty-year-old George Wills, a tall and quiet boy who had grown up on a farm. He wrote home: "Their quantity of land is so limited, that they haven't the woodland to spare for groves, but have a small yard without trees."

These soldiers were warm and volatile people, given to emotional excesses, and their own land reflected their carelessness about bookkeeping. Mr. Hoke was wrong in assuming that the tidy husbandry of his fellows discouraged a more profligate people. The Southerners were impressed by all the grain and vegetables, stock and dairy products and fruits, not because such cultivation suggested the might of the enemy but because the yield promised good eating that day and perhaps the next.

There was some private grumbling about Lee's orders against pillaging, and, despite the strictly enforced orders, individuals managed to evade the cordon and undertake private foraging parties. The more guileful evolved a system by which they stole way during the brief confusion when camp was being pitched and before the night guards were posted.

Away from the eyes of the sentries, they strolled up to any likely-looking house and asked for food. The natives found the soldiers rather frightening. Although Lee's published orders had been intended to reassure the Pennsylvanians, the men were a fearsome-looking lot and appeared less disciplined than they actually were. Most had long since stopped shaving, and camp barbers scarcely brought a "trim look" to their hair. The results, combined with their gaunt, weather-stained faces and rough, nondescript clothes, their swagger and bold eyes, gave Lee's men as individuals a curiously lawless look. Then, they *were* "Rebels," and proud of it.

Usually the house-owners supplied them with food in order to get rid of them, though on occasions the men had to be ravenous to eat under hostile silent stares. Sometimes the inhabitants, finding no harm in the men, became cordial and even friendly. They asked questions about the South and discussed the war. Twenty-year-old Edward Moore, who had enlisted in the Rockbridge Artillery during his freshman year at Washington College, visited a house with three pretty daughters who actually encouraged him on the invasion. "They said," he reported, "they did not dislike rebels, and if

43

we would go on to Washington and kill Lincoln, and end the war, they would rejoice."

In Moore's four-gun battery there was a Maryland volunteer from Hagerstown, Private Merrick, a lawyer who had been educated abroad and who had become the battery scarecrow. Campaigning in Virginia, he had been too far from home to supplement his uniform with old civilian clothes, as did the others, and a particularly skinny six-foot frame made it impossible for Merrick to get a fair fit from the government issue or battlefield gleanings. His coat and pants always failed to meet by several inches, and, in the space between, his soiled white cotton shirt looked like some kind of raffish sash. Merrick insisted on covering his thin hair with a gray cap, and his shoes somehow got to be the color of rust.

On the trip northward the beggarly-looking scholar disappeared from camp without a word. Later a handsome carriage drove up to the battery's bivouac, and three stylishly dressed gentlemen stepped out. One of these fashion-plates was Merrick. He introduced his friends, who passed a bottle around, and the Rockbridge battery—composed almost entirely of former college students from the Lexington, Virginia, area—never spent a more pleasant evening. Then the elegant friends departed, and Merrick, still without a word of explanation but still in his fashionable clothes, returned to his place on the gun-limber as the guns and caissons rolled northward.

Such desperate need as Lawyer Merrick's was required to evade the unusually strict discipline under which the Army of Northern Virginia marched on the invasion. On their own land the men of this most informal of armies had never behaved so well.

With whole communities of their homeland in ashes behind them and thousands of dispossessed families crowding into its cities, they did not burn a single house. They were

44

Lee's soldiers, and his chivalric code decreed that they should fight only armed men. It was a code that would soon belong to the past. Not knowing that, the soldiers took simple enjoyment in the victuals of a countryside which had not been fought over.

With the lowest percentage of stragglers in the army's history, the men marched over the hard Northern roads well closed up in columns of four, in brigade units, which numbered usually from 1,200 to 2,000 men. Officers rode ahead and especially trusted men marched out as flankers. Behind each regiment, averaging around 350, marched a group of personal body servants and a group of stretcher-bearers, and last came the brigade wagons, each drawn by four horses or mules. There were a few bands to play "Dixie" and "The Bonnie Blue Flag," South Carolina's secession song, but there was little singing.

As a Chambersburg citizen saw them, "The Confederate infantry . . . presented a solid front. They came in close marching order . . . [and] . . . their dress consisted of every imaginable color and style, the [government-issue] butternut predominating. . . . Hats, or the skeletons of what once had been hats, surmounted their partly covered heads. Many were ragged, shoeless, and filthy . . ." but all were "well armed and under perfact discipline. They seemed to move as one vast machine."

The men were not, as Northern observers insisted, "trying to overthrow the government." The men had volunteered to defend their land, and now they were taking the war to the invaders. They were really very simple people who loved their own ways and were fighting for the right to preserve them.

The issue of slavery was remote to most of them. Something over ten per cent of the Southern white population were slaveowners, while as many as twenty-five per cent of

45

Southern white families were associated with the institution of slavery. The large slave-operated plantations were mostly in the Tidewater regions, and many of the mountaineers had never seen Negroes until they saw the body servants of the young bloods in their regiments.

George Wills, the North Carolina preacher's son, had one of these personal servants, who acted as chef, valet, and forager. This Wash was one of the Negroes whom well-intentioned Pennsylvania housewives tried to induce to steal away from their masters. One woman, trying to get at Wash's loyalties, asked him if he were treated well. "I live as I wish," he replied politely, "and if I did not, I think I couldn't better myself by stopping here. This is a beautiful country, but it doesn't come up to home in my eyes." Wash spoke fairly accurately for all the men who followed Lee into Pennsylvania's Cumberland Valley, west of the northern extension of the Blue Ridge.

With pauses here and there, the troops had been on the road for twenty-four days when on Saturday, June 27, the two corps, Longstreet's and Hill's, forming the middle and rear columns, concentrated at Chambersburg. Communication lines were established with Ewell farther north at Carlisle and with his division under Early at York. The spirit and the condition of the troops, the casualness with which the men accepted their fine march and safe arrival in the enemy's country, should have gladdened the heart of any commander.

But General Lee was burdened by responsibility for the life of every man who made camp in the strange countryside, and he knew their lives were endangered by the mysterious absence of the cavalry that should be covering the mountain passes on their flank.

46

"We Must All Do More Than Formerly"

5

On Sunday, June 28, while Lee at his camp outside Chambersburg was trying to conceal his apprehension over Stuart's absence, a young staff officer rode northward alone through the enemy's country. He was Captain James Power Smith, once an aide to Stonewall Jackson. When Jackson died, his staff officers selected Captain Smith to escort Mrs. Jackson and her seven-month-old baby to the home of her father in North Carolina. Having completed this mission, Captain Smith, like most of Stonewall's other staff officers, was invited to join the staff of his successor, General Ewell. By the time the "invitation" reached him in Richmond, Ewell's corps was already crossing the Potomac. Captain Smith set out after the army alone.

About sunset on Sunday he reached Greencastle, Pennsylvania, where groups of young farmers and their ladies were gathered on the street corners. Smith was halfway through town before he grew aware of his conspicuousness "in the uniform of a Confederate captain, with side-arms rather ornamental than useful." Suddenly apprehensive, he covered his fear by elaborately bowing to the farmers and lifting his cap, as he said, "to the astonished ladies" until he was on the open road again. There he shook his horse into a quick gallop and did not stop riding until daybreak the next morning, when he saw Confederate sentries guarding the well-built houses in Chambersburg.

Passing the public square, Captain Smith pushed his exhausted horse on the less than a mile to the woods on Mr. Messersmith's farm. There the commanding general's headquarters tents loomed in the grove through the mist of a cloudy Monday morning. Captain Smith was looking for someone to report to when General Lee, drawing on his gauntlets, came out of his tent and approached his gray horse, Traveler, held by an orderly.

Recognizing the staff officer of his late lieutenant, the General beckoned Captain Smith toward him. After asking the young officer solicitously about Mrs. Jackson, he inquired if Smith, so recently from Virginia, had any knowledge of General Stuart.

By chance, Captain Smith had crossed the Potomac the day before with two troopers bearing dispatches for detached cavalry units, and they had casually told him that on the preceding day (Saturday the 27th) they had left the main body of cavalry under Stuart in Prince William County back in northern Virginia. When Smith passed on this information, General Lee, he said, "was evidently surprised and disturbed."

Captain Smith moved away to join friends on Lee's hospitable staff for rest and refreshment before continuing on to report to General Ewell. It became his turn for surprise when the General's A.A.G., Captain Walter Taylor, also pressed him for information about Stuart's cavalry. Then Smith was told that not since Lee wrote Stuart a message on the night of the 23rd, six days earlier in Virginia, had there been any communication between the army and its cavalry.

Even now, Taylor said, A. P. Hill was warily moving his corps through the winding passes of South Mountain in the rain to discover the whereabouts of the enemy on the other side of the low range of hills. Ewell had been ordered back from Carlisle and Early from York, and the separated corps of the army were to recontract east of the mountains in the area of Cashtown and Gettysburg. No one could even guess what had happened to Stuart. General Lee was worried both about the fate of his former cadet and about having to concentrate in unfamiliar country without cavalry.

For not only had Stuart disappeared with the three most experienced brigades, but Lee did not know the whereabouts

48

of any of the cavalry units he had scattered for screening on the northward march.

The brigades of Beverly Robertson and Grumble Jones were to have guarded the mountain passes in Virginia until the army had crossed the Potomac, and then followed it. Before the spy Harrison had reported the night before, Lee could assume that those brigades remained away because Hooker was still in Virginia. Now he knew that Hooker's army, under Meade, was across the mountains from him and that it was Stuart who was still in Virginia. The Union army separated Lee from his own cavalry. This disturbing intelligence only deepened the mystery of why Jones's and Robertson's brigades had lingered south of the Potomac after the enemy had crossed the river.

Even the raiders under Imboden, borrowed for the occasion and ordered to close in from the west, had not appeared.

Jenkins's raiders, another unit that General Lee had pried loose from President Davis's scattered detachments for the invasion, were north with Ewell, and Lee placed little trust in them. They had reported at only half their paper strength, 1,800 effectives showing up. Leading the invasion into Pennsylvania, the lightly disciplined riders had not behaved like veteran cavalry. They were accustomed to long rides, swift strokes, and quick loot, and neither by nature nor training were they fitted for reconnaissance.

With a potential support of more than 12,000 troopers, the largest cavalry force ever at his disposal, Lee spent a dismal Monday hoping for the sight of one unit of them, while Hill's infantry, substituting for the horsemen, pushed eastward through the rough mountain passes. Two divisions of Longstreet's corps prepared to follow the next day. The three-brigade division of George Pickett would wait at Chambersburg as a rear guard until some cavalry showed up from somewhere.

During the anxious hours General Lee kept his thoughts to himself. His report, written later, revealed nothing of his mental torment. Characteristically without the use of a single "I," he wrote simply: "In the absence of the cavalry, it was impossible to ascertain his [the enemy's] intentions . . . [and] . . . it was determined to concentrate the army east of the mountains."

Although he communicated his troubles to no one, the general was manifestly under great strain. He could not stay in his tent. He walked up and down in the picnic grove, powerful and erect, his handsome face clouded. This was one of the few times during the war when Lee's effort to keep self-control was apparent.

During the afternoon he was visited by one of Longstreet's division commanders, General John B. Hood. An immense blond man of thirty-two, Hood, a West Pointer, was a Texan by adoption and a very literal-minded man of action. The presence of General Hood shook Lee out of his brooding. With his innate consideration of others and of the commanding general's duty to give assurance to his men, Lee managed a smile and said half humorously: "Ah, General, the enemy is a long time in finding us; if he does not succeed soon, we will go in search for him."

Then he prepared to leave Chambersburg with two of Longstreet's divisions the next day. Pickett's weakened division, as rear guard, would comprise the only approximation of a line of communication with home.

The next day, Tuesday, June 30, would mark a full week since Stuart had disappeared, and the commanding general could wait no longer for his cavalry.

That night his camp chest was packed for the trip through the circuitous mountain pass that led to the turnpike village of Cashtown and, eight miles beyond, the unimportant crossroads town of Gettysburg.

"All Is Vanity. . . ."

THE TWO troopers on detached duty who chanced to encounter Captain Smith at a river crossing were accurate in reporting General Stuart's cavalry back in Prince William County, southwest of Washington, on Saturday, June 27. The two cavalrymen would have disturbed the commanding general even more deeply if their report had included the sorry condition of men and mounts.

On the 27th the command was forced to halt while the horses grazed and the attenuated men supplied themselves from captured Union sutlers' stores. At this moment Hooker's army was in Maryland with the corps pointed toward South Mountain.

Even this early in the campaign Jeb Stuart was failing in his mission, with apparent unawareness of his failure. Judging from his reports, his mind was sharp and his conscience was clear.

In the details of his actions Stuart showed his usual vigor and initiative. He seems never to have considered that his success in details was totally unrelated to his major assignment: to screen Lee's infantry and to provide the general with information about the enemy.

Somewhere between June 9, when he had been hard pressed at Brandy Station, and June 24, when communications with the northward-advancing infantry were severed, Stuart the man superseded Major General Stuart the cavalry leader.

During the two years before the invasion Stuart's vanity had served him and the army as well as had his devotion and skill. Flamboyant and doting on praise, he possessed the ability to achieve the spectacular, and the dedication to a cause to make his ability useful. People reacted strongly to his vivid personality, and he inspired both the deepest loyalty and the most abiding dislike. This had been true his whole life.

He had been born thirty years before in southern Virginia tobacco-growing country, the son of a lawyer and congressman who served both in Richmond and in Washington. The elder Stuart was too convivial to establish a solid success, although socially he was greatly sought after for his accomplishments as a singer, raconteur, and drinking companion. James Ewell Brown Stuart took after his father in his love of gay gatherings, though he shunned liquor; from his mother he inherited a tougher inner core. She trained him to the iron will that characterized all his undertakings. Stuart's fixity of purpose was always awesome—and in June 1863 it was disastrous.

His youth was typical of the young Southern gentry who lived in style and privilege, with a rigid code of personal honor and not much cash. At West Point, where he was a college mate of the same Pleasonton whom he fought at Brandy Station, he did well in everything military, finishing as second captain in the corps. He even then displayed that attention to dress which was to make him the beau of Lee's army.

Beginning as a regular-army lieutenant in Western garrison life and Indian-fighting, the twenty-one-year-old Stuart made an impression by his vast physical strength and endurance and by his fearlessness. There was no question of his courage: he simply did not react with fear. During his tour in the West he made a love marriage with Flora Cooke, a Virginia girl whose father, Colonel Philip St. George Cooke, was a regular-army man commanding the 2nd U.S. Dragoons. Then, in 1859, while he was a first lieutenant in the U.S. 1st Cavalry, Stuart, by a curious circumstance, became personally involved in an incident that served as a prelude to the Civil War.

He and Flora had children by then, and the lieutenant applied for a leave of absence so that his parents in Virginia might meet their grandchildren. Leaving Flora and the children with the grandparents, Stuart went to Richmond as a lay delegate for the General Convention of the Episcopal Church, of which he was a devout communicant. Army business took him on to Washington, where he happened to be when John Brown led his band of insurrectionists into Harper's Ferry. Lieutenant Colonel R. E. Lee also was in Washington on a leave of absence to settle his father-in-law's estate at the near-by plantation of Arlington. Thus it was that the former West Point superintendent and one of his former cadets collaborated to suppress John Brown's insurrection and arrest Brown himself.

This was the first joint action of Lee and Stuart. They remembered it three years later when, in July 1862, Lee was appointed general of the heterogeneous army defending Richmond and Stuart was commanding its small cavalry force. Lee immediately dispatched the young cavalry leader on a reconnaissance mission to discover what the Federal General McClellan was doing in the marshy, heavily brushed country around Richmond. The inept performance of the

Union cavalry presented Stuart with his first opportunity of the war to satisfy his penchant for the spectacular.

Instead of returning with his information, he decided to ride around McClellan's entire army. It was a reckless venture and militarily profitless, but luck held—he lost only one man and one gun-limber—and his literally hairbreadth escapes made exciting reading for a Confederate people famished for good news.

The timing of the exploit was perfect. Everything was going wrong everywhere in the newly formed nation, and Richmonders lived in hourly dread of seeing McClellan's army enter their city. Suddenly the people had a hero, young and golden, who fitted their romantic concepts:

> *From plume to spear a cavalier,*
> *Whose soul ne'er parleyed with a fear,*
> *Nor cheek bore tinge of shame.*

Then twenty-nine years old, Stuart, with his stocky legs and massive torso, was not a graceful man on foot, but on horse he was an eye-filling figure. In a day of beards his thick red-brown whiskers and luxuriant mustaches were things of splendor, and his light eyes, sometimes as cold as morning light on a saber, could also appear merry and flashing. His gray uniform was magnificently tailored, given dash by a red-lined cape; his boots glistened like dark silver, and on his campaign hat fluttered an ostrich-feather plume. There was an air of audacity about him which won the hearts of a discouraged people.

Ladies garlanded his horse with roses, and music followed wherever he went. He sang in a rich baritone when he was riding, and when he wasn't riding he was dancing. He was a gallant with the girls—too much so, some said. Even loyal troopers complained of him as a ladies' man. At the Dundee plantation, where he headquartered for a spell when his fame was running in, an elderly lady today remembers her father protesting "Stuart kissing all the girls."

He savored every moment of it, but no dance or song or pretty pair of lips ever kept him away from duty. Not even Stonewall Jackson, his dear friend, was a more dedicated Confederate. In action he was all business and sometimes was inclined to be hard on his men, of whom he thoughtlessly demanded his own illimitable energy. In the Second Manassas campaign his screening of the infantry and harassment of the enemy were a classic illustration of the proper use of cavalry. Stuart was a Confederate all the way, on a primal conviction, and winning independence came before everything to him—until June 1863.

2

Men, to be successful, must emerge at the right time. Stuart's star had risen during the early period when the Union cavalry was inferior to the Confederate in skill and performance. Similarly, Sheridan came to Virginia in 1864 and distinguished himself at a time when the Confederate cavalry had passed its physical peak and was in a state of decline.

Stuart's original troopers were trained riders from childhood, and they brought with them their fine—in many cases, blooded—horses. They knew the country they were fighting over as well as they knew their own rooms. Representing the cavalier stock of the South—the young Ruperts who carried ladies' handkerchiefs on sabers—they held in their hearts a contempt for "Northern clerks and mechanics." Stuart's men rode as they fox-hunted, straight across country, taking all obstacles at a full gallop. They went into action shouting as if they could never die.

The Federals began the war with a lot to learn about handling horses in the field, but the U.S. Navy and Treasury departments, and manpower and industry prosecuted the war until in due time the Union cavalry had learned their lessons in the hardest of all schools—survival. After two years they were good riders, physically tough, and they knew the Virginia countryside pretty well themselves. They were smoldering over the indignities suffered at Stuart's hands, and they had produced some first-rate officers who were determined to even the score with the Rebels' beau sabreur. They came close to it at Brandy Station.

On that day Stuart's invaluable volunteer aide, South Carolina's Farley, a gentle Shakespearean scholar and savage fighter, was killed by a shellburst. Rooney Lee was wounded in the leg, and Wade Hampton's son, serving on his father's staff, was severely hurt. Alabama's Major John Pelham, the boy cannoneer whom Lee called "the gallant Pelham" and who was the darling of the cavalry, had been killed in the spring. And the giant Prussian volunteer aide, Heros von Borcke, had been invalided out with a serious throat wound. They were all going, with none to replace them, when newspapers began to attack Jeb Stuart.

References were made to dancing and singing, with guarded hints about his role as a ladies' man. These frivolities were suggested as a reason for his less than spectacular showing against Pleasonton. Actually, Stuart had handled his men superbly once he settled down to the fight. The surprise, caused by the ineptitude of a brigadier who had been forced upon him, and his own overconfidence had got Stuart into the trouble. The improved fighting quality of the Union cavalry kept him in it.

Then while Stuart's own papers were criticizing his personal habits, the Northern papers were provided with a means for holding him up to ridicule.

Stuart had on his staff a cousin, Channing Price, a faithful and efficient officer, and Price had a brother, Thomas, who until a few months before had been a student in Germany. Late in 1862 the plight of his state brought Thomas Price home, and Stuart, to save this second cousin from the rigors of the infantry, gave him a staff commission with his engineers. Coming fresh from European student life into the rough hardships of cavalry life, Thomas Price proved to be an unhappy volunteer, and as a devotee of Old World culture he was impervious to the male charm that emanated from the aggressive Stuart.

To relieve his misery, Lieutenant Price confided his impressions to a diary. Great was his agitation when one afternoon his engineering unit was run down by hostile cavalry and his diary was captured along with his luggage. His excitement was explained when the diary, having made its way to a Northern newspaper office, was published in a newspaper that promptly appeared in the Confederate camp. There, for all to see, were Lieutenant Price's unflattering comments on Cousin Jeb, including such items as "General Stuart, in his usually garrulous style. . . ."

All in all, Stuart must have felt his fame slipping from him at the time when Lee started the cautious movement of his three corps northward into Pennsylvania, and Pleasonton did nothing to help him regain his glory. Pleasonton sent his by now hard-bitten and confident cavalry daily, even hourly, against the gray troopers guarding the mountain passes. He never broke through, but Stuart's riders were hard put to contain the pressing Federals. They were really fought out during those two weeks from June 9 until the misty morning of June 22, when the Confederate vedettes peered warily ahead and found the blue horsemen gone.

Not only had Stuart's cavalry been pressed on the defensive as never before, but also they had not been able to gain a spot of information about the enemy. Stuart, smarting over the cuts to his ego, refused to read the portents. Always the

Federals had had more foot soldiers, more and better cannon, fantastically more and better supplies, but always Stuart had had better cavalry. Suddenly he did not, and he refused to accept the fact.

When Lee completed the movement of his infantry, guns, and wagons away from Hooker and started northward along the Shenandoah Valley, his trusted cavalry leader was preoccupied with re-establishing the supremacy of Jeb Stuart. He was young and very vain, and his pride was hurt—but not his confidence. He would show them. He would show them all, by another "ride around McClellan."

3

Stuart decided that in moving north to screen the infantry he would not take the safe way up the Valley west of the Blue Ridge. Instead, he would ride around Hooker and cross the Potomac to the east, closer to Washington, then join the infantry on its way north. He submitted this plan to Lee, who, with reservations, agreed to it "if practical."

Apparently General Lee was concerned about adding this risk to the whole gamble of the invasion, for on June 23 he had Colonel Marshall, his A.A.G., write Jeb Stuart a worried follow-up letter of instructions.

Without question, those instructions offered Stuart the discretion that Lee customarily granted to his subordinates. His innate consideration restrained him from giving a direct order to those he trusted, and he was always influenced by the individualistic nature of the patriot army. Because this army lacked the machinery of a regular establishment, Lee felt that more could be accomplished by appeals to the officers' initiative and sense of personal responsibility. He preferred suggestion to command when an officer had proved trustworthy, as had Stuart, and Lee was especially fond of young Jeb.

Lee's letter was delivered to cavalry headquarters before daybreak of the 24th. Stuart, refusing the comforts of a house while his men slept in the rain, was sleeping under a rubber blanket on the ground. As always, Stuart came fully awake at the touch of his aide. This is, in part, what the letter said:

> If General Hooker's army remains inactive, you can leave two brigades to watch him, and withdraw with the three others; but should he not appear to be moving northward, I think you had better withdraw this [west] side of the mountains tomorrow night [24th], cross at Shepherdstown the next day [25th], and move over to Frederick.
>
> You will, however, be able to judge whether you can pass around their army *without hinderance,* doing them all the damage you can, and cross the river east of the mountains. In either case [that is, whether Stuart crossed the Potomac west of the mountains at Shepherdstown or at some ford east of the Blue Ridge], *after crossing the river, you must move on and feel the right of Ewell's troops,* collecting information, provisions, etc.

There was no underscoring in the letter clumsily written by Colonel Marshall and endorsed by Lee, but even in Marshall's unclear instructions the words here italicized would leave a trained cavalryman in no doubt about his assignment.

The letter also referred to the instructions sent two days before, in which Lee's orders were clearer: "If you find that he [Hooker] is moving northward . . . you can move with the other three [brigades] into Maryland, and take position on Ewell's right, place yourself in communication with him, guard his flank, keep him informed on the enemy's movement. . . ."

Lee left to Stuart's discretion only the place to cross the river and whether to move northward by the Valley or by circling Hooker's army if he could "without hinderance." Stuart was given no leeway regarding the purpose of the

cavalry's movement. In fact, the repetitive instructions reflected Lee's anxiety over Stuart's big risk, and in the second
letter he showed that he urgently wanted Stuart to follow the
army quickly: "I think the sooner you cross into Maryland,
after tomorrow [June 24], the better."

The last line of the letter, the last words that Stuart received from Lee in Virginia, read: "Be watchful and circumspect in all your movements."

4

Committed to making the ride around Hooker eclipse even
the celebrated ride around McClellan, Stuart ignored Lee's
provisos and accepted the anxious letter as authority for
moving northward to the east of and around the Union army.
"The commanding-general wrote me, authorizing this move
if I deemed it practical"—that was the only mention Stuart
made of the letter in his official report.

To "deem it practical," Stuart was obliged to defy immediately the specific order to cross the mountains and move
north by way of the Valley *if Hooker remained inactive.* To
the best of Stuart's knowledge, Hooker *was* inactive on the
morning of June 24. He had been so informed by the irrepressible scout Major John Mosby. This slight, sandy-haired,
cold-eyed lawyer, then twenty-nine years old and destined
to become one of the most famous of all guerrilla leaders, was
consistently accurate in his personal reconnaissances, and—as
of the time he scouted Hooker's army—Mosby was accurate
in his report on it.

With no reason, then, to doubt Mosby, Stuart disregarded
Lee's reservation and planned to begin his ride around
Hooker's supposedly idle army shortly after midnight. His
concentrated cavalry would begin to move eastward at 1:00
a.m. on June 25, though Lee had written that "the sooner"
Stuart crossed into Maryland after the 24th "the better."

By one of the odd coincidences that occurred throughout the campaign, Hooker began the movement of his army to the river on the same day. But, while Hooker's movement belatedly removed the proviso that Stuart was not to circle the Federals if Hooker remained idle, his marching troops raised the other reservation: Stuart was not to circle if Hooker's troops caused a "hinderance." The Union army indeed caused such a hindrance that the encirclement ceased to be "practical." By then Stuart was committed.

At this point it is necessary to know—as Stuart did not—what Hooker was doing.

Fighting Joe Hooker had experienced a very bad day at Chancellorsville. Some say he lost his nerve because, a chronic heavy drinker, he had forsworn the bottle in order to meet his large responsibilities. Be that as it may, Hooker was an ambitious man and as eager as Stuart to regain his glory. Nobody knew better how fast the ax fell on unsuccessful Union generals, for Hooker himself had maneuvered most unscrupulously to get the commanding general's post from his predecessor, and he realized now that time was running out on him. He could not make mistakes or show indecision against Lee.

Fredericksburg lies fifty-five miles due south of Washington, and from there Lee had made his piecemeal movement to the mountains on a southward-dipping diagonal to the passes due west of Washington. He thus had followed, of necessity, the longest side of a triangle. While Lee was completing his withdrawal from Hooker's front, Hooker had pulled his army back northward so that it remained on the direct westward line from Washington to the mountain passes into the Valley.

As the last of Lee's infantry moved northward west of the Blue Ridge, Hooker separated his corps and stretched his

61

army from the Centreville area (on that line from Washington to the mountain passes) northward to a crossing of the Potomac near Leesburg. The Potomac runs northwest from Washington, and Leesburg lies about thirty miles west of the capital and fifteen to the north. Hooker's scattered army was so placed as to contract for a defense of Washington, an obsession of Lincoln's, or for a crossing of the Potomac at Edward's Ferry, near Leesburg. So far he had done everything right.

On June 25, Lee with the last of the infantry crossed the Potomac at Williamsport, thirty miles farther north and west of the mountain ramparts. Hooker shortly started to concentrate his army for a crossing at Edward's Ferry. From there, east of the mountains, he could parallel Lee's northward progress.

When Hooker started his troop concentration, his southernmost units were still southwest of Washington near a ridge called the Bull Run Mountains. This low range lies east of the Blue Ridge, which it roughly parallels until the two ranges merge at the Pennsylvania border and form South Mountain. When Stuart began his ride at 1:00 a.m. on June 25 his troopers were concentrated west of the Bull Run Mountains—between this range and the Blue Ridge, in the vicinity of a town named Salem. Stuart's first move eastward was to cross the Bull Run Mountains, and it was in the rolling country beyond that he encountered a Federal infantry corps in movement. The "hinderance" to his own movement then began.

The hindrance was sufficiently definite and unmistakable to impose a conscious decision on Stuart. He must either turn back and take the safe way west of the mountains until he caught up with the army, or make a more circuitous swing around Hooker than he had originally planned. According to Stuart's report, it never occurred to him to turn back. However, doughty Mosby assumed that he would and returned to his lone operations, leaving Stuart without his most able scout.

By now Stuart had not only his heart but also his inflexible determination set on the dangerous way. Indeed, every detail of the cavalry's movement had been planned for the audacious ride. The two brigades Stuart had left to guard the mountain passes until Lee was safely across the Potomac were those Stuart liked the least. One was commanded by Beverly Robertson, whom he distrusted with reason, the other by Grumble Jones, whose antipathy for Stuart at least equaled Stuart's for him.

Although unpredictable Robertson was senior to dependable Jones, he commanded the smaller brigade. This disparity Stuart left them to work out between themselves. After all, they needed only to guard the passes and then fall in with the army. It certainly never occurred to Stuart that the two brigades would remain fixed, as if planted there, in an inanition of command which immobilized the men for whom Lee in Pennsylvania was anxiously watching.

Stuart's mind was not on those men. His mind was on the ride. To that end, he had reduced his artillery to six guns and sacrificed his wagons, forcing his already worn horses and tired men to live off the country. To accompany him he had selected his three favorite brigades, and their leaders were always primed for a fight or a frolic.

Wade Hampton, a militarily untrained South Carolina plantation grandee, commanded one brigade with a native ability that was steadily maturing with experience. As tireless as Stuart, the huge Hampton was so powerful and combative that in his youth he went into the woods seeking bears to fight with a knife.

Stuart was going to miss his friend Rooney Lee, the general's son, about whom it was said "he was too big to be a man but not big enough to be a horse." The Harvard-educated younger Lee had to be left behind because of the leg wound he had suffered at the hands of Pleasonton's people. He was later to be taken by Federals from his mother's house, where his leg was healing, and carted off to prison while his beautiful wife died.

Colonel John Chambliss would handle Rooney's brigade, and he was becoming a good man. Chambliss was a West Pointer who, soon after graduation, had returned to work on his father's large plantation in Virginia. Bringing his own stable of horses with him when he volunteered to defend his state, Chambliss, who had known his commanding officer at the Point, soon became adapted to the mold of a typical cavalry leader with Jeb Stuart.

For the third brigade, Stuart was heartened by the return to command of his other Lee friend, twenty-eight-year-old Fitzhugh Lee, the commanding general's nephew. Fitz Lee was the *bon vivant* and the gourmet of the cavalry command. Perhaps not so meticulous in detail as Wade Hampton, he had the background of West Point and the regular army, and his love of fighting was native and joyous. He had been laid up with rheumatism, and Stuart had missed his laughter, but Fitz made it to the concentration for the ride North. He wouldn't have missed it for anything.

These were not the lieutenants to counsel caution. All were of that breed which used to be called "tough gentlemen." They were gentlemen in the tradition, tough by nature and habits of life, and they felt very personally about what the enemy had done to plantations and the horse country. When Stuart called: "Follow me!" they would be breathing on his neck and he would have to gallop hard to keep ahead of them.

It was the *élan* of his officers which Stuart responded to—not that last worried admonition from General Lee "Be circumspect"—as the troopers of the three brigades came gallop-ing into the Salem area all during the day and early evening of June 24.

Their number totaled between 5,000 and 6,000 officers and men, probably closer to the lower figure. Stuart, pre-occupied with his plans, failed to notice two ominous details in his command. The horses that were to move without grain already were gaunt from hard campaigning, and the men, in-stead of attending eagerly to details of preparation, were ly-ing like logs on the ground, sleeping until the last minute.

In the 9th Virginia, of Rooney Lee's brigade, the son of the commanding colonel wrote his mother of the brief camp at Salem. His regiment had been moved southward for the concentration, and he wrote that "this move, considering the direction our army was marching, filled us with astonish-ment, and was one the mystery of which none of us could understand."

Such boys had been too long in the saddle, living on too short rations and exposed too constantly to danger, even to conceive of the adventures that haunted the imagination of their leader. None had his inexhaustible energy. Most of them were ready for a rest before they started. Aroused after mid-night, the troopers moved automatically as they sleepily sad-dled and mounted their lean horses.

None sang that night the war song written to Stuart.

> *Come tighten your girth and slacken your rein;*
> *Come buckle your blanket and holster again;*
> *Try the click of your trigger and balance your blade*
> *For he must ride sure that goes Ri . . . ding a Raid!*

5

At one in the morning the men started their horses east-ward through the pass in the Bull Run Mountains. The night ride was necessary to avoid the eyes of the Federal watchers in the mountain signal stations, and at daylight the troopers emerged unobserved on the blue rolling land called "the horse country of Virginia." The limestone deposits produced grass that made for sturdy bones in the animals, and the meadowlands formed one of the great fox-hunting regions of the world. The people had lived graciously there before the war, with the stylized informality characteristic of hunting communities, and no area in the South produced more passionate Rebels. Also, no area in the South had been more fought over in the last two years, and only a wishful optimism could expect to find forage for horses or food for men in the naked countryside.

The beguiling landscape was dotted with crossroads villages, scarcely more than a country store or a blacksmith shop or a small public house. Each proudly bore a name, and the abundance of place names gives a false impression of density of population. A boy from the Deep South wrote his father of passing northward and dutifully chronicled the name of each place through which he passed. His letter sounded as if he were making the Grand Tour, when he had journeyed no more than twenty miles and beheld no settlement with as many as one hundred inhabitants. As Stuart's men rolled eastward into the climbing June sun, their course was marked by the names of little places whose only significance was as points of designation, and it is confusing to try to follow in detail Stuart's course by names of places no longer on maps.

On the first day out, the cavalry found their road to Centreville and the Potomac blocked by Hancock's Federal corps in motion. Union wagon trains were long, and good soldier Hancock had, as Stuart reported, "his infantry well distributed through the trains." The passage would require hours.

It was late now to turn back, but the Confederates could

not go forward. Fixed on his plan and unable to endure the enforced idleness, Stuart passed the time by shelling Hancock's trains as if to justify Lee's order to do as much damage as possible. He gained only the passing satisfaction of forcing the marching troops to deploy in line of battle. During this pointless exchange his troopers found some grassland and lay on the ground while their horses nibbled.

Late in the day Stuart determined to move a few miles southward, "to deceive the enemy," and to start fresh the next day on a southeasterly swing around Centreville.

As Lieutenant Beale wrote his mother, "That night was rainy and disagreeable, and we spent it without shelter or fires." The next morning, Friday the 26th, not at all refreshed, the cavalry started out on Stuart's revised longer course. That day they did not see a single blue soldier. Stuart observed that the horses were breaking down from lack of grain, and the columns were forced to halt again to graze the animals.

So on Saturday the 27th, when Lee arrived with the rear guard of the infantry at Chambersburg, and Ewell thirty-five miles farther north at Carlisle was preparing to take the capital of Harrisburg, the army's cavalry was creeping ahead in the Washington area, averaging fewer miles a day than the foot soldiers.

That morning the troopers came into Fairfax Court House, and their spirits arose as they sighted several well-stocked shacks of sutlers, those traveling merchants who followed the Union armies with dainties. Confederates regarded sutlers' stores the same as enemy wagons, and before the stricken gazes of the pedlars they pounced on every article in sight. Young Beale wrote home: "There were many things taken there and speedily consumed by *'us ravenous rebs.'* "

Stuart wisely permitted the tired men to indulge themselves, while the horses, still without grain, grazed again.

With enlivened spirits, the troopers pushed on, at last approaching the Potomac for a crossing. As they neared the river late Saturday afternoon, the men came upon the still smoldering campfires of Sedgwick's Federal corps. The Federals had moved out that morning toward the good crossing at Edward's Ferry. Union stragglers, picked up, revealed that all of Hooker's army was northwest of them, crossing the river. Militia units had moved southeast back to Washington.

These were close quarters for tired men on worn-out horses, and in the darkness Stuart sent Wade Hampton ahead with his brigade to find the best of the poor fords available. Rowser's Ford, the least bad, offered a rough crossing from rugged banks out over rocks and quicksands, and when the first brigade made it Hampton sent word back that the crossing was "utterly impossible" for the guns.

There in the blackness Jeb Stuart revealed that iron determination which could never accept defeat in any project. "I," he reported, "determined not to give up without trial, and before 12 o'clock that night, in spite of the difficulties, to all appearances insuperable, indomitable energy and resolute determination triumphed." These are not the words of a modest, self-effacing man, nor a man of sophistication, but in unconsciously revealing his old-fashioned personal credo in that report Stuart was a totally truthful man.

The water came up to the saddle skirts, sometimes over the seats, and to Colonel Beale the river seemed a quarter of a mile wide. One of Stuart's officers wrote his wife: "The guns and caissons went clean out of sight in the rapid torrent, but all came out without the loss of a piece or a man. . . . On the morning of the 28th of June we all stood wet and dripping on the Maryland shore."

Such triumphs of will and cold nerve formed the episodes that colored the career of Jeb Stuart; yet in this particular triumph Stuart's cavalry were, for all practical purposes, conducting a private war of their own.

It was not that Stuart was in any sense unmindful of his mission to fall in on the army and make contact with Ewell's right. But, when the sun rose on Sunday the 28th, Stuart, having ridden around Hooker's army, did not know where Ewell was.

He knew from Lee's instructions that Dick Ewell, with the advance corps of the army, was supposed to head for the Susquehanna, and that one column would "probably" move by the Emmitsburg road. He also knew that, with Hooker moving into Frederick, Maryland, his cavalry's direct route to the Emmitsburg road was blocked. Hancock's corps had caused the time-consuming swing back in Virginia; now Hooker's whole army caused him to ride north, instead of cutting northwest, in heading for the Susquehanna and Ewell's presumed destination.

If Stuart's reports reflect his true state of mind (and he was not given to brooding self-analysis), he quite casually accepted the fact that at best he would not reach Ewell until the infantry had completed its march. Hence, he could not possibly follow Lee's orders to "guard his [Ewell's] flank, keep him informed. . . ." Yet, caught up in his ride, Stuart seems to have been curiously detached from the element of urgency in providing the infantry with its cavalry on an invasion of hostile country. For on that Sunday the 28th, while Lee struggled to hide his apprehension in Chambersburg, Stuart diverted his men to chase an enemy wagon train almost to the outskirts of Washington.

6

The weary men in Stuart's cavalry knew nothing of his orders and no details of their mission. There was a good deal of rivalry, not at all good-natured, between the cavalry and other branches of the service. Whenever the horsemen passed an infantry unit, foot soldiers would point at their spurs and yell: "How long does it take to grow them things out'n yoh heels?" At Stuart's grand cavalry review before the campaign began, the hard-visaged Texans with Hood had to be restrained from shouting: "Here's yoh mule!"

This term of contempt came from a song about a farmer who visited a camp to sell some produce and then spent his time hunting for his vanished mule. The verse went:

> Come on, come on, old man,
> Don't be made a fool
> By everyone you meet in camp,
> With "mister, here's your mule."

On Sunday morning the 28th, after the night crossing of the rough ford, the troopers felt they deserved a breather in Rockville, Maryland, little more than ten miles from Washington and today almost a suburb of the city. Even though the advance brigade had exchanged shots with some enemy horsemen and part of the command remained in line of battle, their nearness to the enemy's capital excited the bravado of the younger men. While they waited for any enemy force that might develop, the young horsemen preened themselves before the girls of a female academy, who displayed the most winsome Southern sympathies.

In the midst of this interlude the officers received the happy news that a large wagon train was on its way from Washington to the Federal army, which that day became General Meade's. (Despite his celerity and soundness in countermovement against Lee, Fighting Joe Hooker had not been forgiven Chancellorsville. Feeling that his superiors lacked confidence in him, he had offered his resignation and it had been promptly accepted.)

Stuart's cavalrymen could be aroused from the deepest stupor at the prospect of enemy rations, and in their relaxed humor at Rockville they went after the wagon train as if on a lark. The brand-new wagons, with harness and fat mules in use for the first time, stretched for four miles. As Colonel Beale of the 9th Virginia said, "Such a train we had never seen before and did not see again."

The train's small guard took alarm at the sight of the tattered butternut uniforms, and got the wagons turned and headed back for Washington before the leading troopers reached it. The chase began. The fresh mules, four or six to a wagon, could move under the whip as fast as the tired cavalry horses. When the troopers fired pistols at the drivers, the crackling shots only urged the mules on faster. Drivers, some of them Negroes, began to jump from the wagons, and the cavalry got to laughing at the spectacle they were a part of. Colonel Beale's son wrote his mother that "the chase was the most interesting, exciting and ludicrous scene I ever witnessed or participated in."

Finally one of the careening wagons failed to round a curve. Wagon and mules, with legs churning in the air, sprawled across the road, and the next dozen wagons piled up before the train could be brought to a halt. Another dozen wagons had already made it around the curve. So caught up in the spirit of the chase were the men that even responsible officers kept going just for the excitement of it. Colonel Blackford, Stuart's staff officer, who had said his poor horse "looked as thin as a snake," wrote his wife that "it was as exciting as a fox chase for several miles, until when the last [wagon] was taken, I found myself on a hill in full view of Washington."

Then began a feast of ham and crackers, with whisky chasers, before the quartermasters could collect the stocks of bread, bacon, sugar, and, most important of all, oats. After the horses were fed grain for the first time in six days, the

71

men crowded oats into their saddlebags along with stores of such victuals as they particularly hungered for.

Next came the chore of reassembling units scattered over an area of five miles, and the time-consuming work of having 400 Federal prisoners sign their names to parole papers (which stipulated that they could not fight again until exchanged for Confederate parolees). Finally, there was the problem of the 125 wagons and the hundreds of magnificent mules.

Looking at these "best United States model wagons" and their teams "with gay caparisons," Stuart decided to take his prize capture to the Army of Northern Virginia. That the well-stocked wagons had been captured at the gates of Washington added a gaudy fillip to the adventure which he could not resist. Having already involved his command in the long ride to the Susquehanna, the cavalry leader now burdened the movement of his troopers in enemy country with the guardianship of a cumbersome wagon train.

This was how Jeb Stuart spent Sunday, June 28, while General Lee waited for news of him in Chambersburg and the spy Harrison was riding hard from Frederick with information of the Federal army's whereabouts.

7

In the backwash of their sport and logy with unaccustomed feasting, the cavalrymen started north that night on horses to which the desperately needed grain had scarcely compensated for the hard gallop of the chase. On the next day, Monday the 29th, while Captain Smith gave Lee the shocking news of Stuart's whereabouts, Stuart ordered another halt so that his tired men could tear up some tracks of the B. & O. Railroad. Considering the excellence of the Federal railroad-engineering units, this brief annoyance to the enemy chiefly served to reveal Stuart's preoccupation with the raiding aspects of his ride. Although he made efforts to discover the whereabouts of his own army from sympathetic Marylanders and Northern newspapers, there was no urgency in his inquiries.

Late that afternoon the cavalry moved into Westminster, where the railroad station yielded more food for the men and grain for the horses. That night, with the van at Union Mills, the men slept for a few hours. They moved out early the next morning, Tuesday, June 30, the day when A. P. Hill's corps—acting as reconnaissance troops—poked through the winding mountain passes into Cashtown and the van pushed on eight hilly miles farther east toward Gettysburg.

Around ten o'clock that morning Stuart came within sight of Hanover, eleven miles east of Gettysburg. At this moment he and Hill were less than twenty miles apart.

Stuart had come upon two-day-old papers which announced that Early's division of Ewell's corps was at York, as indeed Jubal Early had been on the 28th. Now, on the 30th, Early was maching back westward toward Gettysburg. Everybody was heading for Gettysburg except Stuart, and he, who had been playing it by ear until now, definitely made York his destination.

Two factors prevented his pushing ahead. Judson Kilpatrick had cavalry in some force in Hanover, blocking Stuart's way, and the captured wagon train, whose mules were no longer fresh and spirited, was miles to the rear.

Taking first things first, Stuart attacked Kilpatrick, and his men never fought more poorly. Hampton was absent with the wagons, Fitz Lee was out covering the flank, and Chambliss's men were too tired to be alert after an initial success. An unexpected counterattack by the brigade of newly promoted Federal Brigadier Farnsworth scattered Chambliss's troopers, and General Stuart and his staff were nearly captured. Only a fifteen-foot jump over a gully by Stuart's mare took the general away from pursuers who were not quite up to that kind of riding.

Yet that flash of personal heroics added luster to the Stuart legend among those who loved him. Staff officer Blackford wrote his wife: "I shall never forget the glimpse I then saw of this beautiful animal away up in midair over the chasm, and Stuart's fine figure sitting erect and firm in the saddle."

This glory was lost on the exhausted riders. Farnsworth's flurry was contained and Kilpatrick slowly driven westward from Hanover, but Stuart's men grew apprehensive when that night they moved still farther north. They knew that neither they nor their horses were in physical condition for extended action, and they sensed the enemy all around them.

Clinging grimly to the captured wagons, Stuart diverted the train eastward around Hanover before rolling north toward York. He was anticipating Lee's pleasure at receiving the large wagons, with which provisions could be collected from the Dutch farmers.

When Stuart's men, moving in a fog of fatigue, started nervously northward in the darkness, the prelude of the battle had taken place at Gettysburg. Pettigrew's North Carolina brigade of A. P. Hill's corps had encountered Union cavalry about the town. As Stuart had gathered no information about the enforced convergence of Lee's army, he began the night ride that completed the removal of his cavalry from the Gettysburg campaign.

8

To the men on stumbling horses who made that ride in the very dark night, the final phase of Stuart's adventure held the quality of a nightmare. Men slept on their horses, and some fell off without awakening. Young Beale wrote his mother: "It is impossible for me to give you a correct idea of the fatigue and exhaustion of the men and beasts. . . . Even in line of battle, in momentary expectation of being made to charge, they would throw themselves upon their horses' neck, and even the ground, and fall to sleep. Couriers in attempting to give orders to officers would be compelled to give them a shake and a word, before they could make them understand."

Daylight brought no relief. When they approached what had come to loom as the haven of Jubal Early's infantry at York, advance riders brought the shocking information that Early had left York and was proceeding westward. Whatever the effect of this gloomy intelligence on the general, he showed no uncertainty. Impervious himself to the toll of physical strain, Stuart gave the only orders possible in the circumstances. He sent staff officers westward to pick up Early's trail, and started his cavalry northward toward Carlisle, which, according to the latest news, was occupied by Ewell.

Late in the afternoon of Wednesday, July 1, with no food and little ammunition, the creeping cavalry arrived in front of Carlisle. There they learned that Ewell's infantry was gone. Instead, the town was fortified with Union militia and artillery under a major general. To get rations, Stuart demanded the surrender of the town. When this was refused, he opened a blast with his guns while the troopers slumped, aching, in their saddles.

"Weak and helpless as we now were," Lieutenant Beale wrote, "our anxiety and uneasiness were painful indeed. Thoughts of saving the wagons now were gone, and we thought only how we, ourselves, might escape. . . ."

Young Beale indulged in no sentimental reflections about his father's alma mater, Dickinson College, in the town where the shells fired by the dispirited gunners were bursting. He was too busy looking over his shoulder for enemies.

The troopers could not know that the Federals' Kilpatrick, whom they had engaged at Hanover, had little stomach for the rough going and had not pursued them. Nor could the men have imagined that the whole Union army was rapidly converging thirty miles to the south of them, where the two armies had blundered into each other that morning. Indeed, while their horse guns were futilely shelling Carlisle, the first day's fighting of the Battle of Gettysburg was drawing to a close.

Stuart learned about it that night, through the ignominious means of his searching staff officers having found their own army. Lee reported to his cavalry leader the whereabouts of his infantry.

At midnight the sleep-riders started out again, southward through Mt. Holly pass. So deep was their exhaustion that one man fell off his horse at a fence and, sprawled across the wooden rails, slept on. Daylight found the spent columns with miles yet to go. With no pause, on the morning of July 2 the troopers began the final lap across the long landswells to Gettysburg.

For Stuart's cavalry the ride was an epic in heroism that went unheralded in the legends told to the tune of "If you want to have a good time, jine the cavalry."

For the thirty-year-old cavalier seeking a new plume, his greatest personal adventure was the greatest anticlimax of his career. He *had* ridden clear around Hooker's army, had on the way diverted Union cavalry and infantry forces, had caused vagrant alarums and collected fine captures, and his exploits were summed up by Lee, when Stuart reported to him that afternoon, with the coldly spoken words:

"Ah, General Stuart, at last you are here."

"And Then A. P. Hill Came Up . . ."

WHEN Stuart moved north from Hanover on June 30, riding out of the campaign, two thirds of A. P. Hill's corps had negotiated the tortuous passes through the South Mountain range and were going into camp outside Cashtown, the little village lying along the hilly turnpike eight miles west of Gettysburg.

They had not been so hard used as Stuart's men. They had been eating well and were in fine spirits despite the drizzly weather. The division of Harry Heth (pronounced Heath) was in the van, and it was one of his brigades which had pushed on eastward and encountered Federal cavalry near the farming seat of Gettysburg.

This brigade was Pettigrew's North Carolinians, one of the two new units that had filled out the new division in A. P. Hill's freshly created corps. Although his brigade came to the army when President Davis insisted on sending the troops of his preference to Lee, Johnston Pettigrew himself had seen service in Virginia before Lee assumed command and had won deep respect both as an officer and as a gentleman. A scholarly North Carolina lawyer, Pettigrew was one of those natural leaders of a privileged background who, without military ambitions, had been advanced on the application of native intelligence and contagious courage. By the date of his promotion, the untrained Johnston Pettigrew was senior brigadier in the division that he was the last general to join. This fact, too, was to exert a profound effect on the campaign.

When his reconnoitering foot soldiers encountered enemy cavalry, Pettigrew discreetly fell back on his division and reported in detail to General Heth. Neither of the men was disturbed by the presence of blue horsemen among the undulations of the closely farmed country around Gettysburg. The only importance of the town, of 2,400 population, was its situation at the intersection of a number of roads. It was also a minor educational center: a small college, a theological seminary, and a seminary for young ladies were situated there. A railroad had been started westward from Gettysburg, but work had not progressed beyond a deep cut for the roadbed. There was, however, one item in the Gettysburg stores which Pettigrew coveted for his men: shoes.

Pettigrew mentioned to Heth his desire to get those shoes, and his superior officer approved. In one sense, the invasion was a commissary raid, and Heth had kept his men busy requisitioning supplies. In fact, the newly promoted major general had used the hours in Cashtown to obtain a hat for himself. The supplies in the village stores were too limited for Harry Heth to get a fair fit, but one of his headquarters clerks had stuffed folded paper into the sweatband to hold the new finery to his head. Having thus replenished his own wardrobe, General Heth was only too willing to look after his men's raw feet. He told Pettigrew that he would take up the matter with the corps commander, A. P. Hill.

This minor item in the chain of command, from brigadier to lieutenant general, involved three men new to their positions—Pettigrew new to the army, Heth to division command, and Hill to corps command. All of an age (Pettigrew was thirty-five, Hill and Heth both thirty-eight), they typified the background common to general officers of the Army of Northern Virginia. Hill and Heth had been classmates at West Point, graduating a year behind Heth's cousin George Pickett. Neither man possessed any considerable estate for the support of his family after relinquishing a career in the old army.

A. P. Hill, though of a plantation background in Virginia's horse country, was one of the army's intense disbelievers in slavery. But, then, Powell Hill was intense about everything. Slightly built and of middle height, he had a lean, mobile face that, even with the full beard of convention, reflected his high-strung nature. He was more sensitive than the average professional soldier, courtly in his manner, genial, easily approachable. His personal warmth made him well liked in the army and a social favorite in Richmond. He was particularly liked by ladies, though sharing none of Stuart's tendencies to squander his favors.

He had courted the girl who married the Union's General McClellan—whom Hill had known pleasantly at West Point—and he was married to the sister of John Morgan, the Kentucky cavalry raider. Contemporary comments about Powell Hill and the ladies all concerned his quite lovely wife: she stayed too long, too close to the lines, in order to be with him.

After a good record in the old army, Hill started with the Confederate armies as colonel of a volunteer Virginia regiment. His troops belonged to the brigade that first gave the Rebel Yell, going in on the Federal flank late in the afternoon at First Manassas. Promoted to brigadier after the battle, he was soon advanced to major general and at the Seven Days commanded the army's largest division, six brigades, which was inversely called the "Light Division."

He was an indifferent administrator, but, as he was extremely attentive and even indulgent to his troops, the men loved "Little Powell," as they called him, and he handled them superbly in battle. Some of his own intensity was communicated to his soldiers, and the Light Division built one of the most notable combat records in the army. At the Battle of Sharpsburg the previous summer the division had reflected lasting glory on their leader and a curious distinction.

"And then A. P. Hill came up," said the report of his movement that saved the day, and, remembering, both Lee and Jackson called for him in their dying deliriums. "Tell A. P. Hill he must come up," the Old Man murmured on his deathbed in Lexington, Virginia, years after Hill had been killed and his fierce brigades were ghosts in men's memories.

At the army's reorganization in May 1863 it was accepted that one of the new corps would go to Powell Hill on the record of his performance and the general liking with which he was regarded. To his admirers, however, there was one notable exception: the army's senior lieutenant general, James Longstreet.

Antithetical types, Hill and Longstreet had come to an open clash primarily over the difference in their characters and attitudes. While courtly Hill was very punctilious about the forms of the code of personal honor which characterized his class, Longstreet was a bluff man, physically powerful and self-assertive, with little sensitivity to the nuances of human relationships. Although only in his early forties, he had graduated from West Point before the Hill-Heth-Pickett class entered, and he seemed of an older generation. He was slightly deaf, and there was about him the stolid heaviness of a settled man. Forthright in his likes and dislikes, Longstreet was capable of both lasting enmities and lasting affections. He was also more jealous-minded than was known, and jealousy provoked his clash with Hill.

80

"And Then A. P. Hill Came Up . . ."

During the Seven Days a temporary staff officer of Hill's wrote a newspaper article in which, to add to his own luster, he overpraised Hill. Longstreet, at that time nominally Hill's superior, felt slighted and had his chief of staff, Moxley Sorrel, write an answer to the paper. Although it was published anonymously, its authorship was no secret in the army, and the next time Colonel Sorrel brought a routine communication from Longstreet, Powell Hill refused to accept it. Longstreet, ignoring Hill's personal motives for refusing the communication, placed him under arrest. Hill, adhering to the personal element, challenged Longstreet to a duel.

At this point General Lee intervened. Stonewall Jackson had been sent on a semi-independent assignment, and Lee permanently attached Hill's large division to what was evolving into Jackson's Second Corps. A. P. Hill also became involved in a dispute with Old Jack, as did many another, but their differences concerned strictly military matters and were smoothed over. Longstreet, however, was a grudge-holder. During his army career he locked horns with four of his subordinate generals—Lafayette McLaws, Evander Law, John B. Hood, and Robert Toombs; he carried his hatred for Jubal Early to the grave; and he wrote vindictively of A. P. Hill and spitefully of Stonewall Jackson long after they were dead.

What Hill felt about Longstreet is unknown. Killed before the end of the war, he wrote nothing about the period, and his private papers were either destroyed or secreted. With all his affability, Hill revealed nothing intimate about himself in any exchanges that have been recorded, and his carelessness about administrative details made his reports sketchy and impersonal. But Hill was naturally courteous, and by the time the army marched north he and Longstreet were on what might be called speaking terms. There was definitely no more than surface civility between them.

Their relations presented another incalculable element in

81

Lee's new organization. The informal command system and discretionary orders favored by Lee presupposed co-operation among his subordinates. Once a battle was joined, communication by courier presented almost insuperable time hazards on a field of any size. Because no sort of communication system from general headquarters was possible, Lee depended on generals who used their own initiative. Some first-class fighting men had been transferrred out of Lee's army because of their inability to work well with brother officers, and an officer's ability to make decisions was a primary consideration in Lee's appraisal of him.

Powell Hill's decisiveness amounted almost to impetuosity. He was inclined to make decisions too quickly, too independently. He was one of the men really excited by battle action.

In addition to his impulsiveness and his uncordial relations with the First Corps commander, there was one other doubtful element in the general of the newly created Third Corps. His casual administrative methods would be taxed by a new organization in the artillery which placed more responsibility on the corps commanders and at the same time obscured the lines of authority in artillery command.

In the reorganization, Lee abandoned the old system in which each corps had its artillery and the army a general reserve commanded by Brigadier General William Nelson Pendleton. The reserve artillery was abolished. Each corps, with an artillery battalion attached to each of its divisions, was given its own reserve of two battalions. In turn, the colonel commanding a corps reserve supervised the artillery of his own corps. This change, designed for simplification, resulted in more confusion when vastly dignified General Pendleton was upped in title to Chief of Artillery with no guns to command.

This anomalous command was given Pendleton as a mistaken gesture of consideration for a loyal Confederate whom

Lee respected personally. A Virginia contemporary of Lee, fellow West Pointer and fellow Episcopalian, the rather slow-thinking Pendleton had early resigned from the old army to enter the ministry. At secession he had been rector of a church in Lexington, Virginia. There he formed the four-gun Rockbridge battery of neighborhood college students and named the guns (instead of numbering them) Matthew, Mark, Luke, and John. His rise was due largely to his administrative work, in which he was very fussy about details. At Chancellorsville he mishandled the guns under his immediate direction so badly that Lee did not include the Reverend General in the commendations in his report.

Lee's reports were very carefully written, with the assistance of his staff (especially Marshall), and his omissions conveyed as much as what he said. He was fair and studiedly specific in his praise, and, unless writing about an officer killed in action, he seldom used terms of eulogy. Only once did he apply an adjective to an officer below general rank, and that immortalized the young artillerist as "the gallant Pelham." Hence, in his Chancellorsville report, when he listed specific artillerists for citation and described their accomplishments, his omission of Pendleton was clearly a rebuke.

Because of the respect that the sometimes bumbling Pendleton commanded as a person, he was continued in a position of nominal authority without having any specific batteries on which to impose it. Pendleton assumed that he exercised a supervisory control over all artillery, and seemed to feel in no way ousted from command. In turn, the commanders of the corps artillery alternately deferred to him and forgot about him.

A. P. Hill assumed the unaccustomed command of artillery in a confusing and untried situation. However, when he received his promotion to lieutenant general, he foresaw no difficulties with the new arrangement in artillery and received his larger responsibilities without—at least, without revealing —any self-doubt. While not one of the Confederates in whom personal ambition burned, he was gratified by his advancement and happily accepted the congratulations of his friends and comrades.

In assuming command, he showed no effects of having operated under Stonewall Jackson's tight control. In his first assignment he acted with sound judgment, discretion, and decisiveness, vindicating the confidence Lee placed in him.

2

A. P. Hill's first assignment was one of real responsibility for a new corps commander. As if aware of his excitable nature, Hill acted with tensely alert caution when Lee's two corps moved north from Fredericksburg and left Hill to guard the Rappahannock River against thrusts from Hooker.

The country was brushy there, and in June the thick vines in the woods and along the winding roads made concealed movements easy for bodies of infantry. It was up to Hill to guard some twenty miles against surprise from an enemy that outnumbered him five to one, and, equally important, he must not be imposed upon by feints and demonstrations that might hide other purposes of Hooker's army. With Lee beginning the first tentative movements away from his base, it devolved on Hill to discover the enemy's intentions concerning a long-desired objective, the Confederate capital. Actually Hooker wanted to take advantage of Lee's audacious movement and drive on to Richmond, but he was overruled from Washington.

In this assignment Hill was not working with a well-organized corps that had its own systems already established. He was obliged to complete the organizational details of staff work and supply services and experiment with them in the face of a powerful, aggressive enemy. In Hill's three divisions, half of the brigades had never worked with the other half. In a newly formed division, two of the brigades had never before seen the Army of Northern Virginia. And the thirteen brigades, two of them under strength, represented a wide cross-section of the South: there were regiments from eight states.

The one tried division with which Hill was familiar was composed of four brigades from his own old Light Division. This was commanded by dark-bearded Dorsey Pender, a twenty-nine-year-old North Carolinian who, although he hoped that independence for the South would result from the invasion, wrote from Pennsylvania of his personal distaste for invading another people's land.

Only seven years out of West Point and the father of three sons (whom he was never to see again), combative Pender had risen on first-rate ability, steadfast ambition, and a headlong personal leadership in battle which gave a driving force to his brigade. Pender had been wounded four times, and at Chancellorsville he grabbed up the colors and rode at the head of his troops to the Federal works (he did not write his wife about this). In recommending him for promotion to major general, Hill said that he was "the best brigadier in the division."

Pender had hoped eagerly for Hill's promotion to corps command, for he expected his own advancement to follow, and he was troubled by no self-doubts at all. As a division commander he did not immediately win the liking of all his subordinates, and he soon admitted that he found his new responsibility "a heavy burden." An intelligent, reflective man, deeply religious and guided by a strong sense of duty, Dorsey Pender saw his division command essentially as opportunity to help win his country's independence and to establish his family in a good position in peacetime.

85

Of Pender's four proved brigades, all well led, two came from his native North Carolina, one from South Carolina, and one from Georgia.

The other veteran division, new to Hill, had been removed from Longstreet's corps—a fact that did not endear Powell Hill to Old Pete. This was commanded by efficient Richard Anderson, a forty-two-year-old regular-army man from South Carolina. In the old army he had distinguished himself in the Mexican War, and in the Confederacy, early in 1862, he was given a brigade in the division of Longstreet, his class-mate at West Point. The Federals' Abner Doubleday, with whom the Confederates were to have some trouble on July 1, had been in the same class.

After the Seven Days, Anderson's highly capable perform-ance was rewarded by promotion to major general. Judging solely on his performance, Lee regarded Dick Anderson as "a capital officer," high praise for him, and had him marked for future higher command. Personally courteous, Anderson lacked the color of those officers around whom legends grew. In an army with many prima donnas, he was a self-effacing man, neither seeking praise for himself nor winning support-ers by bestowing it on others.

Married to the daughter of a Chief Justice of Pennsylvania, Anderson lived a private life that was remote from the circle of "cousins" in Lee's army. He had been well liked in the First Corps, where he had grown accustomed to operating under the close supervision of his friend and former class-mate Longstreet.

Anderson was a stranger to A. P. Hill's personality and to his methods of operation—which, indeed, Hill as a corps com-mander had not yet established. After Longstreet's methodi-cal insistence that everything must be just so before he would venture into action, Hill's tendency to leap before he looked would probably offer a disturbing contrast. Certainly

Hill would not exercise so strong a control as Longstreet, and the unassertive Anderson's reaction to the new command was another incalculable of the reshuffled army.

Anderson's five brigades came from Virginia, Alabama, Mississippi, Georgia, and Florida.

Hill's third division, commanded by Harry Heth, was newly formed of two brigades from Hill's old division and the two new brigades that Jefferson Davis had forced on the already disrupted army organization. The North Carolina brigade was ably commanded by Johnston Pettigrew, but the newly organized Mississippi brigade was commanded by the president's inexperienced thirty-eight-year-old nephew, Joe Davis. He had never led in battle, and the best that seemed to be said of him was that he was unpretentious and, unlike his uncle, of agreeable personality.

The two veteran brigades from the Light Division were much reduced in numbers from the hard fighting at Chancellorsville. Even more serious was the fact that, while Archer's Alabama-Tennessee brigade was well led and had a fine combat reputation, the Virginia brigade had suffered from changes in leadership. Under Field the brigade had been one of the best in the army, but after wounds took Field out of action indefinitely, its regiments had deteriorated until Heth took them over. On his promotion to major general, the brigade had again come under its senior colonel, John Brockenbrough, and the men lacked the group spirit that characterized a crack brigade.

Harry Heth himself was an instance of the soundly trained soldier of perennial promise. Always seemingly on the verge of becoming truly outstanding, he never—for a variety of obscure reasons, including the luck of the game—lived up to the army's expectations.

He came of a Virginia family prominent in the Revolution and intimate with the Lees, and he was the only officer in

87

the army whom General Lee called by his first name. Eschewing the impressive beards of fashion, Harry Heth was clean-shaven except for a full mustache, and his pleasant face was dominated by a fine, broad brow. An honest man of charming personality, Heth, like A. P. Hill, was well liked for his social graces, and Powell Hill personally held him in great respect. Militarily, Hill thought Pender the better soldier.

It was hard to define the quality Heth lacked in battle, for he was brave, intelligent, and absolutely devoted to his duty. Hill and Lee still had expectations of him when he was promoted to major general, and friendly Heth, not at all assertive, seemed confident enough.

This new corps illustrates the makeshift nature of the reorganization of the whole army. The four best brigades from Hill's own division were kept intact, under the best division commander. The two weakest brigades numerically, one under dubious leadership, were joined to the new brigades to form a division under the second-best division commander, who was himself still unproved.

For practical purposes, the new divisions should have been formed with three brigades each from Hill's old division, and only one each of the new brigades. All the divisions in the army were allotted equal amounts of work and equal shares in responsibility. Confederate military organizations, however, were formed on many non-practical considerations. Political consideration for the several states influenced Jefferson Davis, who, in his mania for troop manipulation, was not aware of the intangibles that built morale necessary for team efforts.

Of Hill's new Third Corps it could at least be said that all seventeen of the general officers had demonstrated devotion to their country and all but two had been disciplined in the service of its best army. On the surface they operated at least adequately as a unit while confronted with no duty more taxing than guarding river-crossings. Hill was responsible for the only decisions to be made there, and these he made confidently and correctly.

Deciding that Hooker's noisy thrusts on the Confederate side of the river were no more than feints designed to feel him out, Hill kept up a bristly front of his own and, without calling for help, permitted Lee to complete the northward movement of his other two corps. This required no great sagacity on Hill's part. Even the battle-wise enlisted men in his command recognized Hooker's demonstrations for what they were. Hill did, however, reveal that sole responsibility for making crucial decisions when faced with a potential threat did not panic him, as it had many other officers. With his three divisions well contained, he waited without apprehension until the morning when the temporary city that was the Union camp (twenty times larger than century-old Fredericksburg) had vanished.

Then, duplicating Lee's piecemeal move, he put his three divisions into motion on successive days. Once on the march, Hill showed the effects of having served with Stonewall's fabled "foot cavalry." His men, well closed up, with colors flying, tramped mile after monotonous mile over the dusty roads, day after day, out of their familiar homeland into the strange country of the enemy, through heat and through rain, with the smallest number of stragglers the Army of Northern Virginia had ever had.

They were lean men in proudly worn tatters, with no more water weight than a prizefighter. Physically and morally toughened by hunger, exposure, hardship, and danger, they were welded together, despite the newness of the corps organization, by the single emotional bond of a common cause. In handling these citizens-into-soldiers on their grueling journey into a hostile land, A. P. Hill acquitted himself admirably. Officers and men of the only new corps in the army were developing a special pride by the time Heth's division went into camp outside Cashtown on June 30, with Pender's division close by and Anderson's a few miles away in the mountains.

Considering their unprecedented assignment to act, in the absence of cavalry, as reconnaissance troops in a country they had never seen, the men were unrealistically relaxed—from the privates in the 1st South Carolina, the oldest unit in point of organization, to the corps commander. When A. P. Hill rode into Cashtown at the end of the day and Harry Heth reported that Pettigrew's brigade had encountered some Yankee horsemen around Gettysburg, the corps commander was no more concerned than Heth had been. There was nothing about a scouting cavalry force to indicate the presence of the main Union army, which reports placed many miles away.

Actually, separated from the Confederates by low hills in the rolling farm country, the van of the Army of the Potomac was gathering in the same area, somewhat farther south of Gettysburg than Hill's corps was to the west of it. Nobody was looking for a battle. The two armies were looking for each other, each to discover the other's intention.

Meade did have his cavalry about him—although two of the divisions were off in the wake of Jeb Stuart, who that night was riding northward away from the gathering armies. The mounted division working out from the Union infantry was commanded by a rough fighter named Buford, and it was Buford's division that had run into the Confederate infantry brigade. A sound cavalry officer as well as a stout fighter, Buford had sent back the intelligence which caused three Union corps to be hurrying toward what might be a point of spontaneous contact. General Meade, with his army widely scattered, ordered these advanced corps to take the defensive if they encountered Lee's people.

Although none of this was known to the Third Corps officers on that summer night outside a Pennsylvania village,
Powell Hill was also under orders from Lee to avoid a "general engagement" if he encountered the enemy, because of
the dispersal of the Army of Northern Virginia. Thanks to Buford's cavalry, however, the Federals did know of the presence of Confederate infantry. Hill and his officers, made carelessly confident by the easy success of the invasion, rather
lightheartedly assumed that the Union horsemen were unsupported by infantry in force.

(As of June 30 they were not. With a night march of nine
miles Hill's men could have occupied what became the Union bastion of Cemetery Hill.)

Because no officer in Hill's corps anticipated real action in
that immediate area, Harry Heth kept uppermost in his mind
the quartermaster aspects of the invasion. Thus it was that he
mentioned to General Hill his desire to get shoes for his men
while discovering what troops might be in their front. Years
later, in remembering that quiet conversation with his former
West Point classmate, Heth quoted Napoleon as saying that
"a dogfight can bring on a battle." But on that summer night
in Cashtown military maxims were far from his mind.

He said to A. P. Hill: "I will take my division tomorrow
and go to Gettysburg and get those shoes, if there is no objection."

Hill replied without a second thought: "None in the
world," and unknowingly gave the order for the Battle of
Gettysburg.

3

The next morning Powell Hill showed the strain of his new
responsibility. He awakened feeling very ill, too sick to
mount his horse. Men noticed his extreme pallor. Although

no diagnosis was made, he was probably suffering from over-strained nerves. This indisposition was to recur frequently after that warm morning of July 1.

Perhaps during the night, after his offhand conversation with Heth, Hill had done some thinking about what might be hidden beyond the rough swells of farmland and woodland rolling eastward from the base of the mountain. He had sent word back to Lee that he was pushing out eastward in the morning, and also to Ewell, then hurrying southward from Carlisle, and said nothing whatsoever about shoes. To Ewell, who might get up to collaborate with him if he struck an enemy in force, he wrote (as he reported) "that I intended to advance the next morning and discover what was in my front."

In this probing action Hill was restrained by Lee's orders from bringing on a general engagement. Restraint was foreign to Hill's impulsive nature and strange to his experience as a division commander who had operated under the clearly specified objectives of Stonewall Jackson. It was not that soundly trained Hill lacked the skill to avoid commitment while making contact, but in some cases that was a hard thing to do. For the first time his was the sole responsibility for twenty thousand men, on whom the rest of the army was forming. In any event, Hill's sudden disability made it impossible for him to assume personal responsibility on July 1, 1863. He gave the field responsibility to Harry Heth because Heth's troops happened to be farthest advanced along the pike.

Hill ordered Heth to move out with caution, prepared for any eventuality. Heth was told that Pender's division also would be ordered on through Cashtown as a reserve to be available if Heth ran into serious trouble.

Between five and six o'clock, at full daylight on a sultry morning, Harry Heth, on his first battle assignment as a ma-

jor general, pushed out his four brigades in routine deployment for contact. In taking elementary precautions, Heth
gave no indication of sensing an impending clash of any consequence.

The brigades were sent into motion according to the positions where the men had slept during the night. Because of
this the troops deployed on the south of the turnpike were
the smallest brigade (1,048 officers and men) in the division.
Heroes of Chancellorsville, Archer's Alabama and Tennessee
veterans had not had their heavy losses made up. Since the
formation of the Light Division, the brigade had been commanded by James Archer, a forty-six-year-old Marylander
with a fine combat record. Archer was a slight man with a
thin face elongated by a dark, narrow beard, and it would
seem that on that July morning he was suffering from some
debilitating ailment.

By the same chance deployment, to the left of the turnpike
went the new Mississippi brigade under the president's inexperienced nephew, Joe Davis. Only two of the regiments
were veterans. One of these, the 11th Mississippi, formed
around the nucleus of a company of University of Mississippi
students, had fought with distinction in Virginia during the
first year, but all of the troops were strangers to Lee's army.

Behind these advanced brigades, Pettigrew's and Brockenbrough's troops deployed in reserve. Along the narrow,
fence-lined road rumbled the twenty guns of a reserve battalion commanded by bespectacled Willie Pegram, a greatly
loved and highly accomplished young Richmonder.

In orthodox Confederate fashion, the two leading brigades
sent out skirmishers in three lines, bouncing on rope-
muscled legs through wheatfields and over stubble, studying
each rise as they approached with their bright rifles ready.
The sun climbed higher, the day grew hot, and the skirmish
lines had covered five miles before the first shots crackled

93

ahead of them. At the whine of Minié balls, the men saw the separate spurts of smoke that come from a line of pickets, and they identified the light firing as carbine fire. This was the cavalry the Confederates expected.

The skirmish lines moved ahead more slowly, more warily, and the deployed regiments came up in closer support. Buford's dismounted troopers, apparently unsupported, fell back firing before the steady advance.

By ten o'clock the lead brigades had moved ahead two more miles and were within one mile of Gettysburg. Then guns began to roar and shrapnel hurtled through the air, tearing past the men and thudding into trees and into the rich earth. There were six guns of regular army artillery, firing in sections. Heth did not know that these cannon were the only ones Buford had with him. The Confederates looked for depressions in the ground, fence posts, any slight cover where they could wait for their own artillery to open up and develop the enemy's situation.

After tearing down the fence railing, Willie Pegram got his pieces unlimbered across the road. His experienced gunners soon found the range of the enemy guns and began raining metal among the Federal gun crews.

The enemy's artillery was posted on a low ridge on the far side of a wooded ravine that cut between the two lines. At the bottom of the ravine ran a brook called Willoughby Run. On the right of the road the hill leading up to the Union position was covered with a thick growth of trees. As a routine precaution, Willie Pegram shelled the woods. The answering fire grew no heavier. General Heth concluded that he was facing nothing more than the Federal cavalry that Pettigrew had encountered on the previous day. He ordered his two leading brigades forward.

The men grew aware of the increasing warmth of the day as they lunged down the hill to Willoughby Run. On the right of the road the men of Archer's thinned-out brigade encountered a fence to be climbed before they crossed the run. Their order became a little loose as the whole brigade started scrambling up the hill.

Ahead the underbrush suddenly blazed out at them. The heavy oyster-white Minié balls tore through the ranks, many lodging in lean bodies. Amid sudden groans wrenched from the wounded and the startled calls of officers, the men burrowed close to the earth, sought shelter behind trees, and began to return the fire.

They were facing the first brigade of Doubleday's division of Reynolds's I Corps, rushed hastily onto the field at the urging of Buford. Appropriately called the "Iron Brigade," the Midwesterners were hard-bitten troops with justifiable pride in their prowess. The Iron Brigade was down to under two thousand in strength, but at the point of contact they heavily outnumbered the one brigade they met, Archer's. The Alabama and Tennessee boys recognized the black hats affected by the men of the Iron Brigade. Whatever the high command of Lee's army thought, the men of Archer's brigade now knew that they had stumbled into the Army of the Potomac.

4

While the Confederate field officers were trying to bring order to the four thin regiments on the wooded slope of the ravine, a reserve regiment of the Iron Brigade worked around in the woods to the Confederates' right, overlapping them. Suddenly they came rushing out of the obscuring brush on Archer's flank, hurrahing and shooting. The experienced Southern soldiers knew that it was time to get out of there.

No veteran troops on either side, by this stage of the war, had any shame about the manner of their leaving an uncomfortable spot. They had often proved the adage about the runner living to fight another day, and they would fight on another day or in another hour, for that matter—as soon as conditions were favorable. Archer's men went pell-mell down the hill and across the brook. Some piled up at the fence.

While the last were scrambling over, the black-hatted Federals swooped down along their flank and captured a number of the disgusted Rebels. Most humiliating of all, Archer, suffering his curious exhaustion, was waiting to have a try at the fence when he was pounced upon by a burly Union private and wrestled into submission. When Archer was led off, as mad as a wet hen, his capture marked another ominous portent for the reorganized army: he was the first general officer taken prisoner since Lee had assumed command thirteen months before. Archer remained in prison more than a year and died in October 1864, shortly after his release.

While Archer's leaderless men scrambled up the safe slope of the wooded ravine, things were going even worse on the other side of the Cashtown turnpike.

There Joseph Davis's Mississippians had made their contact with Union infantry in the open and had not suffered the surprise of Archer's men. Nor had they struck anything quite the likes of the Iron Brigade. As a consequence, they had enjoyed a gratifying local success. They drove before them all except one Union regiment. This, failing to receive orders to retreat, held its ground with the support of a fresh six-gun battery whose gunners simply refused to quit.

In working forward to clear the last remaining obstacles, Joe Davis by ill chance discovered the deep cut of the unfinished railroad bed. This cut ran parallel to the road and passed at right angles to the skimpy remnants of the Union line. It seemed to inexperienced Davis a heaven-sent cover for getting on the enemy's flank without exposure.

General Abner Doubleday, with everything working to his

advantage in the extemporized action, hurriedly brought up a reserve regiment to support his flank. They arrived at the railroad cut, where they found the Confederates lined up below them. It was like shooting fish in a barrel.

The sudden helplessness froze the green troops in the brigade. They huddled against the dirt wall of the cut until triumphant yells of "Surrender!" allowed them to throw down their arms and save their lives. The veterans tried to run the gauntlet to safety. Those who were not shot in the backs escaped, but the unit was too disorganized to be of any further use in the immediate action.

Harry Heth had not exercised the close field command by means of which Doubleday had won the brief, furious action. But when Heth saw his two brigades stagger back up the ravine, with Davis's temporarily wrecked, he acted in soldierly fashion.

He reformed Archer's stung veterans, placed Colonel Fry in command, and shifted them farther to the right, stretching beyond the point where they had been overlapped. Davis's brigade was pulled out on the left and its segments were sent to the rear to reform. Brockenbrough's veterans took their place near one of the huge stone barns that were a constant wonder to the Southerners. These men stretched somewhat farther to the left, or north, side of the turnpike than had Davis. In the center, between the two brigades, Johnston Pettigrew moved up his North Carolinians.

Willie Pegram's guns continued to bang away, and David McIntosh's battalion from the reserve artillery galloped up and unlimbered their pieces.

Caught behind in the initial contact, Harry Heth had taken every precaution against a counterattack by the enemy. His division also stood in strong line of battle for an advance if that became indicated. Beyond that he plainly did not know what to do. Anxiously he surveyed the scene, where sharpshooters blazed away during the uncertain lull, and tried to reach a decision.

The shoes in Gettysburg forgotten, Heth concentrated on that part of his orders which (properly the function of Stuart's cavalry) concerned reconnaissance. There was no doubt that he had found the enemy, though what proportion of the Army of the Potomac was there he could not even guess.

It would be reckless to push against those smoke-veiled woods again without the support of Pender, who was now hurrying his four brigades from A. P. Hill's old division over the turnpike from Cashtown. Besides, there was the other part of Heth's orders which cautioned against bringing on a general engagement. In his dilemma, Harry Heth, a brigadier one month before, became unhappily aware that he was commanding general on a strange field.

With what turned out to be the wisdom of discretion, General Heth did what he had done as a brigadier in Hill's division: he waited for A. P. Hill and orders.

5

Hill had stayed in, camp at Cashtown, through which Pender's division had passed and where the men of Anderson's division were streaming down from the mountain pass. The firing seven miles away came clearly to the sick man, and the roll of artillery seemed all out of proportion to a "feeling-out" of the enemy. Heth had sent back no information about what he had stirred up, and Hill was anxious as to how his corps would perform in its first encounter with the enemy.

In the midst of Hill's pondering, General Lee and his staff galloped down the mountain road into the village. Lee had been proceeding leisurely with Longstreet in the direction of Cashtown, where he planned to establish headquarters, when the sound of heavy firing had sent him hastening through the mountain pass.

The commanding general, mounted on his gray horse, Traveler, was finding it difficult to keep his composure. While his outward calm was impressive, he was clearly suppressing anxiety and excitement as he reined in and asked A. P. Hill what the firing meant.

Hill could only say that he was wondering himself, for Heth had orders not to develop an action. He would go himself to find out. Weakly he mounted his horse and advanced along the turnpike, which became increasingly crowded with ambulances moving up, wounded and stragglers limping back, and Pender's veteran brigades pushing ahead toward the sound of the firing.

Lee showed his desperation for information by summoning Dick Anderson, in whose competence he placed reliance. Anderson's division was then passing over the street where, for a short space, the turnpike became Cashtown, and he confessed that he had no notion of what was going on. He knew only that General Hill had ordered him to hurry toward the scene of action.

In the mountain roads behind them, two of Longstreet's divisions were held up by the passage of Ewell's wagons. At Chambersburg, Pickett was just being relieved of rear-guard duty by the appearance of Imboden's cavalry. These raiders had finished their personal foraging and flank duty, but the belatedness of their arrival prevented Pickett's three brigades from figuring in whatever action was developing. On other roads Ewell's three divisions were pushing toward Cashtown or Gettysburg without urgency. It was not a situation in which to open a battle. Yet plainly it was the volume of full-scale fighting that rolled back from the farmland to the east.

Sitting on his gray horse, General Lee at last admitted in

99

words his apprehension over Stuart's absence. "I cannot think what has become of Stuart," he said to Anderson. "I ought to have heard from him long before now. He may have met with some disaster, but I hope not."

Modest Anderson remained silent.

Lee, his dark eyes staring into the distance, spoke aloud his thoughts. "In the absence of any reports from him, I am in ignorance as to what we have in front of us here. It may be the whole Federal army, it may be only a detachment. If it is the whole Federal army, we must fight a battle here."

He seemed to regard the prospect with foreboding, for his final remark sounded a defensive note unusual in Lee. He murmured: "If we do not gain a victory, those defiles and gorges which we passed this morning will shelter us from disaster."

Then, as if to shake off his apprehensions by movement, Lee nudged his horse impatiently ahead, out of the village. Once on the turnpike, with his staff following, he urged Traveler into a gallop.

The small cavalcade had covered five miles toward the deepening sound when they passed between the ranks of Pender's troops deployed for action. Ahead Lee saw the mists of battle smoke hanging like ground fog over the ravine of Willoughby Run and spreading in an arc north of the turn-pike.

Captain Smith, the former staff officer of Stonewall Jackson who had joined Lee's headquarters at Chambersburg, had remained temporarily with Lee's staff and was in the group riding along the Cashtown pike. Smith reported that Lee surveyed the size of the action with surprise, and that the developing engagement was "something spoken of with regret."

Whatever his exact words may have been, when Lee pulled his horse off the road about three miles from Gettysburg, evidently his intention was to investigate the possibility of breaking off the action.

Harry Heth, writing later of blundering into the Army of the Potomac, said: "Without Stuart the army was like a blind-folded giant." When Lee, with steady hands, brought his field glasses to his eyes, he was probably searching the strange terrain for ways to extricate this segment of his army and complete the convergence of his corps and wagons.

From his remarks to Anderson in Cashtown, it would seem that he was thinking of a defensive stand, as at Sharpsburg the year before. With the enemy coming at his own united army, he would be relieved of the embarrassment of Stuart's absence.

Yet, even as Lee's field glasses focused on the town of Gettysburg and the ranges of hills spreading out from it, messages coming in from subordinates brought the news that troops from Ewell's corps had joined the action and were extending the size of the engagement.

Rodes's and Johnson's divisions of Ewell's corps were the troops that, occupying Carlisle, had been preparing to take the state capital at Harrisburg when reached by Lee's order to contract toward Gettysburg. These two divisions and Jubal Early's division, hurrying southwestward from York, had, with A. P. Hill's old division, composed Stonewall Jackson's Second Corps—the mobile striking force. Under Old Jack the troops had been famed for their marching and their guile-fulness at evading Jackson's discipline to forage for food and forbidden liquors. Under their new lieutenant general, Dick Ewell, the corps seemed to be carrying on the Jacksonian traditions.

In leaving Carlisle, the men of Rodes's division, moving rapidly in a loose, shuffling gait, had marched southeast all day on June 30. On the warm morning of July 1, while some miles from Gettysburg, they heard the dueling guns of Heth and Doubleday. With soldierly instinct Rodes hurried his men to the sound of the firing. Knowing no more of what was happening than did anyone else, Rodes, by the chance direction of his march, brought his men into the rough, rolling country squarely on the flank of the Union troops facing Heth less than a mile west of Gettysburg.

Through the vigilance of Buford's cavalry, the Federal infantry was warned of this threat developing on their right.

The Union force that Meade had rushed toward Gettysburg was composed of two corps of three divisions each. As the Army of the Potomac was not then formed into army groups of corps, Meade had given acting field command of the advance corps to Major General John F. Reynolds, commander of the first corps. Reynolds, a native Pennsylvanian and friend of many Southerners from the old army, was shot by a Confederate sharpshooter while directing the placing of the troops early in the day. Major General Abner Doubleday, commander of Reynolds's first division, had been handling the corps while Reynolds was supervising the whole action. In the absence of any other authority, he assumed command of the field on Reynolds's death.

A regular army man in his mid-forties, Doubleday was not restrained by modesty. He seized the opportunity offered by the sudden responsibility. Perhaps made overconfident by his repulse of Heth's two brigades, Doubleday handled the troops in detail with decisiveness, but he remained in what obviously was becoming a poor defensive position. As new Union divisions hurried to the field, Doubleday held a line facing Heth and, in some confusion of command between himself and a newly arriving corps commander, formed fresh troops at a right angle to his Willoughby Run position to meet the thrust of Rodes from the northwest.

With one force facing west and the other northwest, the Federals were fighting two battles under a single, if unclarified, control. At the same stage the Confederates were fighting two battles under no control. Rodes, also new to division command, was sending in his men too fast, and they were getting the same rough reception that Heth's two separated brigades had encountered.

This situation was gradually revealed to General Lee as he studied the field and received reports from officers. Harry Heth, who had been waiting uncertainly for several hours while he continued desultory firing, saw Lee's group beside the road and went over to the commanding general.

"Rodes is heavily engaged," he said to Lee. "Had I not better attack?"

"No," Lee said slowly, studying the confused, extemporized action. Then he said more decisively: "No, I am not prepared to bring on a general engagement today. Longstreet is not up."

It was now three o'clock in the afternoon. The only heavy fighting was Rodes's action to the left of the turnpike and northwest of the town. There the Confederate troops, unable to gain the position, were in greater difficulties than was apparent to Lee's group. While Lee was pondering resolutions, Powell Hill rode up, his looks reflecting his illness. Hill had been with Pender while his own old division deployed for action. Little Powell, sick or well, always wanted to carry any action to a conclusion, and his mind was on attack.

Suddenly a fresh action developed to the northeast. Lee soon learned that the firing had been opened by Jubal Early's division of Ewell's corps. Early, moving southward from Heidlersburg, had been attracted by the sound of the firing and hurried toward it. His march brought his division onto the field on the left of Rodes's heavily engaged men. Naturally aggressive and a well-trained soldier, Early threw in his brigades on the Federal's right flank, overlapping it.

The Union right angle of defense now stretched from west

of Gettysburg (facing Heth), to north and west (facing Rodes), to north and east of the town, where Early's fresh men came yelling onto the field. Although General Lee had never seen the country before and was still in doubt as to the size of the Union force against him, the Federals' defense situation became too vulnerable for Lee to allow the opportunity of attack to pass.

An opportunist, like all great generals, he had watched the chance of march unfold a battle precisely of the nature he would have planned, and instantly he acted as if he had planned it. Most of his successful offensive maneuvers involved large troop movements to get on or behind an exposed flank of the enemy. Once he had observed that the extemporized troop movements had achieved the same end as his planned maneuvers, he was ready to send in the whole line with all he had.

After Jackson's death, the usually gentle Lee was the most combative general officer in the army, and attack always sent his adrenalin soaring. His rigid self-control relaxed, his handsome face grew animated, the burdening years rolled away, and his eyes flashed like a young man's. All uncertainty fled, and he knew precisely what he wanted each unit to do.

With no time to write orders, he sent his staff officers galloping off. Captain Smith was sent to Lieutenant General Ewell, reporting for staff duty as he delivered a message. Lee's commands for A. P. Hill's Third Corps were given directly to Little Powell.

Pale though Hill might be, direct action sustained him too, and there was nothing of a sick man about the new corps commander as he rode to his own men with the orders for assault. Maybe General Lee had not wanted a general engagement, but, now that it had come, Powell Hill was freed of his unnatural restraint. He was going to send in his troops as they had always gone in—and nothing would stop them.

104

6

Harry Heth was eager to wipe out the morning's mistakes of carelessness. When he urged three of his brigades forward over the ground where they had been turned back earlier, there were no elements of surprise or tactical outmaneuvering to throw his men off stride. They advanced in a solid line, spraying bullets ahead of them in sheets. The blue line they struck was equally solid. It became a soldiers' fight there on the hilly ground—some open land, some wheatfields, some woods, with fences running everywhere.

The Confederates had the psychological advantage of the initiative, the Federals the disadvantage of awareness of heavy pressure on their distant flank. The Federals fought with a cold determination to hold the ground. The Confederates attacked with a hot determination to drive everything before them.

In savagely reckless thrusts, not counting the toll of dead and wounded who fell among them, the Confederates nudged back the defensive line. The Union units gave ground grudgingly, forced back step by step. The Iron Brigade left neat rows of dead lined up on the ground. But the Federals were not breaking. At one point, it was the waves coming at them which were on the verge of breaking against their stubborn line. Casualties among Heth's troops were passing the proportion beyond which attacking units cannot remain effective.

At this point, a shell fragment struck Harry Heth on the side of the head. He fell from his horse in a limp heap. His staff rushed to him, thinking he had been killed outright. He was still breathing. Unconscious, he would regain his senses by nightfall. Heth's life had been saved by the accident of not being able to get a hat that fitted in Cashtown: the paper padding in the sweatband had prevented the shell fragment from piercing his skull. After a poor morning of the blundering contact that brought on the engagement, Heth was removed from action at the climax of his hour.

A. P. Hill, in his first field command of a corps, recognized that the tide of Heth's troops was spent. As his former classmate went down, Hill sent in Pender's division with fresh momentum.

To these four brigades of Hill's old division, thrusts in virtual parade-ground order had become ingrained. They went in fast, screaming their high, eerie battle yell, but they went in solidly. Their regimental units as cohesive as a fist, they poured out the tremendous firepower that characterized all of Lee's best veteran brigades.

Dorsey Pender, who wrote the reflective letters to his wife in North Carolina, had been a hard-driving commander of one of these brigades. Taking a division of four of them into action for the first time, Pender handled the larger force with the same control he had exerted on a brigade. Something of his own dark force fused with the confidence and the discipline of the experienced fighters to send masses lunging forward like indestructible objects.

His troops had been tired before they went in. After their ten-mile walk from west of Cashtown in the sultry weather, they had suffered the mental strain of waiting under fire, of small advances in the open and then waiting again. A private in the 1st South Carolina, formed before Sumter, said that "these advances in the line of battle are the most fatiguing exercise I had in the army. . . . The perspiration poured from our bodies." Waiting, they heard the screams in the ambulances crowding the narrow turnpike, saw the slack-faced wounded staggering past them, huddled under bursting shells and stray bullets with no one to shoot at—and had time to think.

Plunging ahead under Dorsey Pender's fierce resolution

was a relief after the waiting. Down the ravine they went, where Heth's men had marched so lightheartedly in the morning, across the stream, and up the open hill that Heth's men had just won at the cost of fighting themselves out. Nearest the turnpike, where Pettigrew's North Carolinians had carried the hill, the 1st South Carolina moved with their brigade.

This brigade, created as a state unit of hot-bloods before the Confederacy was formed, had originally been commanded by Maxcy Gregg, and they were the first Southern troops to parade in Richmond when Virginia seceded in protest against the invasion of the newly formed Confederacy. They had marched down Franklin Street, their band playing "The Bonnie Blue Flag," on their way to drive the Yankees back North so that they themselves could go home in peace. That had been more than two years before. Gregg had been killed at Fredericksburg, and McGowan, his successor, was absent because of wounds; on the Cashtown turnpike the hard-bitten survivors of the original young chevaliers were commanded by a colonel, Abner Perrin.

Although their elaborate uniforms had long since given way to the frazzled butternut and patched makeshifts worn indistinguishably by ante-bellum princelings and paupers, although most of their body servants had been sent home and their mess chests no longer contained the imported wines that made their suppers social events in the early days, their new commander, Colonel Perrin, rode in front of the troops, sword in hand, wearing a tailored cadet-cloth uniform with shining buttons—a bright target against the background of faded gray.

On the smooth plateau beyond the hill, Perrin's brigade passed through the ranks of Pettigrew's halted men. The two-year veterans observed the spent men of the North Carolina brigade that Jefferson Davis had forced on Lee, and one

107

said: "They had fought well but, like most new soldiers, had been content to stand and fire, instead of charging." That statement was a little less than just to the troops who, under Pettigrew, had pressed steadily forward in the face of galling fire; it was, however, an essentially sound judgment by an experienced soldier of the specific requirements for a successful attack.

Then from across the open plain the brigade came under the fire that had checked the advance of Pettigrew. "The artillery of the enemy opened upon us with a fatal accuracy. . . . Still we advanced, with regular steps and a well-dressed line. . . . Shell and cannister continued to rain upon us. A good many were killed and disabled. . . ." Next "the Federal infantry opened on us a repetition of the fire that had already slaughtered a brigade (Pettigrew's). This was particularly heavy on the two right regiments, for at that point the enemy was protected by a stone wall.

"Still . . . the line passed on, many of the men throwing away their blankets and haversacks to keep up. Struggling and panting, but cheering and closing up, they went, through the shell, through the Minie balls, heeding neither the dead who sank down by their sides, nor the fire from the front which killed them, until they threw themselves desperately on the line of Federals and swept them from the field."

The stubborn Union line did not break all at once. The Confederates kept up the pressure, and the Federals were given no chance to reform. As soon as some units found an island of natural defense for a stand, other parts of their line were forced back and the defenders came under enfilade fire.

Pender's other three brigades were forcing their way through the more obstructed areas on the right with the same unremitting drive. Then, on the left of Pender's division, the right of Rodes's division of Ewell's corps thrust in from the northwest and made contact. Suddenly all the pieces of

108

the Confederates' extemporized action came together, and
the separate battles became one. The weakened Union defensive line was enveloped at the crest of the single attacking
wave, and, the South Carolinian reported, "they then gave
back at all points, and the rebel turn came to kill."

"As the disordered mass fled toward Gettysburg," Pender's
division began to lose order in chasing the Federals who had
inflicted such heavy losses on them. Groups of the 1st South
Carolina raced on tired legs to get the gun crews, toward
whom they felt especially vengeful. The Union gunners got
their pieces out fast, losing some men, and the exhausted
Confederates could get close enough only to finish off one
crew and capture its gun.

With the flesh no longer able to sustain the spirit, the men
of Perrin's brigade stumbled on toward Gettysburg in the
wake of the fugitives. To their right the other brigades had
rougher going on the slopes of Seminary Ridge, named for
the Lutheran seminary whose cupola rose out of the mists of
smoke. By the time they had cleared Seminary Ridge of the
enemy, the men of those three brigades were in no mood to
give chase. They began to look for water for their parched
throats.

Perrin's brigade, gathering prisoners as they went, made it
all the way into the town. The 1st South Carolina Regiment
claimed that theirs was the first Confederate flag raised in
Gettysburg.

General Pender rode into town to survey the new situation, raising his hat to the men of Perrin's brigade as he
passed them. Other general officers were coming in with the
soldiers of Ewell's corps. Unarmed Federals were everywhere, nearly five thousand to be gathered as prisoners. It
would have been hard to decide whether the Federals or the
Confederates were the more surprised by the stampede that
had ended the unexpected collision of the armies.

109

The confusion in the streets grew. Farther back in town, sniping went on from the windows of houses. In the distance, light sporadic fire broke out and ceased. Pender's officers began to collect the men who, disintegrating into small units, were engaged in little more than half-bewildered sightseeing. The more voracious had found frightened families who would hand over food, and the dyed-in-the-wool foragers were searching for henhouses. Some just sat down in the street, resting against the sides of buildings.

Some time after four o'clock they had all been collected and withdrawn to the west of town. There they formed in a skirmish line that extended up onto Seminary Ridge, where the other brigades were resting.

A. P. Hill was up there, studying the condition of his units. There was enough daylight left for a pursuit that would complete the victory, but Hill decided that other units would have to do it. His brigades had suffered fearful casualties. The survivors had been at it since five in the morning and looked done in. Hill felt that no more should be asked of the men today. Actually, it was the time for the cavalry. As he said, "The want of cavalry . . . was again seriously felt."

At half past four A. P. Hill mounted his horse and rode to report to General Lee.

7

The commanding general had established temporary headquarters alongside the turnpike, across the road from a small stone house. As Hill approached, Lee and his staff were standing on the grassy edge of Seminary Ridge, from where the general was studying the movement and terrain below him.

Gettysburg lay about half a mile below, and he could see the confusion of sudden victory in the streets. Southward from the town a street extended for a quarter of a mile up a sharp incline and leveled out at the top of a steep hill, where it divided into the Baltimore pike and the Emmitsburg road. On the plateau an arched brick gateway opened southward into the Evergreen Cemetery, giving the name of Cemetery Hill to that end of a ridge. This ridge ran from north to south, roughly paralleling the rise on which Lee stood.

Through his field glasses he could see the disordered Federal units who, retreating through Gettysburg, were reforming on Cemetery Hill. The position where they were seeking safety was given great natural strength by the angle at which that end of the ridge extended eastward from Cemetery Hill, like the foot of a boot. This rocky extension, called Culp's Hill, presented a precipitous front facing northward. The sloping front of Cemetery Hill faced westward toward Lee. The Federal troops were placing themselves within the right angle of a natural fortress.

The Baltimore pike, crossing the hill from the southeast, was the route by which Federal reinforcements would hurry to check the broken retreat of the van of the army. Lee could see blue troops and guns scurrying southward along the ridge. They were drawing a defensive line from the right angle at Cemetery Hill along the leg of the boot across from him.

This ridge, Cemetery Ridge, ran southward for two miles and ended in rocky peaks called Round Top and Little Round Top. The crest of that ridge was a little more than three quarters of a mile from where Lee stood. Between the two rises, small farms lay on the slopes of the shallow valley, along the floor of which ran the Emmitsburg road.

It was obvious to Lee, and to all the men staring beyond Gettysburg, that either Cemetery Hill or the ridge extending southward had to be taken to complete the victory of the spontaneous clash. Only one of the positions needed to be occupied, since occupancy of either would expose the other to enfilade fire. If neither was occupied, the whole Union army could converge on that natural fortress and take a strong defensive position. The day's success would be reduced to a local action without meaning and won at extremely heavy cost in casualties.

Repeatedly, in Virginia, Lee had failed to reap any fruits from military victories, partly because of the lack of manpower to follow up an action and partly because of the barren defensive lines that Davis's policy of holding ground forced him to adopt. Here, Lee could not afford another such barren victory. He would never have more men than he had now, and never a better opportunity to drive home a stroke for independence. His decision to attack one of the two defensive positions south of Gettysburg was already made: he was considering the details of what units to use for the final attack when A. P. Hill rode up to the group.

According to a British observer, Little Powell looked "very delicate" as he reported to General Lee. Hill too had noticed the Union reinforcements gathering on the opposite ridge, and he admitted that he did not believe his troops were in condition to clear the ridge. Casualties had been heavy, units were disorganized by the furious fighting and the chaotic pursuit, the men were close to exhaustion, and ammunition was running low. In some regiments, all ammunition was gone.

It is possible that the relentless Jackson would have spent an hour reorganizing his units while the men refreshed themselves, redistributed ammunition as far as it would go, ordered the men to fix bayonets, and driven those able across the rough, shallow valley the 1,400 yards to Cemetery Ridge. It is possible.

Hill and his best division had served with Old Jack, and he did not believe that his men were capable of another attacking effort. Some had staggered when they tried to run toward the Union guns barely an hour before, and all were puffing and stumbling on their last climb up Seminary Ridge. It was known that Hill was more indulgent of his men than Jackson. It was also known that in battle he never counted costs, but demanded all that flesh could endure. He was a natural attacker, and if he believed his men incapable of mounting the final attack, Lee must accept his judgment.

The conclusive action must therefore be made against the precipitous right angle of Cemetery Hill and Culp's Hill. Once that position was in Confederate hands, the Federals would find south-running Cemetery Ridge untenable. Union reinforcements and the survivors of the day's fighting would be forced back on the main army before Meade could complete his convergence. Then it would devolve on Lee's old army friend to find a way to get at *him*.

The assignment would go to Ewell's men. Rodes's division had been roughly handled, but Early's division had enjoyed the happy chore of delivering the knockdown to a reeling enemy. They were unworn and eager to finish the job. Rodes's people could reform for a reserve, and Allegheny Johnson was bringing Ewell's third division to the field. That division had once been Old Jack's, and it contained Jackson's original command, the brigade that had petitioned the government after Jackson's death to be officially designated as the "Stonewall Brigade."

The whole corps had been trained and conditioned in the stern school of Stonewall Jackson. The men had thus far given every evidence of carrying on their tradition of almost inexhaustible mobility and a swift and terrible striking power. With two divisions on the ground that was to be attacked, and one fresh coming up, it would be a tribute to Stonewall's memory to allow his Second Corps to complete the day's triumph.

Lee turned to his young A.A.G., Walter Taylor, and gave him an oral order to be carried quickly to General Ewell. According to his own report, Lee told Taylor to tell Ewell "to carry the hill occupied by the enemy, if he found it practicable, but to avoid a general engagement until the arrival of the other divisions of the army. . . ."

As Taylor's independent report used virtually identical language regarding his instructions to Ewell, there is no doubt that the Second Corps commander knew what was expected of him when Colonel Taylor delivered the message around five o'clock. Night would not fall until eight. Ewell had three hours in which to do the job.

8

While Taylor was receiving the instructions and mounting his horse, A. P. Hill joined Colonel Fremantle, of Her Majesty's Coldstream Guards, and told him of the day's fighting. From the sweeping action that had brought a victory, Hill's mind retained most vividly the memory of a Federal color-bearer who had been the last man to quit the field. Even as he retreated, the soldier shook his fist at the oncoming Confederates, and Powell Hill said that he was very sorry to see "this gallant Yankee" finally fall. Hill's training with Jackson could not affect his sensitive nature.

In a similar scene, when one of Jackson's colonels captured three Federals instead of shooting them, because the colonel admired their bravery, Stonewall said: "Kill them all. I don't want them to be brave."

War never became that stern for Powell Hill. The year before, the Federals' indomitable Phil Kearney, a one-armed general, had been shot dead from his horse in the wet woods near a destroyed plantation. When Hill saw his body in the muck, he became very emotional and exclaimed: "Poor Kearney. He deserved a better death than this."

114

"And Then A. P. Hill Came Up . . ."

Hill was instructed by General Lee to place some of his guns in a position to sweep Cemetery Ridge. He was to open a fire that would divert the Federals' full attention from Ewell's forthcoming attack and prevent reinforcements from moving to the Cemetery Hill—Culp's Hill objective. Hill rode back to his own men who were lying along Seminary Ridge.

While Lee was waiting for Ewell to open his action, his group was joined by Longstreet. The burly commander of the First Corps had ridden well ahead of his troops, in order to see for himself the field of the sudden collision. After a brief survey of the terrain across from them, Longstreet surprisingly turned to the commanding general and began to advise him as to what course of action to follow.

According to Longstreet, he said: "All we have to do is to throw our army around by their left, and we shall interpose between the Federal army and Washington." Following this statement, Longstreet began to develop the possibilities of his strategy. It would force Meade to attack them, and after they had beaten Meade (as he assumed they would), "the possibilities are that the fruits of our success will be great."

This curious advice in the midst of a battle came from the one corps commander who had taken no part in the day's action, whose troops were not on the field, and who had glanced only briefly at the results of the fighting.

However, unknown to Lee, this suggestion of shifting to defense sprang from a long-held conviction of the way the invasion should be conducted, and Longstreet believed that he had imposed this conviction on the commanding general. Some days before, when the corps commander first offered his views, Lee had given a customarily courteous reply and dismissed the matter from his mind. He was not aware now that Longstreet on Seminary Ridge was speaking in terms of what he considered an agreement. As for the proposal that advised him to break off the completion of this successful ac-

115

tion and shift around to the enemy's left, Lee was too preoccupied even to answer it specifically. Having blundered into one fight without the mysteriously vanished cavalry, he certainly had no intention of starting out again blindfolded over rough terrain while his wagons and divisions were scattered all through South Mountain.

He replied simply: "If the enemy is there, we must attack him."

Longstreet would not quit his argument. "If he is there, it will be because he is anxious that we attack him—a good reason, in my judgment, for not doing so."

Lee did not answer that at all. He knew that the enemy was on the opposite ridge for the same reason that he was on Seminary Ridge: those were the positions to which the surprising fighting had led them. Concentrating on a study of the terrain, Lee apparently did not even listen when Longstreet went on with what amounted to an insubordinate harangue.

In Longstreet's later apologies he attributed to himself some impassioned dialogue that no one close by on the field remembered him speaking. In fact, the staff officers and military observers were as intent on surveying the enemy's ground as was Lee, and no one seems to have paid particular attention to the corps commander whom they regarded as "Lee's Warhorse." Whatever he actually said, Longstreet was in a strangely disturbed state of mind.

Actually, he had convinced himself that since Jackson's death he had replaced Stonewall as Lee's collaborator. But he conceived of the collaboration in a way that Old Jack never had—as something of an equal partnership. What Longstreet was suffering on that open field on Seminary Ridge was the shock of discovering that the partnership existed only in his mind. Instead of accepting his collaboration, Lee

116

was dismissing his strategy as he would that of any subordinate officer. Bewildered and incredulous, Longstreet simply could not accept the repudiation of the relationship as he had conceived it.

Everybody had talked about the whispered night conference of Lee and Jackson before Chancellorsville. In his intense jealousy of Jackson's fame, Longstreet had always belittled Stonewall's accomplishments, and to his unreflective mind it must have followed naturally that it would be "Lee and Longstreet" with their heads together on the invasion. But General Lee was not even listening to him: he was listening for the guns that would announce the opening of Ewell's attack.

While Longstreet was glumly brooding, Captain Smith rode up on his first assignment since joining Ewell's staff. Like Taylor, whom he had passed without seeing on the way over, Smith brought an oral message.

Ewell had instructed him to say that Early and Rodes believed they could take Cemetery Hill if other troops would support them with an attack on Cemetery Ridge. Oddly, division commanders Early and Rodes, and not corps commander Ewell, had independently decided on the same course of action as had Lee for concluding the day's success.

Lee told Captain Smith that he had no troops on hand for taking Cemetery Ridge. Then, turning to Longstreet, he asked where his First Corps troops were. It was a question the commanding general would have directed to any troop commander. Longstreet, puzzled and agitated, took no interest at all in the field before them. Muttering that one division was about six miles away, he became evasive about the others and dissociated himself from the pressing present.

Lee told Captain Smith that Ewell must attack without supporting action on the ridge, though A. P. Hill's guns would provide some distraction. The commanding general instructed the staff officer to tell General Ewell to take the hill —again adding: "if practicable."

James Power Smith, who had been doing a lot of riding in the past few days, galloped off, and again Lee waited to hear Ewell's guns. Instead, as his watch showed the hour to have passed six, even the scattered firing began to dwindle. Gradually the booming of heavy guns ceased. The farm country took on an eerie aspect of peacefulness as shadows gathered over the valley between the two ridges where armies were forming.

Then Walter Taylor returned and said that since delivering the instructions to Ewell he had observed no indications of any activity from the Second Corps. The complete silence that settled over the countryside more than confirmed Lee's young A.A.G.

General Lee said nothing for a while. He had started this emergency convergence of his three corps because of Stuart's unexplained absence. This morning he had been startled by unexplained heavy action, when Hill's troops stumbled into an engagement. Now that Hill's fighting qualities and the sound instinct of Ewell's division commanders had turned a blunder into a victory, he was confronted in the evening with an unexplained silence in the quarter from which the success was to be solidified.

He would have to discover for himself the reason for the silence, just as earlier he had discovered the reason for the action. He said to Colonel Taylor that they would ride to Ewell's headquarters to see what was going on.

What had happened to Dick Ewell?

"The Good Soldier"

IN THE CONFEDERATE armies there were many "characters,"
natural and self-made, and Lieutenant General Richard
Stoddert Ewell combined both varieties to flourish as the favorite eccentric of the Army of Northern Virginia. His contemporaries gilded the lily with stories about him, and Ewell
himself possessed an aptitude for spontaneous utterances
which contributed to his quaintness.

When the two divisions of his corps occupied Carlisle, they
held the northernmost position of any Confederate force, but
his men did not remember their curious distinction in the war
so much as what Ewell said to a local Episcopalian minister.
In Virginia, Union officers always forbade communicants to
pray for the president of the Confederacy, according to the
rubric of their Prayer Book. In Carlisle, where the situation
was reversed, the rector asked General Ewell if his parishion-
ers might pray for the president of the United States. "Certainly," General Ewell said, "pray for him. I'm sure he
needs it."

In telling the latest Ewell anecdote the men always elabo-

119

rated on his unique appearance—the fringe of hair decorating his bald pate, the absurd mustachios that emphasized his strange assortment of features, the bulging eyes of a defiant bird. Yet in Chambersburg, whose citizens knew nothing of his legend as an eccentric, an observer saw him as a distinguished-looking gentleman of fine deportment. Both descriptions could apply, depending on the viewpoint. There was nothing one-dimensional in the complex of parts which constituted the strange character called "Old Baldhead" or "Bald Dick" or, most often, simply Dick Ewell.

Born forty-four years before of a well-established planter family in northern Virginia, Ewell came along when the family fortunes were in a state of decline, and this circumstance affected his military career—especially as Jackson's successor with the Second Corps—more than has been recognized.

Prepared for West Point on the earnings of his mother and sisters as schoolteachers in the Manassas area, Dick Ewell went into the regular army with an ambition to become a planter and restore his family's estate. He was a shrewd, practical-minded man, but, before he was ready to establish a plantation, his state seceded and he was soon a Confederate general operating in the neighborhood where he had grown up.

Although Ewell had never previously commanded more than a company of dragoons in the rough service on the Border, he rose rapidly on high competence, fearlessness, and selfless devotion. In the spring of 1862, as major general with an 8,500-man division, he distinguished himself in the fabled "Valley Campaign" as the dependable lieutenant of Stonewall Jackson, and in the hard summer fighting he emerged as one of the outstanding division commanders in the war. Then, at Second Manassas, he was badly wounded in his knee and was invalided out for more than eight months. It was during his absence from the army that a profound

120

change, related to his early circumstances and personal ambitions, occurred in the formerly dependable soldier.

While Ewell was recovering from a leg amputation, he fulfilled a longtime romantic aspiration and married a childhood acquaintance, a widow named Mrs. Lizinka Brown—or "the Widow Brown," as the general called his lady, long after she was Mrs. Ewell. There was a saying in the army to the effect that married men fought as well as single men, but rarely was a man who married during the war as good a soldier as he had been before. Along with this generality went the specific fact that the Widow Brown was a lady of considerable property, about which her bridegroom became very solicitous.

The inner change resulting from Ewell's new estate was reflected in noticeable outward manifestations. From his years on frontier outposts Ewell had developed a rough exterior, and associates who were not aware of his essential gentleness and thoughtfulness had often cowered before his intemperate outbursts and epic rages. Even intimates had been impressed by his fanciful, awesome swearing. After his marriage, all that was gone. Ewell embraced the Episcopal Church, and one of his staff said that he became "an earnest and humble Christian."

As to how this new Ewell would cope with his new responsibilities, there were two other questions: How would such a rugged physical type be affected by a wooden leg? How would he operate in the lonely sphere of corps command when all of his first-rate performances had been made under the firm guidance of Stonewall Jackson?

It is probable that this quaint and lovable character was not Lee's choice for Jackson's successor. Ewell's standing in the Second Corps and the sentiment favoring him made his selection inevitable. And, unlike Hill, "Old Baldhead" inherited an established unit that had grown from the nucleus of the Stonewall Brigade. The staff and supporting services were the products of Old Jack's stern demands, the soldiers were hard-tested veterans, and there was only one new brigade—which turned out to be a good one—in the organization. As in Hill's corps, however, there were two new division commanders and several untried men in brigade command.

The corps's original division, Jackson's, which had suffered a high mortality in commanders, went to Major General Edward Johnson, a forty-seven-year-old career soldier from the plantation country near Richmond. Although not the first choice for the division and of brief association with Lee's army, Johnson, who had been at West Point with Ewell and Jubal Early, was a solid and unspectacular soldier soundly trained in fundamentals and a hard fighter. He had been wounded out for a while and was without a command when the army was reorganized. A bachelor, Johnson was called "Allegheny" because of a detached force he had commanded in the mountain country of (then) western Virginia, and in any corps except Old Baldhead's he would have won his own notoriety as an eccentric. In battle he was noticeable for wielding a big hickory club in preference to a sword.

His division, originally composed entirely of Virginians, had its losses replaced by a Louisiana brigade and two fine North Carolina regiments.

Ewell's own division had gone, when he was wounded out the preceding summer, to dark, sardonic Jubal Early, and its quality of performance had been steadily maintained by "Old Jube." He was a cold, uncompromising man of forty-seven, heavy-bearded and hard-eyed, very profane in his speech. He walked with a slight stoop and chewed tobacco incessantly. Never generally liked, and in some quarters actively hated, he was close to Ewell, his acquaintance at West Point, had some passionate partisans, and was always supported by Lee for his fighting qualities and profound loyalty.

Because of a loathing of regimentation, Early had resigned

122

from the army within a year after graduating from West Point, and turned to law and politics. He had grown up in the Virginia farming country rolling east from the Blue Ridge, where the people were removed from the traditionalism of the older plantation regions of Tidewater. He became an active member of the western bloc that prevented Virginia's secession until Lincoln called on the state for troops with which to invade her sister states. Going with his own people, he volunteered his services and, after the ravages of the Federal troops in his homeplace, the bitter man became as passionate in his hate for the Union as he had formerly been in its defense.

As a division commander, Jubal Early was characterized by a tight control of his troops, steely skill, and a resourceful energy in action which he communicated to all his brigadiers save one. This was "Extra Billy" Smith, the only political general who had survived Lee's weeding out, and he was to prove a costly survivor. Early's brigades were entirely state units—Virginia, North Carolina, Louisiana, and Georgia—and all well commanded except Smith's Virginians. The Georgia brigade was commanded by one of the three most promising young officers in the army, John B. Gordon.

Ewell's third division was commanded by one of the younger military generation, thirty-four-year-old Robert E. Rodes. A non-West Pointer, Rodes was another of the developing officers of great promise, and at that stage was ahead of the other two. Born of a seventeenth-century Virginia family, he had graduated from the Virginia Military Institute at the age of nineteen and remained for three years as an assistant professor. When a professor's job he sought went to Stonewall Jackson (then called "Fool Tom"), young Rodes resigned to enter the popular field of civil engineering. When Virginia seceded, he was chief engineer of an Alabama railroad and had just received his coveted appointment as professor of engineering at his alma mater. He volunteered where he was, and reached his home state as colonel of a volunteer Alabama regiment.

He showed his fine gifts for war in the first big battle, First Manassas, and came on fast in Jackson's corps. As a brigadier, Rodes was placed in charge of a division at Chancellorsville and was one of the dominant figures on the field. A magnificent-looking blond, he led his troops mounted on a black horse and fought with the headlong courage that also characterized Pender and others of the younger leaders. In what amounted to field promotion, Rodes was upped to major general and given permanently the division he had handled with such distinction.

The five-brigade division—three of North Carolina, one of Georgia, and Rodes's former Alabama brigade—contained two weak commanders, two good men, and in twenty-six-year-old Ramseur the third of the younger officers of outstanding promise.

Despite the newness of Robert Rodes to division command, the newness of Allegheny Johnson to the army, and a spotting of doubtful talent, the proud Second Corps, with its Stonewall traditions, seemed more a known quantity than Hill's makeshift command—except in its top leadership.

Evidence would indicate that officers and men expected General Ewell to perform capably in the techniques of Jackson, and Lee, as if to assure Old Baldhead of his confidence, gave the Second Corps its customary assignment of striking out alone.

2

Leading the way north, Ewell acted with a decisive efficiency that gave his veterans the assurance of being in good hands. In defeating the Federals' Milroy at Winchester, he acted with a Jacksonian dispatch, and the firmness of his movements scattered Union detachments and opened the Valley as a safe line of communication into Pennsylvania. Ewell had reached the Potomac before Lee irrevocably committed himself to the invasion. Perhaps Ewell's fine performance caused the commanding general on June 23, before Jeb Stuart's disappearance, to give the final halfhearted order: "If you are ready to move [north], you can do so."

Marching through the enemy's country, Dick Ewell was undiverted either by vagrant alarms or by the misbehavior of Jenkins's poorly disciplined raiders, who acted as his cavalry. His attention centered on the supply aspects of the invasion. He victualed his own people and animals in unaccustomed bountcousness, while sending back to Lee's commissary five thousand barrels of flour and more than three thousand cattle on the hoof.

With casual boldness Ewell detached Jubal Early's division with only a battalion of cavalry ("Lige" White's Partisan Rangers) to move on via Gettysburg to York and the Susquehanna, while he led Rodes's and Johnson's divisions into Carlisle on Saturday, June 27. Jenkins's raffish troopers, somewhat settled down with the infantry moving close behind them, pushed on twenty miles to Harrisburg. Some blasts from their horse guns revealed that Pennsylvania's state capital was not to be defended. To Dick Ewell would fall the honor of taking the first Northern capital to fall to the Confederates.

Although not a man marked by undue pride, Dick Ewell took satisfaction in showing the army that he was worthy of the Second Corps command despite the physical handicap of his wooden leg. On the long stretches he rode in a carriage like the patriarchal planter of his aspiration, but when necessary he mounted his horse unassisted and rode as well as the next man who had grown up in a horse country. He was certainly going to ride when his troops completed their triumphant march by swinging down the streets of the Pennsylvania state capital, as so many enemy troops had marched through the streets of Southern towns.

On the Sunday night of June 28, in preparing his move, Old Baldhead rested his troops in Carlisle, some on the campus of Dickinson College and some in the barracks where he had once served. On Monday he was ready to give the marching orders when a courier rode up to headquarters on a lathered horse. The courier was from Lee's headquarters in Chambersburg, and he delivered an urgent written message from the general. Ewell read the words with a mixture of outrage and disappointment. He was to return to Chambersburg in a sudden contraction of the army.

Humanly enough, the army's great eccentric did not think of the total problems that might be confronting the commanding general in the enemy's country. He thought only of the crushing blow to his expectations of winning the greatest Confederate prize of the war. The newly converted Christian found no solace in the thought that he was submitting to the will of God. This was Lee's will, and Old Baldhead did not like it a bit.

With his high humor turned suddenly sour by this disruption of his charted course, Ewell lost his self-control when a second messenger from Lee arrived late on Monday afternoon revising the new orders. Worst of all, an element of discretion was inserted.

General Lee, having had time to think out the details of his army's convergence, redirected Ewell to bear southeastward to the village of Heidlersberg, on the eastern side of the mountain, from where he could proceed *either* to Cashtown or to Gettysburg. Only eight miles separated these places, but no such a thing as a choice had ever confronted Ewell in all his experience with Stonewall Jackson, and his extreme agitation became at once apparent.

He grew testy with his staff, his high voice piped more shrilly, and nothing could please him. After sending orders back and forth, Ewell finally decided on a course by night-fall. As Allegheny Johnson's division, with the long wagon train, had started for Chambersburg before Lee's revised order reached headquarters, Ewell permitted him to continue southward with directions to turn east at a point farther south. Jubal Early's division would abandon York and start westward for Heidlersburg on Tuesday morning. At the same time, Ewell would personally accompany Rodes's division to the same destination.

Outwardly, the arrangements for his part in Lee's convergence were made in soldierly enough fashion. Inwardly, the army's eccentric was seething when he bade farewell to Carlisle and glory.

3

On the clear, warm Tuesday of the last day of June, General Ewell rode in his carriage on Rodes's routine march to Heidlersberg. When camp was made in the dusk outside the small village of seven or eight houses, a third courier from Lee found Ewell. This message confirmed the second: from Heidlersberg proceed either to Cashtown or to Gettysburg. Ewell exploded. This was like the early days with Stonewall Jackson, when cryptic messages had fluttered in like falling leaves: "Stay there"—"Move out"—"Don't move for any reason"—"Be here tomorrow at earliest light."

His flare of temper had hardly faded when at nightfall still another courier came, this one from A. P. Hill. He brought the message Hill had sent from Cashtown after Pettigrew's people had encountered the Federal cavalry at Gettysburg. To promote co-operation between the corps, Hill simply advised Ewell that he was moving out from Cashtown toward Gettysburg to discover what was in his front. This was too much for Ewell.

At Cashtown, *toward* Gettysburg—where would Hill be when he, Ewell, got there? And how did what Hill was doing equate with Lee's purposes? Would Lee want him where Hill was headed or where Hill was heading from? In his mind this decision took on the proportions of an insoluble dilemma. He did not brood over which might be the right choice, only which would be the wrong one. Ewell was afraid of making a mistake.

There in the strange, dark countryside Ewell revealed that possession of the initiative paralyzed him. A. P. Hill, a few black ridges away, had reacted with characteristic impulsiveness, but at least he had seized the initiative without hesitation. Ewell needed someone to tell him precisely what to do.

It would be unthinkably humiliating to ask General Lee to make for him such a simple decision as going to Cashtown or Gettysburg. As he could not make it himself, he called in his generals to make it for him. He could not admit to his subordinates that he was immobilized by indecision, even if he admitted it to himself. Instead, he fell back on one of his dramatic rages as a cover for his indecision, and denounced Lee for sending him such an ambiguous order.

It was a strange trio of general officers who served as witnesses to Ewell's greatest performance since returning, a humble Christian, to the army.

The magnificent-looking Rodes, younger than the others, new to division command and unacquainted with Ewell's spectacular scenes, said little during the meeting.

Dark, bitter Jubal Early, chewing tobacco, also said little, though his hard, bright eyes grew speculative. Early's division, coming down from York, had gone into bivouac a few miles away, and he had ridden over to confer with the corps commander. Early was not confused by Ewell's high-flown invective. Every time Ewell pointed at the damnable message from Lee, he was looking for some loophole for himself. Early offered him none. He recognized his superior officer for what he was: a subordinate who needed a leader. On that night Jubal Early insidiously established an ascendancy over his commanding officer.

The third man present was an oddity: a sixty-year-old major general serving as a volunteer without troop assignment. Isaac Trimble was a West Point-educated Virginian who had been successful in railroad civil engineering. At secession, Trimble was general superintendent of the Baltimore and Potomac Railroad, and Marylanders regarded him as one of their most distinguished citizens. Early in the war he commanded one of Ewell's brigades, and so ferocious was Trimble in action that Stonewall Jackson had him ticketed for future command of his own old division.

Trimble's personalized front-line leadership cost him severe wounds in action, and he lost additional time from troops because of various ailments of the flesh. He was on sick leave when the army was reorganized, and in his absence Jackson's old division went to Allegheny Johnson. Recovered by June when the army was heading northward, Trimble was given command of the forces that were to protect the Shenandoah Valley while the army was away.

When Trimble reached his new post, he found no troops. Imboden's cavalry were enjoying their northern expedition on Ewell's flank, and the Maryland infantry had somehow got misplaced in the juggling of units. Even Lee could only write plaintively: "I do not know what has become of them."

Old Trimble wasted no time in a fruitless search. He took off alone after the army and found Lee in his tent outside Chambersburg on Saturday the 27th. Lee, wishing to make use of his friend's fiery spirit, sent him on to Carlisle to join

Ewell as a sort of general officer without portfolio. He arrived on the Sunday when Ewell was in fine fettle over the prospect of taking Harrisburg, and was received warmly by his former division commander.

Thanks to this sequence of circumstances, Ewell's night conference had one positive, outspoken member. Aggressive-eyed Trimble wore a scimitar-shaped black mustache across his bony features which gave him the aspect of a pirate leader, and he did not hesitate to give his opinion to anybody. Having gone with his native state on a point of principle, Trimble had no intention of suffering mutely failures in a cause for which he had sacrificed a successful career.

He reported that he said to Ewell: "I could interpret it [Lee's ambiguous order] in but one way. After hearing from General Lee a few days before his plan to attack the advance of the enemy, wherever found . . . and that, as this advance was in Gettysburg, we should march to that place and notify General Lee accordingly. . . ."

Even that did not still the disturbance in Ewell's mind, though it did end the weird conference for the night.

The next morning, July 1, he compromised as long as possible by following a road that for seven or eight miles went in the direction of both Cashtown and Gettysburg. When Rodes's advance brigades neared the village of Middletown, where the roads divided and a choice must be made, a message from punctilious Hill reached Ewell. It advised him that Hill's advance was nearing Gettysburg. That decided Old Baldhead. In his report he made no mention of his dilemma. Laconically he reported: "I . . . turned the head of Rodes' column toward that place."

4

When thirty-four-year-old Robert Rodes received orders to direct the head of his column to Gettysburg, the new major general found himself (as had Heth in his attack from the west) in sole command of the field. General Ewell was riding in the rear when in midmorning the big blond Rodes was startled to hear cannon fire reverberating across the hilly farmland in his front. He was then perhaps four miles from Gettysburg, coming from the northwest along the Mummasburg road, and his total information about the situation was that A. P. Hill was moving toward Gettysburg to discover what enemy troops were there.

Like Heth, Rodes was under restraining orders to avoid bringing on a general engagement if he encountered the enemy head-on. The enemy was there, a few miles in his front in strength unknown. Rodes determined to meet him with all he had.

To his right ran a wooded ridge, and from his maps the young general discovered that this, an extension of Seminary Ridge called Oak Hill, passed just in front of the town toward which he was headed and from which the firing seemed to be coming. Without breaking stride he deployed a brigade along the rough going of the ridge and pushed on. Soon cavalry began banging at them with new repeating carbines. These were a few of Buford's busy people, firing as they fell back and sending frantic couriers with the news of Rodes's approach.

Rodes's hardened soldiers took no chances on what those summer woods ahead might be concealing beyond the blue troopers. He got a second brigade up on the ridge, and then part of a third—his own former Alabama brigade, commanded by Colonel O'Neal. Without losing their steady motion forward, the fourth and fifth brigades deployed in line of battle as they marched across farmed fields in the rising heat.

In early afternoon, where a road crossed Oak Hill, Rodes came out on a sharp elevation, and suddenly before him lay the smoky panorama of battle. He was looking at the left of Hill's line, across the Cashtown turnpike and directed toward the ridge that Rodes's troops were astride. The firing between Hill's men and the Federals had grown desultory by the time Rodes viewed the action. It was the period when Heth was waiting for developments and before General Lee reached the field. Rodes, finding himself potentially on the flank of Hill's enemy, saw his position as an opportunity.

Even as he watched, portions of the troops in front of Hill faced about in line of battle toward Rodes about half a mile away. The vague dark blurs of moving units took position in the woods near the railroad cut that paralleled the Cashtown pike, and found the protection of one of the stone fences with which the Pennsylvania farmers divided their small fields. These troops were of Robinson's division, the reserves of Reynolds's I Corps, which Doubleday had been handling against Heth.

At the same time Rodes saw great blots of blue troops moving toward him from the streets of the town itself. These were two divisions of Howard's XI Corps, the Germans, who had broken ranks at Chancellorsville and whom the Confederates particularly hated as "bounty troops." They had hurried fast to the field and were tired, but they wanted to erase Chancellorsville from their record.

The quickly swelling Federal strength in his front had no effect on Rodes's decision to attack. Like Lee, he wanted the initiative himself. Like Powell Hill, he reacted to the opening of action with an impetuosity that counted no costs.

He quickly established field headquarters, with the flag run out over the tent, on a hill across the road from the big farmhouse of the Forneys. Then he sent staff officers galloping off with orders to brigade commanders. Counting on Early's division to come up on his left flank, Rodes placed only one brigade on his left to meet the threat from Howard's troops moving out of Gettysburg. The other three brigades at hand he prepared to send forward along the ridge. A fifth was coming up in general reserve. Considering its audacity, Rodes's plan for battle was sound enough, except that in his eagerness the recent civil engineer took no account of his brigadiers' suitability to the nature of their assignments.

Aggressive young Dodson Ramseur was ordered to place his brigade in general reserve. The defensive position on the open plain between the Middletown road and the ridge Rodes assigned to the Georgia brigade of George Doles, another offensive-minded fighter. This thirty-three-year-old Georgian, without formal military training, had showed solid ability ever since the first fighting. A genial, courteous disciplinarian, Doles had been promoted to brigadier the previous November and was one of Rodes's dependables.

For the crucial pivotal slot between Doles, posted across the road on defense, and the two attacking brigades on the ridge, Rodes unwisely designated his own old Alabama brigade under a colonel new to brigade command, Edward O'Neal.

When the artillery fire began to grow heavy between Rodes's guns and the enemy's, as each felt out the other, Rodes belatedly developed some doubts about O'Neal as commander of the connective brigade between Doles and Iverson. In his excitement and determination to excel, Rodes, without thinking of O'Neal's feelings, reverted to his former authority over the brigade and acted as if he still commanded it. There was no intimacy between the two men to begin with, and O'Neal resented Rodes's orders to his regiments.

Rodes's instructions began when the Federal cannon fire was growing particularly troublesome to waiting troops; he ordered O'Neal's brigade back from its exposed position. To O'Neal's right was Iverson, with Junius Daniel's brigade of North Carolinians in support. Rodes personally placed

O'Neal's right regiment in alignment with Daniel's left, and ordered O'Neal to form his brigade line upon this regiment, the 3rd Alabama.

Then, as Rodes tensed for the moment of launching his attack, he observed a gap between O'Neal's left and Doles's right. To remedy this oversight of O'Neal's, Rodes pulled the 5th Alabama out of line and placed it under his personal command.

Rodes had not assumed personal command of the 3rd Alabama, on the right, but only shifted its position to form the brigade line. However, O'Neal seemed to think that both regiments—extreme right and left—had been removed from his command, and his resentment of the interference with his command seemed to confuse him.

Finally, when Rodes was ready to give the command to advance, he instructed O'Neal precisely on the order in which his regiments should be sent forward. Instead of following the orders, O'Neal choked into complete inanition and did nothing at all.

When the whole line swept forward over the rough country, O'Neal placed himself stiffly with the reserve regiment, 5th Alabama, and three of his regiments pushed forward on their own. In the confusion the 3rd Alabama, on the extreme right, received no proper orders at all. Its colonel, Cullen Battle, simply moved along with Daniel's brigade, on whose left he had been placed by Rodes.

Robert Rodes watched with mounting horror the result of his first engagement as major general. The three unled regiments of O'Neal's brigade compressed when they struck the brutal fire of the enemy, leaving the left flank of Iverson's brigade hanging in the air. Caught in enfilade, Iverson's men were slaughtered. One regiment went down in such a neat row that when its survivors waved shirt tails, or any piece of cloth remotely white, Iverson thought that the whole regi-

ment of *live* men were surrendering. The shaken brigadier
added to Rodes's woes by sending him the erroneous report
that a regiment had deserted to the enemy. That was the attacking unit.

The compression of O'Neal's three advancing regiments
also exposed the right flank of Doles's Georgians, the brigade on defense, and they were being overlapped on both
sides by the Federals coming out from Gettysburg.

Of his four brigades in action, Rodes saw Doles fighting
desperately on defense, O'Neal's pivotal brigade useless,
Iverson's exposed brigade shattered and its commander demoralized, and Daniel on the extreme right going on in an
extemporized independent movement that was entering a
zone of acute danger. When Iverson's enfiladed brigade
drifted leftward for cover, Daniel, instead of coming up on
Iverson's right as planned, went on in lonely isolation on the
right flank. Perhaps Rodes remembered then that he knew
nothing about Daniel's fitness for command nor about the behavior of his troops. These North Carolina regiments had
been brought to the Army of Northern Virginia only after
Chancellorsville, as replacements for losses.

Although new to Virginia, the troops had been long in
Confederate service. Composed mostly of volunteers for militia companies, they had achieved an early pride by fighting
in the first battle of the war, Big Bethel, on the Virginia Peninsula. The men had come to regard that action as no more
than a skirmish, and during the later great events of the war
they had been restricted to local fighting in North Carolina.
When the brigade was ordered to Virginia, some of the men,
grown soft in peripheral fighting near home cooking, immediately deserted. Others were eager to test their mettle with
the big army in the main theater, and their pride was stung
by fellow North Carolinians among Iverson's veterans who
jeered at them as home guards. Junius Daniel, a tall Carolin-

135

ian, had his personal pride at stake. He was a West Point graduate who had enjoyed little chance of showing his skill.

When the formerly boastful men of Iverson's brigade huddled and lost direction under the galling fire coming from a stand of green timber, Daniel and his regiments were approaching the grassy edge of the railroad cut that had been so ruinous that morning to Heth's new Mississippi brigade.

The men had passed through fields of golden wheat, and on their left they could see the tower of a college building (then called Pennsylvania College). Ahead of them through the drifting fogs of smoke Daniel saw clumps of Confederates. Assuming, correctly, that they must belong to Hill's corps, he hastily sent a courier to find their officers and ask them to join his right. Combined, they could get at the Federals firing from the railroad cut. But those Confederate troops happened to be the survivors of that earlier experience with the railroad cut. With their commanding officers lost, the men would have nothing to do with Daniel. The *arrivé* with Rodes's division was left to resolve his situation as best he could.

It was at this period when Rodes's gaudy reputation faced wreckage that Harry Heth, on the Cashtown pike, asked General Lee if he should not advance to relieve the pressure on Rodes. Lee said no. At that time he could not have known of the peril to Rodes's division.

Jubal Early, hurrying toward the firing, did not know of it either, but he came out on Rodes's left flank as if part of a battle plan. His lead division, which by chance was commanded by his best brigadier, John B. Gordon, deployed and struck on Rodes's left in one continuous movement.

Without waiting for covering artillery and without throwing out skirmishers, Gordon's Georgians fixed bayonets and moved in a steady line through a cornfield and a field of ripening wheat toward their old adversaries, the Germans of

Chancellorsville. The swift pace slowed momentarily when the long lines of men passed through the willows of a little creek. Then, under fluttering red flags, the troops rushed in to close with the waiting enemy.

Not many of Howard's XI Corps waited to come to grips again with the men of Stonewall Jackson's corps. Those who stood bravely had no chance in the disintegrating units. Some fell back steadily enough until they were caught up in the rush of others who dropped their guns in order to run faster.

As for the commanders of the two divisions, General Barlow was wounded and left on the field, and General Schimmelfennig took refuge in a shed in town, where he hid during the rest of the Battle of Gettysburg. In minutes the attack from Gettysburg was broken, and Doles's flank was secure.

Astride the road on the open plain, Doles had taken the brunt of Howard's attack, and the steady fighter had shown no nervousness even when the XI Corps troops threatened to engulf both flanks. But the close call got the young man's dander up. As soon as Gordon's attack relieved the pressure on him, Doles, without orders from division command, sent his men thrusting ahead in lunging counterattack.

At the same time on his right, where O'Neal's lost regiments and Iverson's brigade were broken, tempestuous young Ramseur threw his fresh brigade forward with a high yell across the corpses and the moaning figures of their fellows.

With the momentum of battle suddenly reversed, newcomer Daniel, isolated on the extreme right, was finally rewarded for his cool courage. His men got an angle of fire on the railroad cut, and it became their turn to shoot in enfilade.

On Daniel's left, Colonel Battle, whose 3rd Alabama had never got proper orders, sent a request for instructions. Beleaguered Daniel, in his first action with the army, sent back word that he had no authority over the 3rd Alabama. This happened when Ramseur was pushing through the debris of O'Neal and Iverson, and Battle on his own authority sent his regiment in on Ramseur's right.

On Ramseur's left, Doles, with the enemy recoiling from his front, sent his well-bunched units in pursuit of the Federals. A solid arc of a Confederate line was formed from north of Gettysburg to west of the town, where Daniel finally made juncture with A. P. Hill.

When Junius Daniel stood up under his own test of battle with the army, his troops got a gratifying revenge on their fellow Tarheels with Iverson. One of Iverson's regiments lost its battle flag in the fight, and the 45th North Carolina in Daniel's brigade enjoyed the satisfaction of capturing the Yankee who had the flag, and turning both over to the men who had taunted them with being home guards.

The 1st of July would never be remembered as a great day for Robert Rodes. Nervous in his zeal, he had immobilized O'Neal and set in motion a chain of costly repulses. Personally, Robert Rodes never lost his self-control when his battle seemed a grotesque failure, not even when Iverson sent the message about a deserting regiment, and he was quick to take advantage of the turn in his favor. He kept his men on the ridge driving forward until they made juncture with Hill, and on the flats his left joined Early's right to form a continuous line rolling into Gettysburg.

Because his troops stood up under killing, because Daniel and Doles kept their poise, and because Gordon of Early's division threw in his brigade without any fiddling around, the field was won. But the ex-professor felt none of the exhilaration of victory which had come to him at Chancellorsville.

In his heart he must have recognized the errors caused by his overanxiousness and every detail of his salvation from disaster. On his black horse, the exhausted Rodes was a subdued victor when he rode into the confusion of the streets of Gettysburg.

He looked at the heights of Cemetery Hill, on which the retreating Federals were forming a hasty line, and decided that his troops had suffered enough casualties for the day. In the main street he laid out a skirmish line against counterattack and, for the first time since hearing the guns in the morning, waited for orders.

5

Sometime between three thirty and four o'clock in the fading heat of the afternoon General Ewell reached the field. Riding down the road that led from due north toward the town, he paused on a slight elevation near where Doles's Georgians had stood so steady to their guns. From there he could see, over the small farm fields, the clotted streets of Gettysburg and beyond, the rampart-like rises of Cemetery Hill and Culp's Hill.

Between him and the town, the only blue uniforms were worn by the dead and prisoners. Beyond the town, from which the broken blue masses were receding, he could see little knots of Federals scurrying for cover on the hills. The late sun's rays glinted on a few enemy guns up there. Even a civilian, without reports, would have recognized across the debris of battle the size of the victory in the making. Ewell had reports too.

The men of Rodes's division and A. P. Hill's corps had driven everything before them through the town. Although Rodes's and Hill's troops had suffered heavy casualties and the men were hard used, Gordon's and Hays's brigades of Early's division were only stung. The men were fresh and eager, and Gordon personally was pressing his people to take the hills before the enemy reformed there.

Ewell listened, looked, and then gave an order that was

shocking to his staff. He sent a message to Gordon to break off the pursuit.

It was not past four o'clock, and close to four hours of daylight remained, when Jackson's doughty former lieutenant gave the incomprehensible order. Then, as if bemused, the handsomely dressed gray-clad general with the quaint mustaches sat silently on a horse as still as its rider, a picture of inanition. The old dragoon, in the test of decision, had suffered a paralytic stroke to his will.

So he remained, with the bedlam of sounds in Gettysburg echoing around him, when young Gordon with flushed face galloped up on a stallion.

John B. Gordon, then thirty-one, was a Georgia lawyer of plantation background with no military experience, though he came of a long line of warriors and his family had distinguished themselves in the Revolution. Like Pettigrew in Hill's corps, Gordon had risen steadily on his natural leadership of men and capacity to learn the rudiments of warfare.

Curiously, his erect carriage and stern features sharpened by a chin beard gave the impression of an old war-school martinet, and he looked, as his men said, "every inch the soldier." He had trained them, learning as they learned, largely by the force of his personality, and in action he always had that indefinable quality called magnetism. Part of his appeal to Southerners was his chivalric attitude, which he had demonstrated during the afternoon's fighting.

Just after his men had won their sector of the field and were forming for pursuit, Gordon came upon the wounded young Union General Barlow, who had been abandoned in the stampede to Gettysburg. Gordon immediately dismounted and offered his personal assistance. The Federal "boy general," believing that he was dying, asked Gordon to get his effects to his wife, who was traveling with General Meade's family. As Gordon's wife also stayed close to the

140

lines, he was pleased to be able to grant the dying request. This solicitude encouraged Barlow to ask Gordon to read him aloud his wife's last letter and then destroy it. The captured Barlow recovered, and after the war he and Gordon established a friendship that lasted for the remainder of their lives.

Gordon was a highly intelligent man and, having applied his intelligence for more than two years to handling units of men in armed conflict, he did not need to be a Napoleon to recognize that the natural fortress south of Gettysburg must be taken to complete the day's victory. However, in learning the rudiments of warfare, he had of necessity learned the protocol of command.

When Ewell's first order to break off the pursuit reached him, Gordon's military intelligence wrestled against protocol, and the intelligence won. He continued fighting. He wavered when a second order came, but still he did not break off the action: his men were going too well. When the third emphatic order came, Gordon recognized that a brigadier who ignored a lieutenant general was playing a losing game.

Yet, with the invasion at stake, he could not supinely obey. He sent orders to his colonels to check the pursuit, forming their lines, and went hunting for General Ewell to discover for himself what exactly was going on. In the presence of the corps commander—fifteen years his senior, a trained soldier out of West Point and Old Jack's great division commander —Gordon could say nothing. He sat his own unquiet black horse hoping that his excited presence would stimulate General Ewell to explanations.

Ewell paid no attention to him. Gordon looked at the frenzied young staff officers and they looked at him.

Those young men had all served with Jackson. One of them, Sandie Pendleton, a V.M.I. graduate and son of the chief of artillery, had been a particularly valued member of

141

Old Jack's military family. In the quick intimacy of camp life
Sandie Pendleton had formed a friendship with Henry Kyd
Douglas, the volunteer aide from Maryland who had been
transferred to the staff of Allegheny Johnson.

While Gordon's feelings were battling his acquired military manners, good-looking Harry Douglas rode up to the
group with a message from division commander Johnson.
"Old Allegheny," having completed his chores with the
wagon trains from Carlisle, had crossed South Mountain and
was hiking his men toward Gettysburg on the Cashtown pike.
He wanted it known that he would arrive late in the day, but
that he was on his way and his men would be ready when
they reached the field.

Harry Douglas's message from Johnson conquered John B.
Gordon's self-control. No protocol could restrain him from
saying that he was all ready to go in with Johnson's fresh division, and that there was plenty of light for taking the hill
before the enemy's main army came up.

If Ewell heard the impassioned presumption of the young
brigadier, he gave no sign. In his strangely muted manner, he
answered Douglas's report by saying that General Johnson
should proceed on his journey toward Gettysburg until other
orders were sent him.

Even Douglas was appalled by the absence of urgency in
the command. Johnson's unused men were not directed to
hurry forward to support Gordon or co-operate with him in
taking the hill that was manifestly the key to a complete win-
ing of the field. The atmosphere was as calm as a day in winter camp.

When Douglas (who was to be wounded and captured the
next day) turned his horse slowly around, his face must have
reflected his bewilderment. Sandie Pendleton saw it and said:
"Oh, for the presence and inspiration of Old Jack for just one
hour!"

142

Douglas nodded, sharing the memories and the sickness, and rode off toward Johnson's trudging troops.

Ewell took no more notice of his staff officer's remark than he had of Gordon's importuning. Lost in his own torments, Ewell could only reach the simple decision to go into Gettysburg, from where he heard sporadic firing. At least action was preferable to sitting his horse outside the Blocher house surrounded by accusing faces. Gordon rode along with his commanding officer, still hoping for a change of orders which would let his troops go on to Cemetery Hill.

6

The fighting in the town was growing fitful when Ewell and Gordon rode into a side street from the north. A sniper's ball hit Ewell's wooden leg. The general was philosophical about missing that wound, and for a moment he seemed more like his usual self. Still he made no decision as he and Gordon rode on to the square in the center of the town, where the ragged men in gray were celebrating. In the confusion of gathering thousands of prisoners, of hunting down snipers and wine cellars, of organizing their own units, soldiers congregated around a lieutenant general, the corps commander.

Ewell checked his horse under the shade of a tree and sat there receiving salutations from jubilant Rebels who thought that they had won an easy victory and that the battle was over. A young officer was so exhilarated that he accepted a bottle of wine from a brazen forager and offered it to the general.

But general officers, who knew that the victory had not been secured, were thinking of Cemetery Hill crawling with reforming Federals. Harry Hays, whose Louisianians had come up alongside Gordon's brigade, so far forgot himself as to ask Ewell if he could not go forward.

That the troubled man was incapable of making a decision

143

was observed by Captain James Power Smith. "Our corps commander," he said, "was simply waiting for orders when every moment of time could not be balanced with gold."

The Federals' indomitable Hancock, who was sent by Meade to assume charge of the remnants on the hill, said later: "If the Confederates had continued the pursuit of General Howard on the afternoon . . . they would have driven him over and beyond Cemetery Hill."

The conviction that Lee's army had the game in the bag pervaded the air of the fading afternoon, and the electric atmosphere began to get on Ewell's nerves. His outward calm was shaken. As the scattered firing in Gettysburg receded toward the southern end of the town and the last of the Federals began climbing the steep hill for safety, the general and his agitated staff made their way through the confusion back to the comparatively quiet farmland where the action had reached its climax. There, off the road, he ran out the headquarters flag on the rear of the Blocher house and made his way to the back porch, facing a cool arbor.

He was to get no peace from importunists. Old Isaac Trimble, the volunteer major general, found him there. "Well, general, we have had a grand success," Trimble said. "Are you not going to follow it up and push our advantage?"

Ewell answered in his squeaky voice: "General Lee has instructed me not to bring on a general engagement without his orders, and I will wait for them."

Trimble said: "But that hardly applies to the present state of things. We have fought a hard battle already, and should secure the advantage gained."

Ewell did not answer, and Trimble saw that he "was far from composed."

Trimble persisted, saying: "This is a critical moment for us."

Still Ewell made no reply.

144

As it became obvious that he would do nothing, Trimble impatiently turned away, mounted, and rode toward town to make a personal reconnoitering of Cemetery Hill and Culp's Hill.

At that time no fresh Federal forces had arrived to support troops so shattered that even the famous Iron Brigade, which had started the day happily against Archer, was never again to be effective as a unit.

No Confederate needed to have followed the Federals up the slope of Cemetery Hill to know the condition of the broken commands. They needed only to observe the disorganized and battered state of their own victorious troops. Although the Confederates engaged supposedly outnumbered the Union forces, only four Confederate divisions of the two corps had been on the field against six Federal divisions, and their numerical superiority could not have been overwhelming. But as three of those four divisions (Rodes's, Heth's, and Pender's) were too fought out for further action, it was obvious that the enemy must be in far worse shape, with many of his survivors demoralized. Ewell had a fresh division, flushed with the *élan* of victory and in the momentum of pursuit.

When old Trimble, on his own initiative, went riding along the outskirts of the town, looking for a place to send the fresh troops, he observed something even more interesting. The eastern extension of Cemetery Hill, which culminated in the wooded, rocky knob of Culp's Hill, rose higher than Cemetery Hill and was not occupied! Trimble didn't even know the name of Culp's Hill, but he knew it commanded the nearer hill on which the Federals were gathering.

Ewell could send fresh men without bringing on the general engagement he talked about. In fact, merely by troop movement he could bring the inconclusive day's fighting to a definite and happy end. Trimble spun his horse around and galloped back to the Blocher house. With this information he would surely shake his old friend out of the strange apathy.

It was nearing five o'clock. Ewell had been on the field more than an hour when Trimble found him doing nothing in the arbor back of the house. Trimble advanced excitedly. Through the clear light of the falling sun he pointed a finger dramatically toward Culp's Hill and shouted: "General, there is an eminence of commanding position, and not now occupied, as it ought to be by us or by the enemy soon. I advise you to send a brigade and hold it if we are to remain here."

This was strong language from a subordinate who did not even hold a regular assignment.

Ewell only looked more worried. "Are you sure it commands the town?"

"Certainly it does, as you can see," Trimble shouted back, "and it ought to be held by us at once."

This was too much even for the suffering Ewell, and he made a sharp reply. It was a personal response to the affront, however, and not to the military situation.

Trimble lost his own control. "Give *me* a brigade and I will engage to take the hill."

Ewell only stared straight ahead, his bulging eyes glazed.

"Give me a good regiment and I will do it," Trimble thundered.

Dick Ewell managed to shake his head. He said no more.

Immobilized though he was, Ewell was agonizingly aware that he should do something. From all around him came the sounds of battlefield action—the creak of worn ambulances and the rumble of ammunition wagons hurrying to the front, the thin crack of distant sharpshooters' rifles and the sudden roar of heavy guns, the stumbling of stretcher-bearers, the groans of the wounded and their cries for water, the hard gallop of staff officers' horses, and the hoarse-voiced commands of junior officers.

Some shouted words reminded Ewell that Johnson's division was marching toward Gettysburg, and that his one definite order (besides halting Gordon's pursuit) had been for Johnson to come on until he received further instructions. What were the further instructions to be?

His solution to that simple problem amounted to a confession of the weakness that Jubal Early had observed the night before. Ewell needed a leader. He sent Colonel Smead, the corps inspector, to find General Early and ask *him* where Johnson's division should go.

The reason he gave was that Early had passed through Gettysburg the week before on his way to York, and would know the terrain. The real reason was that the corps commander was now unable to make any decision at all.

7

Smead returned with Early's advice a little past five o'clock. There were upwards of three hours of fighting light remaining. Early urged Ewell to send Johnson's men to take Culp's Hill, as Trimble had suggested, because it dominated the hill protecting the Federals.

Colonel Smead added that Early had sent out Gordon and his brigade in response to a warning that a Federal force was advancing down the York road toward the Confederate rear. As this warning came from Early's one "political" general, Extra Billy Smith, who was most noted for his irrepressible tendency to make speeches, Early put no credence in the alarm. Simply to avoid needless risks, he had sent Gordon to assume command, and he mentioned the matter at all only to make a full report of his division.

This alarm, though wholly discounted by alert Early, struck to the heart of Ewell's fears of doing something wrong. For the first time in that slow-dying hour he was shaken out of his apathy. He sent for Jubal Early.

When Early reached the back porch of the temporary headquarters, he quickly dismissed the possible threat to their left and rear, and talked about taking Culp's Hill. Although he had sent Smead with his advice that Culp's Hill was the place for Johnson when his division arrived, Early did not want to wait for Johnson's men before renewing an assault. He believed that Cemetery Hill, rising southward from the town, could be taken now by his own division with some help from A. P. Hill from the west.

Here at last was a course of immediate action defined by the man whom he had tacitly appointed as his adviser. Ewell was depressed by the prospect of committing any action, but this plan at least offered the relief of shifting the responsibility to General Lee. By James Power Smith he sent the commanding general a message of his plan to attack Cemetery Hill if General Lee would send A. P. Hill in support on the right.

While Ewell was fidgeting through the wait for Smith's return, he was shaken anew by the arrival of handsome young Walter Taylor, Lee's A.A.G. As Colonel Taylor reported it, "I . . . delivered the order of General Lee . . . that, from the position which he occupied, he could see the enemy retreating over those hills, without organization and in great confusion; that it was only necessary for him [Ewell] to press 'those people' in order to secure possession of the heights, and that, if possible, he wished him to do this."

Ewell nodded in acknowledgment of the oral order. Walter Taylor, who knew nothing of the general's long hour of indecision, accepted the nod as agreement that the order would be executed. He rode off to report this to General Lee, who was with A. P. Hill on Seminary Ridge. Ewell, apparently hoping that Captain Smith's reply from Lee would reprieve him from the order to attack, did nothing until his staff officer returned.

148

But Smith, staring bleakly at the successor to Jackson, brought no reprieve. A. P. Hill, he reported, could give no support, and General Lee wanted Ewell to take the hill "if it were possible." Then Smith added that the commanding general would ride over and see him shortly.

This was an order, and General Lee must not find him sitting supinely in a safe arbor while the sun went down on the field. Keeping Jubal Early beside him, miserable Ewell mounted again and went for another personal reconnoitering into Gettysburg.

By now the firing had dwindled. Only a few snipers were shooting from houses on the southern edge of town, at the foot of Cemetery Hill. The bullets ricocheting through the streets did not bother Ewell, but the Federal batteries posted on the hill did. In their anxiety to present a brave front, the Federal gunners were blasting away as if preparing an attack. This was a sound that had stirred Ewell's blood in former days. But there in the fading light these few courageous demonstrators were sufficient to snuff the faint flicker of decisiveness in him.

Seizing on any excuse to postpone the commitment to action, he told Early he would wait for Johnson's arrival before attacking. Even the protests of his adviser could not move him out of that procrastination. With the sun sinking behind South Mountain (while Lee on Seminary Ridge was waiting anxiously to hear Ewell's men going into action), the corps commander turned his horse around and rode back to the arbor.

He and Early were joined there by Rodes. Having received no orders after posting his men in skirmish line from the middle of town out toward Seminary Ridge, Rodes had come for instructions. Ewell had none to give.

With Early growing frantic at the approach of sundown, Ewell seated himself to wait for General Lee's visit. Ewell could think of nothing he had done wrong. Most certainly he had avoided bringing on "an engagement." Yet, in his fretting over avoiding mistakes, he kept worrying about that report from Extra Billy Smith which Early had dismissed. Suppose there was a sizable force of Federals on his flank and rear. He could not sit and think about it. He had to see for himself.

Accompanied by the raging Early and the subdued Rodes, Dick Ewell rode to the eastern side of town (the side opposite to where the fight had begun in the morning). From a rise, in the final clarity of light before sundown, they looked down the York road, which, Early said, "was visible for nearly or quite two miles." By chance, as they stared into the distance, figures that looked like a skirmish line began to move in their direction. They were too far away for the generals to distinguish the uniforms. The usually intrepid Rodes now showed the effects of the day's battle. Believing the alarm from Extra Billy Smith and convinced that Federals were on their flank he cried: "There they come now!"

Not having forsworn profanity as had the converted Ewell, Old Jube cut loose in a torrent of disgust. To it he added a logical remark: "Gordon is out there, and if the enemy was advancing, he would certainly be firing on him!"

Poor Ewell was torn between the two opinions. Rodes voiced the fear that was his own, and Jubal Early voiced the obvious logic. Ewell resolved the dilemma by sending a staff officer to investigate. The movement turned out to be the skirmish line of Extra Billy Smith, facing his phantoms; Gordon had been moving Smith's skirmishers to a position he preferred.

Jubal Early, without waiting for the staff officer to confirm his own opinion, abandoned hope of influencing Ewell to any action and rode to his two brigades nearest Cemetery Hill. Probably he had held some wan hope that the Federals might be preparing to abandon their refuge and continue to retreat back on the main army, for, after surveying the hill, he reported that "it was very apparent he [the enemy] was determined to hold the position on Cemetery Hill."

His personal reconnoitering was sound. Redoubtable Hancock, sped on by Meade, had reached the field and assumed command, and troops commanded by Hancock were not likely to run. Also, Hancock had observed at once their vulnerability from Culp's Hill, and ordered troops to occupy that huge rockpile.

With Early gone, Ewell kept Rodes with him and returned to the back porch of the Blocher house. It was now sundown, and on Seminary Ridge Lee was asking: "What has happened to Ewell?"

Ewell was waiting for Lee's visit. He had hardly settled himself when a staff officer arrived with the report that Johnson's leading brigade had reached the outskirts of Gettysburg.

Ewell had promised Early that he would open his attack when Johnson arrived with Stonewall Jackson's old division. Away from Old Jube's aggressive influence, he was not of a mind to open any action at all. He sent a message directing Allegheny Johnson to proceed through town and go into position opposite Culp's Hill. He said nothing about any action when Johnson arrived there, and did not even suggest that he hurry the troop movement.

Even this late, with more than two daylight hours lost, Johnson's men could have made a race for Culp's Hill against the Federals sent there by Hancock. With no urgency in the message, Johnson allowed his tired troops, who had marched more than twenty hot miles that day, to proceed leisurely through town via a railroad cut. Walking along a railroad necessarily slowed the movement, but, even so, the middle of the strung-out brigades passed through Gettysburg around

151

seven o'clock, when there was still enough light for a young soldier to read a letter delivered to him on the march.

Ewell now was thinking only of Lee's impending visit and of the report he must make. As twilight gathered over the arbor outside temporary headquarters, he heard the commanding general's party halting alongside the house. Suddenly Dick Ewell felt that he could not face Lee alone. He sent off a staff officer with his first urgent message of the day: Jubal Early must come back and be with him.

8

Dismounted, Lee moved slowly toward the arbor, his dark eyes appraising the listless headquarters scene. On his way over, he had observed the lack of purposeful action in all the units he passed. The men were cleaning the rings of powder grime from around their mouths. This disfiguration came from biting off the powder charge in their paper cartridges. Clearly they had no notion of using their rifles again that day.

Instead of preparing for attack, the men were relaxing and beginning to gather fence rails for campfires. The last of hoarded spoils from the march were being dug from knapsacks, and many messes had already returned to the regular skimpy rations of cornmeal and fatback. Individual soldiers and small groups, the indomitable foragers, were stalking off into the shadows, as unmindful of danger as if strolling in their own back yards.

By the time the commanding general reached Second Corps headquarters, he knew that Ewell had not tried to mount an attack. After one look at the sick depression on Ewell's face, he knew why. Paralysis of will marked Ewell like a fatal disease. Just as others in lesser posts of importance had failed in the test of command during Lee's thirteen months with the army, Lee saw that Jackson's great subordinate had failed in his hour of decision.

The two men greeted each other courteously rather than warmly. They were but slightly acquainted, and their close military association during the past weeks had been conducted entirely through messages. Lee was fifty-six, ten years older than Ewell, and while Ewell had been an obscure captain of Border dragoons Lee had been perhaps the most famous and most highly regarded soldier in the old army. Now he was the most famous active soldier in the world. Correspondents from foreign papers and military observers from foreign countries followed him around, and wherever he went people wanted to get a likeness of him.

When Lee greeted Ewell with reserved graciousness, he was deeply fatigued by the strain of the day, and his face showed it. He looked older close up than at a distance, much older than a year before. Then he had seemed young for his years; in the dusk of the arbor he seemed greatly aged. His beard, which he had grown in the fall of '61, had been gray when he took command: now it was turning white. His hair, too, had whitened and had receded at the forehead. Brushed sidewise across his skull from a part on the left, it was worn long over his ears, where it had grown fluffy.

As he followed Ewell into the shadowed arbor, Lee offered none of his usual pleasantries. Although his manner was composed, his face was tight in concentration and his gaze turned inward. During the day one corps commander had drawn him into an action he had wished to avoid; then, when the collision was salvaged, the commander of the mobile Second Corps had robbed the army of its chance to win the field. Unreflectively, Lee accepted this as a fact, as a new element in the problems to be solved.

Unlike other observers of Dick Ewell, he did not try to ascribe reasons for his inanition. Evidently he had had reservations about Ewell's fitness for corps command from the beginning and Ewell had simply confirmed Lee's worst fears.

Lee did not reproach him, did not repine over lost opportunities. His mind was totally absorbed by the details of the next move.

With the whole invasion a tentatively extemporized movement, Lee had at no time sought the enemy for the purpose of attacking him. His seeking of the enemy for the purpose of discovering his whereabouts was essentially a protective measure forced by the absence of Jeb Stuart. From what Lee had said that morning to Anderson in Cashtown, where Lee originally planned to establish headquarters, it would appear that he preferred to establish a position and let the enemy come at him.

There was nothing defensive about this. Lee was one of the great natural counterpunchers of warfare. He induced his opponent to lead, and when the enemy had opened himself in attack, Lee found an exposed spot for a counterthrust. His most decisive victories, Second Manassas and Chancellorsville, had been counterpunches to the enemy's lead. His way of fighting was to catch the enemy off balance, and only once in the war had he driven straight in on a power thrust.

At Malvern Hill, the last battle of the Seven Days, when subordinates' failures had repeatedly allowed the Federals to escape his traps, Lee, goaded beyond clear thinking by continual frustration of his plans, simply threw in everything he had. Malvern Hill was his worst-fought battle. Only Lee's retention of the initiative caused McClellan to continue to retreat after giving a costly and clear-cut repulse to the Confederates.

In the deepening dusk in the arbor north of Gettysburg, Lee was balancing in his mind the same type of failure he had contended with before reorganizing the army. A. P. Hill had not been an ideal choice for corps command; the best man available, he had performed about as expected, although

154

his illness suggested instability. Ewell's initiative was evidently inadequate to cope with his new responsibility.

The Powell Hills and the Dick Ewells were symptomatic of the breakdown through attrition which was undermining the South in its fight for independence. Its physical resources and manpower already were showing conspicuously the effects of the unequal struggle, and now the effects of the prolonged strain were appearing in the quality of command. Too many had been lost, and the pool of replacements was too small.

The men whom the ordeal had proved to be good were now asked to be great, and they were not. They were devoted and loyal, trained and experienced, but beyond these qualities they showed no X of the unusual. Lee must make do with what he had, and he must hurry. He must find ways to get at the enemy before Meade solidified his positions on those hills.

His thinking was shaped by the background of the South's waning strength, by the present illustration of the attrition in high command, and by the need for a decisive victory away from home. Apparently it never occurred to him to concentrate and wait for Meade. His men were driving the enemy, and, though Ewell had kept them from clinching the victory today, Lee thought only of how to complete it the next day.

To that end, he asked Ewell and Rodes about the condition of their troops. Surprisingly, Rodes was very defense-minded. Still subdued by his near approach to disastrous defeat, Rodes stressed his 2,500 casualties and showed no optimism about what his units might do in another assault. Ewell supported his division commander's attitude and added discouraging details about the number of men detailed to handle prisoners. While these two officers were talking as if they had survived a crushing defeat and were thinking only of saving lives, Jubal Early joined the party in answer to Ewell's summons.

Lee now asked the question that had been forming in his mind. "Can't you," he said to Ewell, "with your corps, attack on daylight tomorrow?"

Ewell froze again. He said nothing at all.

His silence encouraged Early to take the floor as spokesman for the corps. But, during the hours of waiting for an attack that never came and watching the entrenchments of the Federals grow on their hill, Early had decided that the time for assault was past. The aggressive general of the afternoon told Lee that his reconnoitering had convinced him that no attack could now be made successfully on Cemetery Hill or Culp's Hill.

Then, carried away by his ascendancy over the corps commander, Jubal Early was emboldened to advise the commanding general on battle plans. He had observed the high knobs of the Round Tops on the southern end of Cemetery Ridge, and he believed an attack there would be successful.

As this attack would involve other corps, Ewell heartily agreed on the wisdom of his subordinate's suggestion.

Their attitude was more disturbing to Lee than the simple fact of Ewell's failure to attack. The day's omission was, as Lee saw it, remediable. A defensive attitude was something else. This defeatism, coming from veterans of Old Jack's fierce strokes—three of the four responsible officers in the striking corps—momentarily shook his confidence in the army's ability to attack.

Speaking aloud his fumbling thoughts, he said: "Then perhaps I had better draw you around to my right, as the line will be very long and thin if you remain here. The enemy may come down and break through it."

"Oh, no," answered Jubal Early. On defense, the men could not be moved. The harsh terrain was favorable for defense either on top of the hill or at the bottom. Lee, he implied, could attack on the right, toward the Round Tops, in complete confidence that his left would be held.

Again Ewell seconded his subordinate, enthusiastic about any plan that demanded no decision from him in regard to his men. Even Robert Rodes spoke with conviction about holding the position they had.

Lee's mind, visualizing the enemy's ground and the position of his own troops, reverted to his desire to press home the attack.

All of Hill's men were on the field, Dick Anderson's division having come up late in the afternoon, but two thirds of the units were cut up and there were the personal limitations of Powell Hill to be considered. He had looked as white as a ghost all day.

The only fresh troops near at hand were two divisions of Longstreet's corps—McLaws's and Hood's, approaching Gettysburg after a long though not forced march. At Chambersburg, Pickett had been released from rear-guard duty. He was a good marcher and eager to get his well-led, seasoned brigades into action, but he could not bring his men twenty-five miles over mountain roads in time for early-morning action. That left the attack to Longstreet, with his two near-by divisions.

In considering these circumstances, Lee revealed his deep disturbance by speaking unguardedly in the presence of subordinates. "If I attack from my right, Longstreet will have to make the attack," he said, as if to himself. "Longstreet is a very good fighter when he gets in position and gets everything ready, but he is *so slow*."

None of the other three men present had ever before heard the commanding general give an opinion of another officer. In their own fixations, however, they were less impressed by the inner agitation Lee revealed than by the shifting of the attack to other units. Jubal Early, still speaking for the will-less corps commander, became very forceful in assuring Lee of what the corps would do in support of others. He reported that he promised "to follow up the success that might be gained on the [Confederate] right and pursue and destroy the enemy's forces when they had been thrown into disorder by the capture of the commanding position on their left."

Lee heard the assurances with some skepticism. In any case, he said, the corps might demonstrate against the enemy's hills, to distract them from the defense of their left. Then, as if unable to accept the supineness that had come over his attacking corps, he added that they might turn the diversion into a real assault if it seemed practical.

On Lee's usual proviso of "if practical," even Ewell and Rodes joined Old Jube in agreeing to make a fine demonstration that *might* grow into an actual attack.

After a moment Lee arose and, with outward calm, bade the gentlemen good-night. He was profoundly unsettled as he turned from the now shadowy trio in the arbor. As soon as he rode off from the strangest conference in his time with the army, Lee's mind began churning again in re-examination of the decision he had gropingly reached in fatigue, in necessity, in desperation.

9

It was full night when he rode along the Chambersburg pike from Gettysburg to the house on Seminary Ridge across the road from which temporary headquarters had been established. His tired staff were making their camp in the orchard.

Around him the army in bivouac was unusually quiet. Men lay down among the unburied corpses, and under the light of the rising moon the sleepers could not be distinguished from the dead, so still they lay. Few letters home were being written. The surgeon with Perrin's South Carolina brigade, wearied from his work, looked at the photograph of his little son, George, before falling asleep with the men.

John B. Gordon was among those to whom sleep would not come. He kept getting up and listening to the Federals' picks and shovels digging in on the hills, and then listening to the contrasting silence of the Confederate camp.

In the troops east of Gordon, the newly arrived division of Allegheny Johnson, there was a private in the 19th Virginia of the Stonewall Brigade who also could not sleep. His name was Wesley Culp, of the family for whom the hill had been named, and he was excited by his homecoming. On the next day he hoped to see the house in which he had been born. He got to see it. On the next day the soldier was buried in the fields of his childhood.

James Longstreet, the First Corps's sturdy "Old Pete," had not tried to sleep. Leaving his hard-marched men plodding through the night toward the field, he rode ahead to find General Lee, to learn the plans for the next day.

Unknown to Lee or to anyone else, the long-dependable corps commander was in the process of trying to establish over the commanding general the same type of ascendancy which Jubal Early now exerted over Dick Ewell. The difference was that Longstreet had kept silent since afternoon, when Lee on Seminary Ridge had dismissed his suggestion of avoiding battle where they were and moving around Meade's left. None of his inner agitation over the burst bubble of his dream of sharing a partnership with Lee showed in his impassive, heavily bearded face.

Lee gained some reassurance from the familiar, stolid presence of his orthodox fighter. Slow Longstreet might be, but his troops were near, they would get some rest, and all the units were composed of trustworthy veterans, officers and men alike.

Very doubtful of Ewell after his visit with the odd trio, Lee began to shift to a plan that demanded nothing of the Second Corps. For if Ewell's chiefs failed to make a convincing demonstration, as their defensiveness indicated they might, the Federals in their natural works would be free to pour enfilade fire along the ridge that the Confederates must take before Meade could concentrate on it. Lee aroused one of the staff officers from his rest and sent him with a message intended to be the final order to Ewell.

General Ewell was to shift from his present position—at an angle to the left of the Confederate line, facing south as the troops of Hill and Longstreet faced east—and move around to his right. This would shorten the Confederates' long exterior line and remove its hinge at Cemetery Hill. Ewell's corps would thus be put, under Lee's observation, in position to support an attack from the Confederate right.

The worn Old Man, in his eagerness to avoid losing the fruits of the unwanted collision, was planning to work with what he had. Yet he was not satisfied even with the rearranged plan. He did not go to bed, nor give Longstreet any positive orders. Worries kept gnawing away behind the composed façade.

Late at night he was surprised to see Ewell dismounting—awkwardly because of his wooden leg—outside headquarters. The general approached the group with more self-control than he had displayed in the arbor conference. He appeared to have regained at least the power to make a decision, and he spoke out forthrightly.

Evidently worried (though he did not say so) about the terrain of the rocky cliff on which he was to demonstrate the following day, Ewell had sent two staff officers to reconnoiter Culp's Hill. They had reported to Allegheny Johnson, and had received a startling report themselves. General Johnson, forgotten by Ewell when he called Early to join Rodes and himself for Lee's visit, had in soldierly fashion reconnoitered the enemy's ground in front of him. His reconnoitering party had brought back the information that the wooded spikes of Culp's Hill were not yet occupied.

In the still of the night, with the day's agonies of command behind him, Ewell had responded to this condition which offered him assurance of success. Unquestionably he had suffered shame in his depressed apathy, and he recognized Lee's change of plans—to shift him around to the right in support—as evidence of loss of confidence. But unoccupied ground to be seized relieved him from uncertainty, and his natural pride asserted itself. He wanted to regain a position of respect in the army by making the attack that the commanding general manifestly hoped for.

He finished his report to Lee by offering to attack Culp's Hill in conjunction with Longstreet's attack on the enemy left.

This was more like the Ewell his colleagues understood. At last the elements with which Lee was dealing became positives. He immediately threw off his fretful vacillation.

General Lee was not known for any favorite expression, like Jackson's "Very good, very good." He showed his satisfaction by a relaxation of his tired tautness of self-control. The haggard mask fell away and his eyes brightened as his mind shaped the plans with firm clarity.

Longstreet and Ewell would attack the enemy's line on opposite ends as soon after daylight as was practicable. Because Longstreet must get his men into position, Ewell would await Longstreet's opening guns before making his attack. The enemy's attention would be distracted and his defense divided. A. P. Hill would make a demonstration in the center, further to confuse the Federal command and immobilize units.

Every member of the staff recognized that Uncle Robert was finally finished with fumbling for a decision that held conviction for him when he spoke with a quiet, resonant finality: "Gentlemen, we will attack the enemy as early in the morning as possible."

To the exhausted staff officers the words meant that at last their day was over. In the orchard under the thin moonlight, the young men, fully dressed, lay down on blankets and fell into heavy sleep.

"Lee's Warhorse"

Dᴜʀɪɴɢ the night of July 1 in the vicinity of the sleeping
town of Gettysburg only Meade's Federal troops acted
with urgency. While the defeated survivors of the day entrenched themselves on Cemetery Hill, new arrivals hurried
through the windless night to occupy the ridge southward
from Cemetery Hill all the way down to the Round Tops,
where Lee planned to attack.

In Longstreet's two divisions near the field, the men who
were to make that attack went into bivouac from two to six
or more miles from Seminary Ridge. It was not thoughtfulness for his men which caused Longstreet to allow the unfought troops to sleep before reaching the position from
which they would attack. The reason lay within the strangely
disturbed mind of James Longstreet.

Regarded as the army's one dependable corps commander,
an old reliable who continued the character of the pre-
Chancellorsville army in the reorganization, Longstreet had
given little hint of the agitated state in which he prepared
for the second day's fighting. His later explanations for his

163

behavior, written years after the war in an atmosphere of bitter recrimination between Longstreet and his former brother officers, revealed that Old Pete himself possessed no clear understanding of the nature of his turmoil at Gettysburg.

Then forty-two years old, James Longstreet had been born in the Edgefield district (that "red hill and cotton" country) of South Carolina, though his roots were not in the aristocratic republic. His people, of Dutch background, had come to the South from New Jersey, and in Longstreet the strain of Dutch characteristics ran more strongly than environmental influence. On his father's death, Longstreet's family moved to Alabama when he was twelve, and all during his youth he visited much in Georgia, where his uncle, Judge A. B. Longstreet, was a scholarly and highly esteemed citizen. Without an ancestral place-identification, Longstreet was more or less attached to the Lower South and was not a typical product of any Southern state.

This least Southern of Confederate leaders was a prudent man, methodical and cautious by habit, blunt-spoken and stubborn in manner, with a disregard for the social graces. Yet his personality was by no means unattractive. Powerful of chest and shoulders, very strong, without fear, he possessed that uncomplicated nature which makes for an easy adaptability in undemanding societies. There was a stalwartness about him, a quality of reassurance in his bluff presence, and he had a hearty sense of humor. He liked to banter with other men and, when amused, laughed loudly. Men of his own type were strongly attracted to him, and he formed enduring friendships. One of his oldest friends was General Grant, an intimate since West Point, who was married to Longstreet's cousin.

Longstreet's wife was a Virginia girl, daughter of his former brigade commander, and the ten children of their union had caused him to exchange military glory for security in the old army. A line captain at the age of thirty-four, Longstreet transferred to the paymaster department with the higher rank and higher pay of major. Without the war, he would probably have lived out his days in this mundane niche at the Albuquerque post, enjoying the fine outdoor sports offered by the New Mexico country. Even when he went with the South, he still wanted security first. Saying that "I had given up all aspirations for military glory," he applied for a commission in the Confederate pay office.

A circumstance changed his mind and course. Because of the long trip by way of Texas, where Longstreet deposited his family, he did not reach Richmond until the end of June 1861, long after most other returned Southerners had received commissions as colonels. When Longstreet appeared at the war office, there was a desperate need for a brigadier to assume command of three raw Virginia regiments on the main defense line at Manassas. By this chance his date of rank, July 1, gave him seniority to the majority of brigadiers of his age, some with more distinguished records in the old army.

As a result, he was upped to major general in October 1861, when his contemporaries were making brigadier. This temporal seniority, along with his stolid self-assurance, caused Lee to entrust considerable responsibility to him when Lee first took command of the army. As Longstreet thrived on it, he was the inevitable choice for corps commander when Lee organized his force into the Army of Northern Virginia.

As corps commander, Old Pete gave complete satisfaction to everyone. Although sometimes slow, and preferring to have everything just so before committing himself, he was always sound. Despite a starvation diet, he kept his troops well conditioned and in fine unit spirit, and as a fighting force in straight-on action they were probably unsurpassed in the modern history of warfare. Wearing a heavy, bushy beard and looking at the world with unblinking blue eyes, the sturdily built general looked the part of the ultimately dependable lieutenant, "Lee's warhorse."

This open record of person and performance comprised the Longstreet that the army and the Confederate people knew. Inside, there was another man, known only to Longstreet—and not too well known to him. This inner man was born sometime in the eighteen months between the war's first battle at Manassas and his good day at Fredericksburg in December 1862. During that period, when Longstreet was between forty and forty-two, he experienced a rebirth of the "aspiration for military glory." As he kept it to himself, the ambition fed a growing delusion that his gifts were commensurate with his aspiration, and the good corps commander convinced himself that he possessed a genius for high command.

After the Battle of Fredericksburg, Longstreet tried in various ways to have himself detached from Lee's army, where he felt the chance would never be given him to win the fame he deserved. Stonewall Jackson stood in the way. Old Jack was the one the songs and poems were written about ("Stonewall Jackson's Way"), and people began to refer to "Lee and Jackson" and then to the rest of the army. In the public mind Longstreet was the warhorse, merely a trusted subordinate.

It was partly Longstreet's desire to stay away from Lee's army which removed him and two divisions from Chancellorsville, where his rival won his supreme glory. While Longstreet was maneuvering for a transfer with his divisions to the West, Jackson died and everything changed. In the reorganization of the army, Longstreet would be next to Lee.

Longstreet's jealous brooding over Jackson apparently led

him into a misconception of the relationship between Lee and Jackson; and Old Jack, more than has been recognized, became a motivation in Longstreet's behavior in the Gettysburg campaign.

Lee and Jackson were not equal collaborators, as they must have appeared to Longstreet. As Lee said, he, the commanding general, had merely to suggest to Stonewall. Suggestions from Jackson were not precluded, but always these were fundamentally tactical suggestions made within the context of a strategy on which the two generals shared that curiously intuitive understanding.

In contrast, Longstreet's short-range defensive thinking was antithetical to Lee's concepts of war, and he was by demonstration a limited soldier. To be a top-flight corps commander was in itself no small achievement (few were in the whole Confederacy), and it was a big leap for a contentedly physical type who two years before had been satisfied to serve as paymaster on an army post. In making that leap to the status of high-ranking subordinate Longstreet had employed his fullest potential. His ideas on strategy were vaporous and primitive, as he proved in his essays at independent command and in his suggestions to Lee.

Longstreet arrived at Gettysburg believing that he had already established his concept of a Jacksonian collaboration with Lee. He had even deluded himself into thinking that, in the collaboration, he had imposed his ideas of strategy on the commanding general. He was deeply shocked and bewildered when Lee, on Seminary Ridge during the afternoon of the first day, dismissed his suggestions. But he was a stubborn Dutchman. That night, while his troops were resting before moving up in the morning, Longstreet was making no plans for beginning the early movement that General Lee had requested. He was pondering ways of bringing Lee around to his own preferred plan of action.

167

Just as his secret stirrings of ambition had gone undetected, not one person in the army suspected that the Longstreet they depended on to solidify their victory was a stranger to them—and, in a way, to himself.

2

From the time that Longstreet arose just before daylight on the 2nd, no one can ever know with any certainty what went on in his mind or what transpired between him and Lee and other officers. In the reports, each hour of the next two days became obscured by the entanglements of the "Gettysburg Controversy" that was waged between Longstreet and his former brother officers for from five to thirty years after the war.

Even the origin of the controversy was disputed, with each side claiming that the other had thrown the first stone. However, no evidence appears of any public attack on Longstreet prior to his derogation of Lee as quoted in a book published in 1866 and in a letter of his which was apparently in circulation around the time of Lee's death in 1870. The first public criticisms of Longstreet in 1872, by Jubal Early and the Reverend William Pendleton, seem to have been primarily a defense of Lee. To attack Lee in that period would have been considered unchivalrous in anyone, and in Longstreet personally it was most unbecoming.

For Longstreet had committed what ex-Confederates considered the apostasy of "turning Republican." Appointed to a post in New Orleans by his friend, President Grant, in 1867, he took an active part in the Reconstruction government there. By 1872, according to Claude Bowers, "in Louisiana . . . Longstreet was ostracised." In September 1874 he commanded an occupation force that fired into a group of former Confederates who came at him with a Rebel Yell. The tensions and loyalties among disenfranchised Southerners created a climate of bitter passions in which the controversy over Gettysburg developed between Longstreet and men who became his enemies.

The high-ranking and highly placed officers who attacked Longstreet in print concentrated on his failures to the point of making him the villain of Gettysburg. In rebuttal, Longstreet expanded on his initial criticism, which claimed that Lee had failed because he refused to follow Longstreet's advice, and made of himself the potential hero of Gettysburg. In these post-war writings, Longstreet's attempts to prove his superiority led him into a rearrangement of his part in the battle to accord with a rational pattern of behavior based on his ignored strategy. But this after-the-fact version of the campaign revealed both a hazy memory of the events and a disregard of available facts.

Longstreet invented things that never happened, distorted recorded incidents, told outright lies apparently without realizing it, and contradicted himself in his various accounts. In reporting his undeclared duel with Lee, the stolid soldier attributed to himself some high-flown oratory which seems most unlikely in the circumstances and which not one officer present remembered hearing. However, the point of his conflicting versions is not so much that they are untrustworthy accounts of what he said and did, but that the self-vindications indicate Longstreet's confusion about his own state of mind.

The state of mind derived from his misconception concerning a collaborative status with Lee, and from his delusion that before they came North the commanding general had agreed to fight according to his plan.

From the moment that Old Pete stepped into the Jackson role, he urged Lee to remain on the defensive in Virginia and wait for another Fredericksburg. Longstreet's idea of military heaven was the Battle of Fredericksburg repeated in-

169

definitely, with his men standing in nigh impregnable positions and receiving clumsy lunges from the enemy. As all Union generals could not be depended upon to perform as ineptly as had Burnside, and as such repulses accomplished nothing toward victualing the army or winning the war, Lee dismissed the advice with his usual courtesy. He explained that he was not launching an invasion to seek the enemy's army. He hoped to draw the enemy out of Virginia after him and, while supplying his troops, he would receive battle where conditions offered opportunity for a decisive victory.

Satisfied that the army was not assuming the offensive, Longstreet regarded Lee's plan as an extension of his own determination to fight *only* on the defense. He recommended to Lee that, "after piercing Pennsylvania and menacing Washington, we should choose a strong position and force the Federals to attack us. . . . I recalled to him the battle of Fredericksburg."

With his mind burdened by the problems of operating in the enemy's country, Lee had offhandedly agreed to the general principle of defensive tactics in a strategic offensive. He certainly did not eliminate what Bismarck called "the imponderables" of war and commit himself to a fixed plan that would restrain him from taking advantage of any opening.

Longstreet, with his insensitivity to the nuances of human relationships, convinced himself that the polite gentleman had actually promised that he would fight only as Longstreet had suggested. In fact, Old Pete later contended that he had "consented" to the invasion only because Lee promised that he would fight on the defensive. The use of the word "consented" by a corps commander shows the depth of his delusion about the equality of the collaboration.

Such a promise was so remote from Lee's thoughts that after the war, when he was told about Longstreet's contention, he could not believe that Longstreet had ever said it.

A friend recorded that Lee said "that the idea was absurd. He never made such a promise and never thought of doing any such thing."

That General Lee did not even remember the conversation about the defensive invasion would explain his distracted dismissal of Longstreet's importunities when Old Pete joined the commanding general's party on Seminary Ridge late on the first afternoon. The collision between the two armies had then dictated the nature of the action, and, except for Longstreet, every general on the field recognized that solidifying their gains was the one urgent necessity for the decisive battle sought by Lee.

But in his fixation on fighting a defensive battle, another Fredericksburg, Longstreet ignored the condition of the battle that had evolved its own pattern. Despite the circumstances that he found at Gettysburg, he clung to a course which could not possibly apply to the existing situation.

Longstreet could not have been in full possession of his military faculties when he determined on changing winning tactics, to which the whole command of the army was committed, in the midst of an engagement. Nor could the after-the-fact rationale he attributed to his behavior have been present when he began the day of July 2 with the purpose of thwarting the plans of the high command which the rest of the army was preparing to execute.

After a breakfast while the stars were still shining, he left his temporary camp along Marsh Creek and started the four-mile ride to Seminary Ridge. His mind was demonstrably not on getting his troops up as early as possible. He was hurrying to Lee to find means of persuading the commanding general to shift the battle to make it Longstreet's fight. Offense had been the strength of his late rival, Jackson. He had no intention of trying to replace Stonewall by operating in the sphere of Old Jack's strength.

171

3

Robert E. Lee was not at his clearest in ordering Longstreet on an unsupervised offensive movement with only the general type of orders which he had used with Jackson. The year before, at Second Manassas, Longstreet had delayed so long in delivering the heavy counterstroke designed by Lee that Jackson's men were fought to the narrow edge of collapse and probably would have lost their pivotal position under more skillfully delivered Federal attacks. But at Gettysburg Lee, forced to use the only fresh troops at hand, depended on the only system he had perfected, even though the personalities involved no longer fitted that system.

In perspective, it would appear that in the beginning cautious Longstreet would have been a wiser choice than impetuous Hill to lead an advance force doing the work of cavalry. However, all post-facto reflections reveal that Lee was suffering from, and in a way reflecting, the strain that attrition was bringing to his whole country and its best army. As his command personnel was not what it had been at its Chancellorsville peak, so the overburdened general did not have on an invasion of vast consequence the self-command that had been his in a more limited and more strictly military situation.

He was trying to do too much himself. Solving the South's problem of self-defense was properly the function of the government. Lee had assumed responsibilities beyond his normal capacities because he alone conceived in terms of the whole. Consequently, the failures in his command, beginning with Stuart's mysterious absence, inevitably made a constant drain on his nervous energy, despite the face of calm strength he presented to his men.

Thinking of everything from Vicksburg to North Carolina

172

ports, further distracted and enervated by having to struggle against the constituted authority to achieve even such compromise measures as the invasion represented, the aging Lee (like Heth and young Rodes on the first day) *did not think of his generals' suitability to the nature of their assignments.*

Of course, once the battle was joined on July 1, he was allowed little choice. To him, "duty" was the "sublimest word" in the language, and he extemporized battle plans in the expectation that each officer would do his duty as he did his. The soldiers would do the rest. That his reasoning was fallacious is not the point: his reasoning reflected the mental condition created by a strain too great for a mortal to carry. A powerfully built man, always very fit (his son said: "I never remember his being sick in his life"), he aged more physically than any other commander on either side.

At Gettysburg, then, Lee perfectly represented the failing condition of his army and his country.

Having allowed impetuous Hill to make the reconnaissance, Lee "suggested" that congenitally slow Longstreet move up for an early attack on the morning of the 2nd.

With Pickett only that day released from rear-guard duty back at Chambersburg, Longstreet had with him only one division with a consistently glowing record in attack. That was Hood's. In striking power the four brigades (two Georgia, one Alabama, and Hood's former Texas Brigade) were more typical of Jackson's old Second Corps than of Longstreet's reliables.

They all bore the imprint of Hood's own native aggressiveness and absolute self-expression in combat. Many finely trained general officers in both armies excelled at those aspects of warfare which were necessary adjuncts to the actual commitment of men to the business of killing. John Bell Hood was among those who were at their best when armed

173

forces came to the ultimate test of battle. As brigade commander and division commander, he never lost his head in action, and he handled his fierce units with a sure touch.

Hood's reputation was marred later when he essayed strategy after he was unwisely promoted beyond his capacities to army command. He was a fighter, not a thinker, and on July 2 he was at the top of his potential as a division commander and at the fullness of his tremendous physical powers.

The tall, magnificently built Hood was then thirty-one, ten years out of West Point, though his hound-dog eyes and the drooping expression of his long tawny-bearded face gave the impression of a much older man. A native of Kentucky, he had fallen in love with Texas when he went there as a lieutenant with the Second Cavalry and it became his adopted state.

Hood first came to Virginia as a cavalry officer with "Prince John" Magruder's forces on the Peninsula. In March of 1862 he was made brigadier in command of the Texas regiments, who were to make him as famous as he made them. In the bitterly fought battle of Gaines' Mill, in the Seven Days Around Richmond, the blond giant led his Texans to the break in the Union line which marked the beginning of the first great Confederate victory since Bull Run, the year before.

"Hood's Texans" became a synonym for an irresistible attacking force. When he was promoted to major general (October 1862) his brigade set the pace for a division as tough as the nucleus. In 1863 the brigade included the somewhat unsung 3rd Arkansas Regiment, whose hard fighting and uncomplaining endurance made the Arkansans indistinguishable from the original troops. The brigade was then well commanded by J. B. Robertson, originally colonel of the 5th Texas.

174

In 1863 Hood had not yet married, though he was later to become a great homebody.

With the division of predictable Hood was the well-seasoned division of Lafayette McLaws, who was to have his troubles with Longstreet. Forty-two years old and a native of Augusta, Georgia, McLaws had been graduated from West Point in the same class with Longstreet, Richard Anderson, the Union's Abner Doubleday, whose troops the army had fought on the first day, and George Sykes, whose troops McLaws would fight on the second.

In the old army he had fought in the Mexican War, served in the Southwest and, married to a niece of his army commander and later President, Zachary Taylor, held the rank of captain—average for his class. Coming into the Confederate army with Georgia volunteers, McLaws began as a major, advanced to brigadier after First Manassas, and in May of 1862—when the badgered Rebel forces were preparing for what seemed a last-ditch defense of Richmond—was promoted to major general on proven capabilities.

McLaws looked what he was, a solid sort of man. He was broad of face, wore a thick, wide beard, and had a heavy head of hair. His gaze was forthright, reflecting determination and intelligence but, like Hood's, no humor. His record of personal relations in the army was good, and he was generally well liked, though he had no passionate partisans.

As a soldier he was sound rather than brilliant. His good troops were not associated with spectacular episodes such as Hood's breakthrough in the Seven Days and the attacks of Rodes and Pender at Chancellorsville, and there would never be a line about him like "And then A. P. Hill came up." Yet, on seniority and steady performance, McLaws merited consideration for corps command in the army's reorganization in May, after Jackson's death.

At Chancellorsville, however, he had not enjoyed a good

day. There, with Longstreet and two divisions away, the capable Georgian had fought directly under Lee, and Uncle Robert was critical of McLaws's failure to make an attack. In a touch-and-go situation McLaws had counted the costs, hesitated, and decided against the thrust. He may have been right, but Lee did not want his leaders to compute the casualties in advance.

Despite his disappointment at being passed over, McLaws was a dedicated Confederate. He kept fine control of his brigades (two from Georgia, one from South Carolina, and one from Mississippi), who had worked together since before the Seven Days. His division had been fortunate in having few casualties among the general officers: Kershaw, Semmes, and Barksdale had been with him from the beginning—though Paul Semmes and William Barksdale were in the last days of their life.

McLaws's division was a typical Longstreet outfit. Not such good marchers as Hood's men, but outstanding on defense, and led by a competent soldier, they were thoroughly dependable. With the self-reliance of old pro's, they did what they were told, stood up under heavy casualties, and produced tremendous firepower. Their unit spirit was high, their self-confidence complete. There was never an army in the world which would not have welcomed them.

On McLaws's and Hood's divisions the second day would depend—on them and their commanding officer, General James Longstreet.

4

The men of the two divisions, around 15,000 or less, had marched into Pennsylvania, sharing the unaccustomed banqueting with the other corps, and reached Gettysburg without having seen a live enemy soldier. On the morning of July 1, fighting was so remote from their thoughts that the camps of the Texans—the most accomplished foragers in the corps, perhaps in the army—resembled a country poultry exchange opening for the day's business. When the two divisions were started on the road to Gettysburg in the early afternoon, "the Texans moved lazily and plethorically into line." Climbing the pass across South Mountain, they were "too heavily burdened, inside and out . . . to make active exercise a pleasure."

Along the road they were delayed by a tedious halt to allow the passage of the miles of wagons belonging to Ewell's Second Corps, and it was full night when the van moved down the steep road toward the Cashtown village. Crossing the mountain, the troops had heard the distant firing of Hill's men and had recognized the high-pitched yells of their own people, and, despite their lethargy, they had lifted a spontaneous cheer. When darkness settled over the hilly countryside, however, the only human sounds were wheezes and puffing as the men trudged over the narrow road in the comfortless aftermath of their gormandizing.

As was habitual in Longstreet's command, the two divisions had made a late start. The march was not one of their more inspired troop movements, and it was around midnight when the head of the column—Kershaw's brigade of McLaws's division—turned off the road two miles from Gettysburg. The rest of the division stretched back to Marsh Creek, two miles farther west. Without making camp, the men sprawled out on the ground and fell into stupefied slumber.

Those in the rear of the strung-out column reached all the way back to Cashtown, and they kept shuffling for another hour or so. Then Hood's division were allowed to fall out with their van at Marsh Creek, four miles from Gettysburg. His men simply dropped beside the road where they halted.

After two hours' sleep, Hood's troops were aroused around three in the morning, and within ten minutes the half-awake men were again shuffling along the dark-shadowed road under the stars. They had not been ordered to hurry.

First light came shortly after four thirty, and they began to see the countryside where Hill's divisions had fought the day before. They passed farmhouses and Herr Tavern, a schoolhouse and a tollgate, and then they reached the wooded western slope of Seminary Ridge, where the cupola of the Lutheran Seminary rose above them. There the van turned off the road and moved across country until the last regiment had reached the point of the turn-off from the Chambersburg pike. It was then around seven o'clock, with two and a half hours of daylight gone.

Hood's good marchers had taken more than four hours to move from four to six miles. The true capacity of these marchers was shown by the division's fourth brigade, under Evander Law, which had also started out at three o'clock from its rear-guard position twenty-two miles west. Before noon they had come up and moved two miles southward, covering twenty-four largely mountainous miles in nine hours. It was the best marching of any unit in either army during the campaign.

Not only had these troops, directly under Longstreet's own supervision, received no hurrying orders, but Longstreet personally gave a curious order whose significance was unnoted at the time. Lafayette McLaws, whose division had been nearer Seminary Ridge and had bivouacked at least an hour sooner than Hood's, had his marching orders changed from four a.m. to "early in the morning." Thus, the nearest and most rested troops moved last, at full daylight, after Hood's men had passed. Then they passed Hood's division, behind Seminary Ridge, and halted farther south around eight o'clock. McLaws's division had used three hours to move from three to five miles.

The men in these doomed divisions were innocent of any

failure in celerity. No one had urged them forward, and the unseen enemy was silent. Although the sun was growing warm, as if the day might turn into a scorcher, the countryside offered a scene of bucolic tranquillity. In fact, the Texans were thinking of food again.

They had moved into "a little valley where water and fuel were easily accessible," and soldiers began building fires when the skillet wagon drove up and unloaded each regiment's share of cooking utensils. It had been rumored that the commissary wagons were going to issue some of the flour gathered in Cumberland Valley. The men were greasing their skillets and hauling water when, on the edge of the low hill on the other side of their little valley, they saw Generals Lee, Longstreet, and Hood, with their staffs, pause and look toward the east. The three generals were talking earnestly in low voices.

It happened that Private Ferdinand Hahn had served all three as a clerk in the Menger Hotel in San Antonio, and enjoyed what might be called a speaking acquaintance with the generals.

"Go on up there, Hahn," his companions urged him, "and hear what they're saying."

Hahn nonchalantly climbed the slope at a respectful distance from the group, and gradually edged closer. Suddenly he came scrambling back down the slope.

"You might as well quit bothering with those skillets, boys —it'll not be twenty minutes before we're on the move again."

His messmates crowded around the eavesdropper, and Hahn said he had heard General Lee tell Hood that Meade's people were already up there "and if we do not whip him, he will whip us."

Being veteran soldiers, the men put the skillets back in the wagon and readied themselves for going in.

Fatalistic about casualties, each man hoped, as before each

179

battle, that he was to be among the spared. None suspected that their dependable-looking corps commander was in such a disturbed state that he was to send them to their doom.

5

By the time Longstreet's last troops came up, their general had spent three daylight hours with Lee and had reached a point of total frustration. General Lee, intent on learning the extent to which his old friend Meade had occupied Cemetery Ridge, scarcely listened to Longstreet's harangues about changing his battle plans.

With his collaboration rejected a second time in twelve hours, Longstreet began to grow surly. Sometime in the early morning he made the—probably unconscious—decision to shift from words to action to get his own way. He began to procrastinate as a means of obstructing the execution of Lee's strategy.

His loyal chief of staff made a guarded reference to Longstreet's antagonistic attitude and deliberate slowness. Colonel Moxley Sorrel, observant and thoughtful, reported that: "As Longstreet was not to be made willing, and Lee refused to change or could not change, the former failed to conceal some anger. There was apparent apathy in his movements."

As this procrastination did not jibe with his post-war interpretation of the battle, Longstreet subsequently tried to prove that he had not delayed in getting his troops into action. He stated that Lee had not ordered him the night before to attack at daylight, as some of his enemies claimed. In this contention Longstreet was technically sound. Lee never gave such direct orders to corps commanders. But the knowledge of Lee's desire for an attack as early as possible after sunrise was general throughout the army at staff and command level. Even if it were possible that the commander of the First Corps had been ignorant of the plan the night before, he knew it at five a.m. when he reached Seminary Ridge in the area of Hill's troops.

Colonel Lindsay Walker, chief of A. P. Hill's artillery, said: "We [Hill's corps] were ready at daylight . . . and waited impatiently for the signal." Brigadier General Pendleton, in his anomalous position as chief of artillery, was at the southern end of Seminary Ridge at sunrise, tracing positions for guns across from the Round Tops. Even while Longstreet stood with the commanding general's group on the shaded area of flatland that served as a sort of observation post, Lee was waiting for the return of an engineering officer sent out at sunrise to reconnoiter the southern end of the Federal position.

But the most conspicuous evidence of Longstreet's procrastination is the fact that, with his van six miles from Seminary Ridge at five o'clock the preceding afternoon, and sharing the common knowledge that Meade was hurrying the concentration of his army, Longstreet took fifteen hours to get his men to the field—and then not deployed for action.

In his explanation, Old Pete attempted to obscure this poor performance by advancing the superiority of his advice which General Lee ignored that morning. According to Longstreet, he urged Lee to try "slipping around" to Meade's left, southward, and interposing their army in a strong position between Washington and the Federals. The number of latter-day supporters of this alleged plan is amazing in view of some elementary considerations.

There is a scarcity of strong positions between Gettysburg and Washington; there were the hazards of supplying the army while in contact with the enemy; and there was the extreme difficulty of making such a maneuver effective with Ewell's corps deployed for action three miles to the northeast, the cavalry not up, and the army spread out. One of

Longstreet's own divisions was a day's march away. With the armies in plain view of each other, there was nothing to prevent Meade from shifting to a strong position when Lee shifted and himself awaiting attack. Finally, Meade, even while rushing his troops to Cemetery Ridge, was taking precautions against such a turning movement, which he knew to be a favorite maneuver of Lee's.

Unquestionably Lee, in considering the alternatives to his two-pronged attack on the Federals' flank positions, had considered what Meade would do. Although he was not trying to outthink the Union commander, Lee always projected himself into his opponent's position. He planned to beat Meade to the obvious move. In the fresh morning light, before the disrupted citizenry were stirring about their farms, he began to evolve the details of attack on the extreme Union left.

This was to come about two miles south of the threatened Federal position on Cemetery Hill, below which Ewell was preparing to renew his halted attack. The rugged boulders of the Round Tops anchored the left end of the line, and Lee reasoned that Meade, in his haste to fortify his right against Ewell, would neglect those natural bastions. Lee visualized a diagonal thrust from the southwest, with his brigades attacking in oblique line to overlap the enemy's left flank and roll him up to the north of the Round Tops. When the enemy flank was completely turned, the Confederates would push on to the high ground of the ridge and take and hold the plateau. The Federal troops farther north on the ridge would be caught in enfilade and forced to abandon the position.

With threats at the other end of the Union line on Cemetery Hill and Culp's Hill, and with demonstrations in the center, the maneuver was soundly conceived. Not brilliant nor reflective of Lee at his imaginative best, the operation was within the potential of his troops and contained the elements of success.

Longstreet, in his claims for his own plan, attributed Lee's rejection of it to a bloodthirstiness that caused him to think only with adrenalin when he was fighting. There is no question that Lee, like all great fighters, was a killer once the battle was joined. That should not be taken as meaning, however, that blood lust inundated his brain when he stared through his field glasses at "those people" gathering on the opposite ridge.

His blood might have been up after the taste of victory the day before, but, according to the enemy's reports on his movements, Lee was "coolly calculating." However, several of the officers standing with him while he waited for the reconnaissance report observed his tension. As of eight o'clock Lee believed the southern end of Cemetery Ridge to be unoccupied in the vicinity of the Round Tops, but he needed the report of the engineering officer for confirmation before he could order the execution of his battle plan.

Contrary to general impressions, Lee's nervousness during this waiting period was unrelated to Longstreet. Although Longstreet's two divisions were not ready to go in and his artillery was not up, Lee did not know this. Longstreet personally waited on the grassy knoll with the other generals and staff officers, and, within the limits of Lee's observations, all of his lieutenants were prepared for action and waiting on his command.

Lee's strain came from the accumulation of responsibility which he bore alone, all focused that morning in the wait for an engineering officer to do the work of the absent cavalry. As usual, he tried to conceal his tension. His face was outwardly composed in what a staff officer called "the quiet-bearing of a powerful yet harmonious nature." As always, he was extremely neat about his person. His cadet-gray coat was buttoned to his throat, around his trim waist he wore a sword belt without sword, his dark boots were polished, and his light-gray felt hat, of medium-width brim, sat squarely on his head. His nervousness revealed itself in an inability to keep still.

A. P. Hill, partially recovered from his mysterious ailment of the day before, had joined the group, looking very slight among the large men. With Hill came Harry Heth, wearing a bandage around his head, and too shaken from the shell blow to assume command of his division. As the group was increased by arriving generals and their staffs, Lee paced up and down in the shade of a line of trees as if alone. Occasionally he interrupted his pacing to peer through his glasses across the valley where the Union troops were still gathering. Then he sat down on a fallen apple tree and began to study his map.

Although his ridge rolling southward from the seminary was lower than Cemetery Ridge, it was wooded for most of its length, and Lee seemed convinced that approaches to the attacking-point could be found which would conceal the troop movement from the Federals. According to the incomplete details of the map, the land between the two ridges at the southern end would favor his envisioned enveloping movement, once the men were in attacking position.

The Emmitsburg road ran diagonally across the shallow valley between the ridges, beginning within the Union lines. At about a thousand yards south it was still no more than two hundred yards from the crest of Cemetery Ridge. There the fence-lined road bent sharply to the southwest, toward the Confederate position. At the end of its course between the lines, the road passed below the point where Seminary Ridge faded off. In that area Lee had no troops at eight in the morning. But there the Emmitsburg road climbed the crest of a low rise, and Lee had selected this stretch of the road—

184

where it was more than a mile from Cemetery Ridge—as an anchorage for his assault troops.

Around eight o'clock in the morning General McLaws rode up and reported that his troops were up. Lee greeted him and directed his attention to the map.

Pointing to the high part of the Emmitsburg road, Lee said: "General, I wish you to place your division across this road," and with his finger showed that he wanted the troops placed in a line perpendicular to the road. Then, explaining that he wanted the troops to get there, "if possible, without being seen by the enemy," he asked the direct question: "Can you do it?"

McLaws replied forthrightly that he knew nothing to prevent him, and added that he would "take a party of skirmishers and go in advance and reconnoiter."

Lee told him that Captain Johnston had been ordered to reconnoiter the enemy's country and said: "I expect he is about ready."

Lee meant that the engineering officer was about to report, but McLaws, thinking Lee meant that Johnston was ready to start, said: "I will go with him."

Longstreet, who had been pacing near by, turned and said quickly to McLaws: "No, sir, I do not want you to leave your division."

Lee, in his absorption, apparently paid no attention to this exchange.

Longstreet then stepped up beside the seated commanding general, leaned over him toward the map, and said to Mc-Laws: "I wish your division placed so," and ran his finger in a line parallel to the road.

Lee raised his head and said quietly: "No, general, I wish it placed just perpendicular to that, or just the opposite."

Longstreet turned away without answering. McLaws, perceiving that Lee had no further orders, then asked Longstreet for permission to accompany the reconnoitering party. Longstreet flatly forbade it, and to McLaws it "appeared as if he was irritated and annoyed." McLaws rode off to his troops and made a personal reconnaissance of the woods south of Seminary Ridge in search of a concealed approach to the point of attack.

Some while after he left, Captain Samuel Johnston rode up to Lee's group with what turned out to be the most fateful misinformation of the Gettysburg campaign. The engineering officer's reconnaissance report also represented one of the costliest consequences of the cavalry's absence, and the desperate expedients to which it forced General Lee. In the emergency, Lee placed his reliance on a single staff officer to perform the mission of mounted troops.

At best, Captain Johnston's information of the Little Round area was incomplete. There were no detailed sketches of the hazardously rough ground at the southern end of the Federal line. Information obtained by an apprehensive individual crawling about on wooded precipices would naturally give an inadequate picture of the obstacles to mass troop movement. Johnston was intent on what he was to survey when he reached the top.

In addition to this incompleteness, the report of the engineering officer who personally reconnoitered the Round Tops was nullified by a stroke of incredibly bad luck. Captain Johnston had scrambled through the thickets to the choppy rock summit of Little Round Top just after the guarding troops of the night had been withdrawn and just before their replacements arrived. He started his risky journey back with the accurately observed information that Cemetery Ridge in the vicinity of the Round Tops was unoccupied by Federal troops.

Those projecting peaks had not yet been occupied, as Samuel Johnston reported to Lee. But the Round Tops were not the objects of Lee's attack. He aimed inside of them, to the north, where his men could climb the sloping ridge and get in command of the ground before Meade concentrated there. That area of Cemetery Ridge was likewise free of blue soldiers when the engineering officer glanced along the ridge, but only because of a freak accident of timing.

To that area Meade was even then sending the bulk of Sickles's corps, with artillery support, to extend southward the line that Hancock's corps was forming in the center. Onto the ridge between the flank *at* Little Round Top, not *on* it, and what might be considered the center of his line—a distance of about a mile and three quarters—Meade rushed between 15,000 and 20,000 men by nine o'clock in the morning.

That was the hour when Longstreet's reserve artillery, temporarily under young Porter Alexander, arrived at the field and at last completed the concentration of the attacking forces—except for the one brigade, Law's that was hurrying toward Gettysburg from its rear-guard post.

By nine o'clock the time when Lee could attack with advantage had already passed. The numbers and guns of the two armies were becoming equalized on the southern ends of the ridges, and Federal troop units were constantly pouring onto the field while Longstreet's men still lounged in groups around their stacked arms.

But, due to the report of Captain Johnston which confirmed his own appraisal of the situation, Lee assumed a condition on the Federal flank which no longer existed. He also assumed that Longstreet's troops were ready to move out at once. After he listened to the engineer officer's report, Lee nodded slowly, as if he had made the final decision to commit his battle plan to the test.

Then he turned to Longstreet and said quietly: "I think you had better move on."

This first direct order to Longstreet to move out was given

somewhere between eight and nine o'clock. After giving the casual order, the general mounted his iron-gray horse and rode the arc from Seminary Ridge around Gettysburg to Ewell's headquarters north of Cemetery Hill.

By leaving the field to Longstreet, Lee showed that nothing had happened to cause him anxiety about Longstreet's performing with his usual dependability. If, in his concentration on Cemetery Ridge, he had noticed Longstreet's surliness, as others did, Lee ignored it. He certainly did not associate the sullenness with deliberate procrastination, nor did anyone else at the time.

Such was his trust in Longstreet that the commanding general left his command post in the expectation of a coming attack. He personally went to investigate the man who, because of his failure the day before, Lee regarded as the unpredictable corps commander.

6

Since the night before, when General Ewell had come to Lee's headquarters with a resolve to attack *un*occupied Culp's Hill, the situation there had changed drastically. The tumbled mass of thicket-grown rock had been fortified by fresh men hurried to the field, who had dug defense lines and placed heavy artillery on the crest. On East Cemetery Hill, where Early's men had been halted the night before, the reformed fugitives had also dug themselves in and brought more guns to support them. General Lee needed no conference with Ewell to know that changed conditions could cause the brave resolves of midnight to be dismissed at daylight like a dream.

Adjusting as he must, Lee changed Ewell's plans, assigning him to make a strong demonstration in conjunction with Longstreet's attack. However, trusting in the younger field officers and the fighting spirit of the men, Lee made it plain

188

that he hoped the demonstration might grow into a full-scale assault. He underscored his wishes by not too gentle reminders of Ewell's failure to take the positions the afternoon before. The demonstration was to begin when Longstreet's guns were heard.

From Lee's viewpoint, capture of one end of the Union line would be as profitable as capture of the other. If both went, Lee would carve a victory of great magnitude. At the least, vigorous action by Ewell could distract Meade's attention from his left and prevent troops from reinforcing the Round Top end of the line.

In A. P. Hill's order to demonstrate against the center, Pender's division had directions to exploit any advantage. Anderson's unfought division was to support Longstreet's left as part of the attack. Heth's division, now commanded by scholarly, militarily untrained Brigadier General Pettigrew, was in general reserve.

That was the plan. It seemed, on the one hand, to restrain Hill's impetuosity and, on the other, to place no excessive demands on Ewell's initiative. The key was dependable Longstreet.

When Lee started back toward Seminary Ridge, *and not before,* he began to listen expectantly for Old Pete's guns to open. As he had left Longstreet not appreciably more than an hour before, it seems clear that Lee—unmindful of any attitude that would cause deliberate delay—had believed that Longstreet was ready to go in when he left him. So confident had he been of this that when he returned to the crest of the ridge around ten o'clock Lee could not conceal his surprise at finding the two armies precisely as he had left them.

Pender's division stretched southward from the Seminary, with the men resting behind the artillery placed at intervals in four-gun batteries. Southward beyond them, out of Lee's vision, the men of Anderson's division, who were to support

Longstreet's attack, were similarly resting. Farther back, westward, on the ridge, lounged the men of Heth's division, the reserve troops under acting commander Pettigrew.

Periodically during the morning the hills had echoed with the quick rattling of skirmish lines firing, as units of troops on one side or the other maneuvered for ground positions to their liking. When the astonished Lee rode slowly down Hill's lines, the only sound was the thin crackle of individual rifles, indicating no more than sharpshooters practicing their skills on the unwary. The guns were silent.

In consternation Lee turned to his aide and said: "What *can* detain Longstreet?"

Only the day before, he had asked Dick Anderson the same kind of question about Stuart: "Where *can* Stuart be?"

When Colonel Long gave no answer, Lee said: "He ought to be in position now." It was as if he were saying: "*Even* Longstreet ought to be in position by now."

This newest and totally unexpected failure in his plans intensified Lee's inner disturbance. As he rode along the ridge, staring from the enemy's thickening lines to Hill's idle troops, Lee in his agitation mistook a group of guns in position for one of Longstreet's artillery battalions.

The sixteen guns were commanded by young William Poague, a V.M.I. graduate who had been captain of the Reverend General Pendleton's Rockbridge Battery of college students from Lexington. Poague was as able a cannoneer as his dead friend Pelham had been, though less spectacular, and during the Battle of Fredericksburg Pelham had said to Poague: "Your men stand up better under killing than any gunners I've ever seen." Promoted to colonel commanding a battalion attached to Pender's division, the young cannoneer had his pieces well placed in four batteries, and great was his consternation when the commanding general lashed out at him for not hurrying on to the right with Longstreet.

190

Poague mumbled that he was not attached to Longstreet; since the abolishment of the reserve artillery, his battalion belonged to Hill's Third Corps.

Instantly apologizing, Lee showed his shaken control by asking this colonel of an artillery battalion: "Do you then know where General Longstreet is?"

The bewildered young man shook his head and called for his commanding officer, Colonel Walker. Lindsay Walker, bored with waiting five hours for the attacking signal, had found a bank where he could lie in the shade, shielded from the hot sun. He hurried forward and offered to guide his commanding general to Longstreet.

Colonel Walker recorded that on the way through the hilly woodland, detouring around wagons and ambulances and stray groups of soldiers, "General Lee manifested more impatience than I ever saw him show upon any other occasion; seemed very much disappointed and worried that the attack had not opened sooner, and very anxious for Longstreet to attack at the earliest possible moment. . . ."

Around eleven o'clock Colonel Walker and the commanding general came upon Longstreet. He and his staff were gathered in complete idleness.

Except for getting his artillery out, ready to take positions, the burly corps commander had made no movement in the two and a half hours since Lee had given the order. Nobody knows how he passed the time.

Longstreet had confided in no one. In fact, as if to give a logical explanation of his tacit disobedience of Lee's order "to move on," he had said to Hood: "The general is a little nervous this morning; he wishes me to attack; I do not wish to do so without Pickett. I never like to go into battle with one boot off."

Knowing nothing of this exchange, Lee was impatient at what he asssumed to be a slowness excessive even for Longstreet, and his only concern was to prod the stolid man into action. His controlled anger was apparent to the other officers.

His words of command are not recorded, but they must have been very firm—nothing discretionary about them. Lee himself reported that "Longstreet was directed to place the divisions of McLaws and Hood on the right of Hill, partially enveloping the enemy's left, which he was to drive in."

When Lee, who never used an "I" in his reports, said "Longstreet was directed," he meant that Longstreet was *ordered* to execute his assigned duties immediately.

Longstreet recognized the difference in Lee's tone and phrasing. Old Pete still had one legitimate excuse for further delay. Saying nothing to Lee about Pickett, who was hours away, he asked that he be allowed to wait until Hood's division was completed by the arrival of Law's brigade. As Law was reported to be wthin half an hour of the field, Lee agreed, and Longstreet's wait continued.

7

There are those who believe that this exchange over Evander Law never happened. Longstreet himself gave several versions of the episode, and Lee none. The circumstance of Lee's known impatience makes it seem likely that some reason was advanced to persuade him to countenance further delay, and Longstreet's request would have been reasonable. The Federals' Brevet Major General Henry J. Hunt, highly observant and articulate chief of artillery with Meade, accepted this version, and said that Lee would have done better to use Anderson's fresh division from A. P. Hill's corps rather than wait for Law's brigade. As Lee saw it, merely another half-hour would be added to what had already become a more than two-hour wait, so he accepted the condition that, according to Longstreet, would make him ready to go in.

As for Anderson, recently transferred out of Longstreet's corps, Lee seemed uncertain as to his proper placement in the command situation. As if to avoid offending sensitive Hill by removing a division that had not yet fought with his corps, and yet to allow Longstreet to call on Anderson without going through Hill, Lee instructed Anderson "to cooperate . . . in Longstreet's attack." This order was the vaguest he ever gave. He did not specify whether Anderson was to act under the orders of Longstreet, commanding the attack, or of Hill, his new corps commander, or Lee's own. He seemed to be reverting to the loose structure of his early days in command.

Longstreet later went so far as to reproach Lee for not personally accompanying the attacking column. Not only would this have been contrary to Lee's custom of allowing corps commanders to fight their own battles, but the criticism overlooked—as others have since—the sizable point that Lee was in command of the whole army. Its two attacking columns would be separated by five miles, with the potential threat of a counterthrust of the enemy at its center. Lee operated from an informal general headquarters at that center, almost directly across the valley from Meade's headquarters. There Longstreet, Hill, and Ewell could send for consultation or guidance, though there was no obligation on them to do so. The afternoon of July 2 was to put to the test Lee's familiar pattern of field command, with two new corps commanders and one rebellious dependable.

General Lee did ride with Longstreet for some distance at the beginning of the covered march to the Emmitsburg road. Probably he wanted to see for himself that the long-delayed movement had begun at last—it was then around one o'clock. In parting with Longstreet to return to his command post, most certainly he did not suspect that his most dependable commander was riding into battle in what amounted to a mutinous state of mind.

For that matter, the other officers and even soldiers who began to observe Longstreet's unconcealed ill-humor did not suspect its nature. Lafayette McLaws said it for them all: "The cause I did not ask." They accepted Longstreet merely as a man out of humor.

Actually, his usually immobile face was reflecting the torments of his frustration and outrage. He had been rejected as "another Jackson" in council, his advice had been finally dismissed with a brusque order, and his delaying tactics had succeeded only in arousing the Old Man's impatience. Prodded on to this attack of which Lee knew he disapproved, he had been treated like any other subordinate.

As he rode southward in the hot shadows of the woods south from Seminary Ridge, Longstreet, perhaps unconsciously, resolved to be no more than a subordinate who mechanically does as he is bid, regardless of circumstances. His native stubbornness gave him the capacity to turn himself into something like an automaton. As such, he doggedly followed Lee's order even *after* he learned that the conditions which had prompted the order no longer existed.

As a corps commander, Longstreet was allowed the initiative to shift the details of the battle plan in his sector according to the conditions he found. If he did not wish to assume this responsibility, he could send a staff officer to Lee and report the changed conditions. Longstreet did neither. He obeyed the order precisely as it had been given, and this he did dully, in the self-imposed stupidity of renouncing all initiative.

However, except for his slowness, Longstreet had given no hint that his bad humor reflected a disturbance so profound that he would be reduced to a state of incompetence for command.

8

From the beginning of the movement out, in which Longstreet managed to consume another hour even after the arrival of Law's brigade, there is nothing except disagreement among the men who recorded it—Longstreet, McLaws and his brigadier, Joseph Kershaw, and the luckless Captain Johnston, who led the way. A composite of the reports seems the best chart of the strange course of the troops going into battle.

Nobody can ever know exactly what happened between one o'clock, when the two divisions started from the western slope of Seminary Ridge, and four o'clock, when the first troops went into action across the Emmitsburg road. Kershaw's brigade of McLaws's division led the march along a lane on the western side of Herr Ridge (west of Seminary Ridge), with that rise obscuring them from the enemy. They all agreed that they moved slowly and that it was awfully hot. The stone fences to be climbed, the post-and-rail fences and worm fences to be torn down, were a constant hindrance and annoyance. Few farmhouses were passed, and even the Texans had no mind for foraging. The gunfire on the other side of the ridge, while still desultory, grew heavier and more constant. The men's canteens emptied, and the sultry heat created an apprehension about water.

The core of the disagreements concerns a point where their concealed lane climbed a hill on which the troops would come in view of the Federal signal station established on Little Round Top. Captain Johnston called attention to their exposure. Up until his warning, there is no serious disagreement among the accounts. Thereafter the hard-worked Samuel Johnston became involved in Longstreet's recalcitrance.

Longstreet's mind was now so controlled by his denial of any responsibility in Lee's plan that he, a general in command of a corps, turned over the movement of his leading division to an engineering officer lent him as a guide. This he did without telling anyone, least of all Captain Johnston.

For his part, this engineering officer assumed no more authority than would, say, a friendly local civilian who offered merely his knowledge of the country. In his account the conscientious captain said that he "had no idea that I had the confidence of the great Lee to such an extent that he would entrust me with the conduct of an army corps moving within two miles of the enemy's line, while the lieutenant-general was riding at the rear of the column."

General Longstreet was not actually at the rear. He rode in the middle of the column because, he said, "I was relieved for the time from the march." He reported with a straight face that he accepted a guide sent by Lee as "relieving" the corps commander from the march.

The general riding with Captain Johnston was stocky Lafayette McLaws, at the head of his division. According to his version, when they reached Black Horse Tavern the temporary guide, in some surprise, pointed out their exposed position to him. McLaws said that, from where he paused, "the Round Top was plainly visible, with the flags of the signal men in rapid motion."

McLaws ordered his division halted, and rode with Captain Johnston in search of an alternate route. They could find no unconcealed way that led to their attacking-point a mile or more farther south. On their way back toward the head of the column they encountered Longstreet, who was riding forward to discover why the march was halted. McLaws reported that he showed Longstreet the route that exposed them to the enemy, and suggested a countermarch as the only alternative to revealing the troop movement.

Longstreet, very evasive about the incident in all three

196

of his conflicting versions, summed up the halt in one account by saying "after some delay. . . ."

Captain Johnston, later a friend of Longstreet's, said that he "called General Longstreet's attention" to the exposed rise. His report was skimpy on physical detail and inclined to ignore McLaws's presence.

Joe Kershaw, commanding McLaws's leading brigade, said: "We were halted by General McLaws in person while he and General Longstreet rode forward to reconnoitre. Very soon these gentlemen returned, both manifesting considerable irritation, as I thought."

Forty-one-year-old Kershaw, a cool-headed officer, was neither enemy nor particular friend to any of the other three. Of a Revolutionary South Carolina family and son of the Mayor of Camden, Kershaw—a lawyer, like his father—was a state legislator. His only previous military experience had been with volunteers in the Mexican War when he came into the Confederate army with a volunteer regiment that he raised. Natural leadership and applied intelligence had advanced him to brigade command, and he was tabbed as future material for division command. A resolute, scholarly-looking man, Kershaw was clean-shaven except for a drooping light mustache; he had a bold nose and intense eyes under projecting brows.

His version did not conflict in essentials with the others, though only he and McLaws said that from the point of the halt the troops did countermarch. Longstreet in one of his vague references said: "There were some halts and countermarches." This does not substantially contradict McLaws and Kershaw, and a countermarch as described by Kershaw would account both for the time known to have been lost and for the confusion that all agreed occurred between McLaws's and Hood's troops.

197

As Kershaw remembered the countermarch, "in so doing, we passed Hood's division, which had been following us. We moved back to the place where we had rested during the morning, and thence by a country road to Willoughby Run, then dry, and down that to a school-house beyond Pitzer's [house]. There we turned to the left [east], moving directly toward Little Round Top. General Longstreet here commanded me to advance with my brigade and attack the enemy in the Peach Orchard, which lay a little left of my line of march, some six hundred yards from us."

Kershaw's description accords with existing maps and places his brigade exactly where all battle reports place it in relation to the other troops of both sides, once they were on the field. He seems a reliable witness for the details of the march, of which Longstreet was determined to remember as little as possible.

McLaws was less concerned with the general direction of the march than with the details that delayed him—"the fences and ditches we had to cross." But his description of the deployment of his whole division to the positions where all battle reports placed the brigades confirms the course outlined by Kershaw. Only this countermarch could explain why the lead brigade of the two divisions required more than two hours to cover less than three miles.

It was passing three o'clock when Kershaw's South Carolina regiments emerged from the stifling woods southwest of Seminary Ridge into an open field. There he headed for the Emmitsburg road, as Kershaw said, "in full view of the Union position."

From the time of Kershaw's first look at that Union position, there is no disagreement among the generals as to what they saw. They beheld a situation that required them, if they executed their assigned tasks, to commit their men to mass slaughter.

198

9

McLaws, the first general above brigade command to view the enemy's position, said: "One rapid glance showed them to be in force much greater than I had, and extending considerably beyond my right. . . . I rode forward, and getting off my horse, went to some trees in advance and took a good look at the situation. . . . The view presented astonished me, as the enemy was massed in my front, and extended to my right and left as far as I could see. . . ."

While McLaws was making his personal reconnaissance and trying to hurry his troops forward, Hood's men passed southward beyond his division, going into position to open the assault on his right. McLaws wrote that "as his [Hood's] troops appeared, the enemy opened on them, developing a long line even to his right. . . ."

That was supposed to be the open end of the Union line, north of the Round Tops, which the assaulting columns were to take in flank. Instead, the defensive lines overlapped their own flank. "Thus," recounted McLaws, appalled at what he saw, "was presented a state of affairs certainly not contemplated when the original order of battle was given. . . ."

The plan of battle contemplated when Lee instructed McLaws that morning, tracing the course with his finger on the map, was for the attacking brigades to strike in echelon at a northeast angle from the southwestward road, with their left resting on the road. To move out in that order, their right must overlap the Federal left, or the line of attack would be suicidal. As it was, McLaws's line would be crossing the enemy front at an angle to expose its own flank and rear.

McLaws's personal responsibility in this "state of affairs" ended when he conveyed the grim intelligence to Longstreet. He assumed that Longstreet would appraise General Lee of the conditions that made his battle plan impossible.

It was McLaws's opinion that Lee, had he been informed of the true situation, would have called off the attack. Although it is nowhere stated that McLaws waited for countermanding orders, his actions indicate that he expected or at least hoped that the attack would be countermanded.

Even bold Kershaw halted after one glimpse of the rifles glistening in the peach orchard on the rise that Longstreet, in his agitation, had personally ordered the brigadier to attack. On his own initiative, Joe Kershaw sent his men straight ahead into a defensive position. He saw a stone wall running between the Flaherty house on his left and the Snyder house on his right. Sending forward a line of skirmishers as a screen, he hurried his brigade to the cover of the stone wall facing the peach orchard.

Closer, he observed that the infantry in the peach orchard was supported by artillery, with an entrenched line of battle in their rear, extending "far beyond the point at which their left had been supposed to rest." As soon as his men were drawn in battle line in a relatively protected position, Kershaw sent back word to McLaws of what he had discovered in his front and what he had done about it.

McLaws, either forgetting or never having known that Longstreet had given a direct order over his head to one of his brigadiers, manifestly believed that Kershaw was acting with wisdom and discretion. His other brigades were strung out for more than a mile back on the narrow road, and as they came up in regiments, he began sending them north in a leftward extension of Kershaw's defensive position, and in support in the rear.

While he was placing his troops, between three and four o'clock, a Longstreet staff officer, Major Latrobe, rode up and demanded to know why McLaws had not attacked. Latrobe said: "There's no one in your front but a regiment of infantry and a battery of artillery."

McLaws replied he would attack as soon as his whole division was formed, but explained that the enemy was in great force in his front, with artillery, and extended far to his right.

In a short time, or so it seemed to harried McLaws, the staff officer returned and repeated the order to open the attack. Again McLaws explained that the strength of the enemy in his front "required careful preparation for the assault."

All too soon Latrobe was back again, with the order this time, McLaws said, "peremptorily for me to charge."

Still he delayed giving the order. Without conscious intention, the major general was pulling a Longstreet on Longstreet. But Old Pete, having finally reached the point of attack designated by Lee, had his mind set on sending those troops in precisely as Lee had ordered hours before. He acted as if the Union left were as lightly occupied as Lee believed and as if the Confederate right overlapped the Union flank instead of being themselves overlapped. No message was sent to Lee.

10

About one air-mile away the commanding general was waiting for the opening of the attack on the impregnable position of a line he had never seen. The unusually careless reconnaissance was the result both of his normal system and of the special circumstances, but his reliance on troop action beyond his supervision reflected Lee's more fundamental mistake of operating with separated columns on a wide front in a technique founded on Stonewall Jackson's collaboration. The truth was that Lee, from the beginning placed under unnatural stress by having to grope without cavalry, did not react to evidence that the system of the Jackson era was unworkable without Old Jack.

Later he adapted himself to this absence. As the Prussian

military observer Major Scheibert noted, Jackson's place finally "was filled *by Lee himself,* who, like a father when the mother dies, seeks to fill both her place and his own in the house." At Gettysburg, the first test by arms without Jackson, Lee had not assumed this dual role.

Trying to *supervise* everything, he actually *led* nowhere, and the army felt the lack of a strong hand at the controls. The overlong Confederate line consisted of three separate small armies mismanaging three separate battles.

During the whole afternoon only one message came to the commanding general. His command post was more like an isolation post, and he had no notion of what was happening at Longstreet's end of the line. There nature had outdone even the Cemetery Hill-Culp's Hill end in natural defenses. The ground of Cemetery Ridge became rough and rocky at its southern end before terminating in the two huge columns of Round Top and Little Round Top. Their perpendicular faces were strewn with boulders and covered with almost impenetrable thickets. Five hundred yards to the west of Little Round Top, toward the Confederate side, rose a somber mass of huge boulders called Devil's Den. When McLaws and Hood moved into position, these forbidding fortresses were still not occupied by Union troops.

Devil's Den rose at an angle between two branches of Plum Run. North of the boulder formation, little Plum Run Valley was marshy and dotted with more stray boulders. To the west of Devil's Den a ridge extended toward the Confederate side where Hood's men were forming in concealment for their attack across the Emmitsburg road. This ridge, low and sloping, was important because at four o'clock in the afternoon there were no Federal units to the south of it—beyond the range of the projected attack.

Two divisions of Sickle's III Corps were placed northward from the Plum Run terrain. Supposed to connect with

Hancock's II Corps, which were in the center on Cemetery Ridge, Sickles had placed his troops six hundred yards in advance of Hancock's left. By four o'clock the V Corps of George Sykes were also hurrying toward the left.

Commanding General Meade had not particularly wanted to fight there, where an essentially defensive position offered little opportunity for counteroffensive. Certain, however, that Lee would follow up the first day, he had risked a race of troop concentration rather than risk demoralization by retreating to a preferable position. Longstreet allowed him to win the race.

Not expecting such collaboration, Meade had spent an anxious morning, expecting attack hourly, and he had not aligned his troops as he might have if he had known he would be allowed eleven hours of daylight to strengthen his position. Concomitantly with Meade's hurried disposition of troops and guns from his headquarters house, the general at the southern end of the line had also taken some liberties.

This corps commander was Major General Daniel Sickles, an unsavory, showy, and pugnacious character from New York who went further on brassy self-confidence and politicking (in civilian life and in the army volunteers) than many a better man went on ability. Dan Sickles, in his egotism, decided to advance the Union line a half-mile westward from the rocky ground of Cemetery Ridge to a part of the Emmitsburg road that followed the crest of a rise. A large peach orchard there faced the high road that formed his front. His left reached toward the extension of the low ridge from Devil's Den to the road, thus placing his lines at an angle between two ridges. Sickles perceived only the natural strength of his salient, and not the dangers to which such a projection exposed his flanks.

East of Sickles's peach orchard, after some scattered fields of corn and oats, were a rocky stand of timber and, south of it, a large wheatfield—"The Wheatfield," it became. South of this field a thick woods stretched down to the northern slope of the Devil's Den ridge. The boulder-strewn marshes of Plum Run Valley spread between those woods and Cemetery Ridge near its termination in Little Round Top. In that rough terrain Birney's division of Sickles's corps formed a flank for Humphreys's division in the peach orchard. It was Birney's brigades that formed the line which overlapped the Confederates. In turn, behind Humphreys's right, up on Cemetery Ridge there were Hancock's guns to spray the road, as well as troops from Hancock's left which could be used in support.

Without knowing the exact details of the ground or of the troops facing them, this alignment of Federals on commanding ground, bisected by stone fences, was the sight that greeted first McLaws and then Hood when he brought his division out on McLaws's right.

There had never been a day when Hood, like McLaws at Chancellorsville, had hesitated to attack. The tawny-bearded giant liked to wade in, and the men he commanded suited his taste. His crack-shooting troops brought tremendous firepower to the target of assault; they were as tough as the legends represent plains Texans to be, and individually highly skillful and fiercely combative in action. But Hood took one look at the enemy's position north of Little Round Top and reacted precisely as had McLaws.

He recognized that the battle order, written more than two miles away on the mistaken information brought back by Captain Johnston, did not fit the existing conditions. He saw that, as Joe Johnston once said, "it was not war, but murder."

His conclusion was the same as McLaws's: Lee never contemplated an attack in echelon at a northward angle to envelop the enemy's southern flank when that southern flank overlapped his own. Not only would his men present their backs to the enemy, but, attacking in echelon, they would present targets in successive waves, like ducks going across in a shooting gallery.

Hood, showing more initiative than McLaws, kept his men concealed in the cover of the woods and sent picked Texas scouts to reconnoiter the country south of the ridge that, projecting westward from Devil's Den, marked the end of the Federal line. After a very quick, though wholly accurate, reconnaissance, the trained scouts reported to Hood that the country south of the Round Tops was open. Offering no more physical obstacles than the usual stone fences, it was then unoccupied by any enemy troops. At this southern end of the Round Tops, Hood could get on the Federal flank as contemplated by General Lee.

For the first and only time in his army career Hood suggested a change of orders to his commanding general. Turning to a staff officer, the Texas convert dictated a quick oral report to be made to Longstreet. In the existing conditions, it was Hood's opinion that "it was unwise to attack up the Emmitsburg road, as ordered." Instead, he pointed out the exposed southern end of the Round Tops and urged Longstreet to allow him "to turn Round Top and attack the enemy in flank and rear."

Hood sent Captain Hamilton galloping off and began planning a movement that would fulfill the intent of Lee's battle order. The commanding terminals of the enemy's defense line would be in his hands before dark.

Two batteries of his guns were blasting away, developing the enemy's position, when the staff officer returned with a reply from Longstreet. It consisted of a single, unequivocal sentence: "General Lee's orders are to attack up the Emmitsburg road."

11

When Longstreet later wrote about overruling Hood's sound plan, he said "that the move to the right had been proposed the day before and rejected."

As the purpose of Hood's proposed tactical movement to the right was merely to get on the Union flank and rear *at Gettysburg,* Longstreet's explanation amounted to a gross distortion. His proposal that had been rejected the day before was for a strategic withdrawal of the Confederate army around to the right *away from Gettysburg* to another position altogether. The only element common to Hood's suggestion for a movement of one division within the battle and Longstreet's proposed movement of the army away from battle was that the direction of both was to the right. In basing his rejection of Hood's extemporized plan on the rejection of his own strategy, Longstreet revealed the depth of the wound to his ego and the consequent undermining of his judgment.

When Longstreet's reply reached John Hood, even so instinctively obedient a soldier could not accept it. As had McLaws, he explained the conditions a second time. Then, in a masterful understatement, he said "that I feared nothing could be accomplished by such an attack" up the Emmitsburg road "and renewed my request to turn Round Top."

Again the staff officer galloped off, and again he returned with the single sentence in reply: "General Lee's orders are to attack up the Emmitsburg road."

Like McLaws, Hood still could not bring himself to commit his men to an attack in which, he recorded, "I could not reasonably hope to accomplish much. . . . In fact, it seemed to me that the enemy occupied a position so strong—I may say impregnable—that, independently of their flank fire, they could easily repel our attack by merely throwing and rolling stones as we approached."

Hood was then joined by his senior brigadier, Evander Law, whose Alabama regiments had done the great marching that morning. Law, from the reconnoitering of his own vedettes, had reached the same conclusion as Hood about attacking around Little Round Top. He had independently written out a formal protest against executing the existing order and offered it for Hood's endorsement. Hood signed Law's protest and grew emboldened to make a final, more urgent appeal.

Seeking out his adjutant general, Colonel Harry Sellers, he directed him to try to convey to Longstreet the impossibility of attacking according to the morning's order. Sellers rode off to implore the commanding officer to shift the attack to the rear of the Round Tops.

A third time (as with Peter's "I know not the man") came the answer: "General Lee's orders are to attack up the Emmitsburg road."

Then, as in McLaws's experience, a Longstreet staff officer arrived with a peremptory order to begin the attack at once.

Hood had no alternative unless he surrendered his sword. Resignedly he said to Law: "You hear the order?"

Law turned away. In his account he recorded only the fact that "I at once moved my brigade to the assault."

When his five Alabama regiments came whooping out of the woods, they were joined by Hood's old "Texas Brigade" —three Texas regiments and the 3rd Arkansas, under Brigadier General Robertson.

The Georgia brigades of Benning and G. T. Anderson began to form as reserves.

As the regiments deployed for their fatal action, Longstreet rode up to see that Hood began the attack. Even with

207

his troops in motion, Hood paused to show Longstreet the difficulties of following the orders and to stress the advantage of striking the open flank at the end of Round Top.

Longstreet said: "We must obey the orders of General Lee."

Without answering, Hood rode ahead with his troops. The big man was riding with his old brigade when a piece of metal struck his arm with such force that he was unseated. Stretcher-bearers hurried forward to lift the huge frame onto a litter. They moved back with the fallen leader under the flying fragments and in the rising din of contact established by the first two brigades.

Longstreet had already ridden northward toward McLaws.

The command of Hood's division devolved on Brigadier General Law.

12

Evander Law was in looks a southern "gallant." Handsome in the romantic fashion, the twenty-seven-year-old South Carolinian had a lean face, sensitive and strong. His clearly defined features and fine mouth were framed by a thin mustache and a closely trimmed dark beard growing down from the edges of his lips. His hollow cheeks were clean-shaven, and his eyes looked at the world with a certain gentle intensity.

Evander Law's only military training had been as a student at The Citadel, where in his senior year he doubled as an assistant professor of *belles lettres*. Graduated at twenty, he became an educator, and before he was twenty-five the dreamy-looking Law founded a military high school in Alabama. He came into the Confederacy with a volunteer company that he raised, and he rose on natural ability. In the March before Gettysburg he married the daughter of a wealthy planter, and, promoted after Gettysburg, Law was

208

to live to be the last surviving major general of the Confederacy—dying in 1920.

Applying his intelligence to warfare, Evander Law—unlike that other natural soldier, John B. Gordon—refused to allow the system of command to negate the course of military logic. In one of the least-mentioned aspects of whole "Longstreet drama," Evander Law flatly disobeyed orders.

He caused the second day of Gettysburg to be fought in defiance of Lee's battle order to which Longstreet gave stubborn obedience.

Before the command of the division came to him, Law, on his own responsibility, sent his brigade straight toward the base of Little Round Top, in violation of the orders to move obliquely northward. If the division was not to be allowed to take the bastion from the rear, then he would try it straight on. He refused to march the backs of his men to enemy guns.

In a sense, the battle on the right became Law's battle for Little Round Top. Strangely, Little Round Top was defended, at the time Law's brigade got there, by a Federal general who also acted on his own responsibility.

Meticulous Meade had sent General Warren on a late inspection tour of the lines, and this alert Federal detected the sunlight on the rifle barrels of Hood's concealed troops waiting to spring out of the woods. With no time to consult Meade, Warren personally directed brigades from Sykes's corps to change their course from supporting Birney's division in Plum Run Valley and take up positions among the thickets on the rocky ground of Little Round Top.

At the moment of contact, while Longstreet was literally obeying orders that he knew the commanding general had issued without knowledge of the actual conditions, Warren was anticipating orders that his commanding general would have given had he known the conditions.

From then on, it became a soldiers' battle. To John West

of the 4th Texas it seemed "more like Indian fighting than anything I experienced during the war." Private Bradfield of the 1st Texas said: "Every fellow was his own general. Private soldiers gave commands as loud as the officers—nobody paying any attention to either."

The confusion began when Law sent his Alabamians straight ahead instead of obliquely, as ordered. Although his plan was sound, its extemporaneous adoption threw a burden of alignment on Robertson's Texas Brigade to his left. Robertson, like all the others on the ground, knew what they were up against and what Law was doing, and tried to adjust his regiments to keep contact with Law.

The heavy Federal fire of near-by rifles and artillery from the ridge made the going difficult over craggy ground where ravines sliced across ranks and boulders separated units of troops. Alert Federal officers seized every opportunity to enfilade flanks even momentarily exposed, and Federal units, in their turn cut off, made incredible counterattacks to throw the advancing line off balance.

General Robertson, by his own account, finally abandoned Longstreet's senseless order of holding to the Emmitsburg road and fully committed his four regiments to Law's attack toward Little Round Top. By then his regiments were separated.

His two left regiments, the 1st Texas and 3rd Arkansas, became enveloped in fire, and their left flank was attacked from the north. Colonel Manning, of the 3rd Arkansas, turned two companies to face left and protect the flank with fast firing. The rest of the force plunged on up the hill along Plum Run Valley and drove the enemy from a troublesome battery posted there.

The two companies on the left were being engulfed. Leaving two companies from the 1st Texas to hold the captured guns on the hill, Robertson rushed the rest back to the 3rd

Arkansas companies that were on the flank. The hill was lost and then retaken. General Robertson sent a staff officer through the terrible field of fire to recall the 4th and 5th Texas. They had drifted to the right in trying to keep closed on Law's left.

By the time Robertson's order reached them, the 4th and 5th Texas had become mingled with the center of Law's regiments, and the whole line was hacking its way to the stronghold of Devil's Den. Both their colonels, Key and Powell, were down—Powell's body was riddled with bullets. Then their lieutenant colonels fell, Bryan heavily wounded and Carter dying. Majors sprang forward to lead the regiments to the rock masses of Devil's Den.

In the savage hand-to-hand fighting among the rocks, men shot at one another from the opposite side of the same boulder, sometimes so close that clothing caught fire from the blaze of an enemy's rifle. The high-pitched Rebel Yell and the full-throated Federal huzzahs echoed through the rocks as first one side and then the other gave way. Bursting shells whined into the most secret crevices. In trying to climb on Devil's Den, one Texan found that "there were places full ten or fifteen feet perpendicular . . . in which a mountain goat would have revelled. . . ."

In the worst of it, the men again had their minds called to food. The stuffed haversack of Dick Childers, their most formidable forager, was struck by a shell that "scattered biscuits all over that end of Pennsylvania." The soldier was paralyzed by the blow, but his companions contended that it was the destruction of the biscuits given him by a Dutch lady which shocked Dick into paralysis.

A slight nineteen-year-old Texan named Will Barbee had been detached to act as a courier, but when Hood went down, Barbee sneaked off in the confusion and galloped across the rough country toward the Devil's Den fighting.

211

His little sorrel was shot from under him, and Barbee landed running. He made it to sheltered space behind a boulder "as big as a 500-pound cotton bale," where half a dozen wounded were lying in the temporary shelter.

Little Barbee scrambled on top of the boulder, the only man in sight unprotected, and began firing as fast as the wounded men loaded and passed rifles up to him. He fell back when a Minié ball caught him in the leg, but immediately scrambled back on his one good leg. Another shot got his good leg and back he fell again. A third time he crawled up and hardly fired a shot before a body wound dropped him on his back in the crevice. He did not die. He lay there cursing because no one would push him up onto the rock again.

Order was lost as groups sought shelter in one place while other groups rushed ahead to new positions. With no wind stirring, the dense smoke hung in veils over the thickets, and officers could scarcely distinguish their own men at any distance. And too many officers were numbered among the appalling casualties.

Colonel Manning, of the 3rd Arkansas, was wounded as his men, restoring their left flank, drove the dark-clothed enemy into the woods to the north of the Devil's Den ridge. Then brigade commander Robertson fell from a Minié ball below the knee. When he was carried from the field the brigade command devolved on Lieutenant Colonel Work of the 1st Texas, the only one left of the five field officers who had led troops into the action.

13

Word reached Evander Law that he was in command of the division. Making his way back from the boulders around Devil's Den, he surveyed the whole field. Then he sent in the reserve brigades of Benning and G. T. Anderson to plug the gap between the lines and to support the exposed left of the virtually surrounded remnants of the 1st Texas and 3rd Arkansas.

With the stimulus of these reinforcements, the whole division drove straight ahead. Even the soldiers recognized that Longstreet's order to attack at an angle had to be abandoned unless they were to be annihilated. The arrival of the fresh troops freed the first fighters of attacks on exposed flanks, and all the men advanced with high yells. Birney's Federal division began to fall back before them all along Plum Run Valley.

The Lone Star flag was planted on Devil's Den. Then Benning's reserve brigade came up and the Georgia flag floated beside the Texas. Even before the ground was secured, decimated regiments of Law's brigade, with odd units from the 4th and 5th Texas, had plunged on eastward up the steep south slope of Little Round Top. With Colonel Oates's Alabama regiment in the lead, the troops themselves were struggling toward the point that Law and Hood had wanted to attack from the beginning.

In this race with the Federal's Warren, of which the lean-faced Law was unaware, his men almost got there first. Climbing and slipping among the rocks and boulders, the men were nearing the crest when they came under the fire of a fresh brigade, Vincent's from Sykes's corps. Oates's men paused, seeking shelter as they gauged the volume of metal coming at them, and then began a final desperate clambering up the slope. One more lunge would win the position that was the key to the whole Union line.

A fresh regiment made a wild charge at them. The men did not know it was only a regiment, and they were exhausted. They had marched twenty-four miles between three in the morning and noon; after a rest, they had engaged in countermarching below Seminary Ridge for hours more; they had been fighting for more than two hours over the roughest imaginable country, with shells bursting over their heads and enemies springing out so close to them that officers went down from bayonet thrusts. There was no energy left for another charge up the mountainside, even if the scattered regiments could have been organized for a final concerted action.

The final action had been the climb up Little Round Top. When a second fresh brigade from Sykes's corps began pouring shot down on them, the men sought shelter where they were. Some were near the crest of the spike, some at the base, the rest scattered between. This last fresh Union brigade had, urged on by Warren, arrived in regiments, so that in the smoke fog it seemed to the Alabama and Texas fellows that Yankee reinforcements were inexhaustible.

They could hear other fresh Federal units going in on their left, trying to support the broken lines of Birney's division in the marshy little valley between their precarious mountain-hold and Plum Run Valley below them. From the little groups close to the coveted crest and those among the boulders around the base, the impetus was gone, and the hurrahing of freshly arriving Yankees turned their thoughts to possible counterattacks from the enemy.

Around half past six Major Rogers, now in command of the 5th Texas, mounted an old log to make "a Fourth of July speech." He was urging the men to hold to the ground they had won when one of Law's couriers, Captain Haggerty, came sidling up among the boulders.

"General Law presents his compliments," said Haggerty, "and says to hold this place at all hazards."

Interrupted in his speech, Rogers shouted: "Compliments, hell! Who wants compliments in such a damned place as this? Go back and ask General Law if he expects me to hold the world in check with the 5th Texas regiment?"

Major Rogers was wrong in thinking he represented the

214

5th Texas. Men from every regiment in Robertson's brigade were clustered around him, and many survivors of the 5th were clinging to thicket clumps near the crest of Little Round Top.

By now the fatigue of the heavy action had begun to show up in individuals. Private Giles of the 4th Texas, disgusted when his ramrod jammed in his dirty rifle barrel, banged in the ramrod, cartridge, and all by striking it against a boulder. Then he raised the gun in the air and, hollering "Look out," pulled the trigger. The rifle roared like a cannon, leaped from his hands, and struck a companion on the ear. While the companion was reviling him, Giles selected a new rifle. "The mountainside," he said, "was covered with them."

Through it all a small fellow from the 3rd Arkansas, firing carefully from behind a stump, was singing at the top of his voice:

> *"Now, let the wide world wag as it will,*
> *I'll be gay and happy still."*

While he sang, the rifles continued to bang away, and the Confederate sharpshooters in Devil's Den took a steady toll of the gunners on Little Round Top. With their own artillery not up, it was the only way to silence cannon.

No counterattack was coming. The Federal troops were holding by the skin of their teeth, themselves awaiting another assault. The men of both sides were fighting literally— and only—for their own lives, and the toll continued to mount in the savage personal combats among the rocks.

So the day was ending for Hood's division, with only General Law aware of the failure to take the key position. The men had done all that could be asked of mortals.

Attacking a position of forbidding natural strength, under enemy guns out of reach of their own and in the confusion of improvised battle plans, they had wrecked Birney's division while fighting off flanking movements from other troops. With great stretches of almost impossible ground taken, they had halted only when fresh brigades on the top of the mountain came at them after they were physically spent and disordered from the prolonged action. That they had lost one third of their number in taking barren ground was not their responsibility.

Nor was Evander Law responsible for the fact that he had been delayed so long in taking the barren ground that his men were late, just too late, in reaching Little Round Top.

The battle plans had called for Lafayette McLaws's division to sweep forward on their left, through the peach orchard, when Hood's men advanced. But Hood's division had attacked alone.

Its open left, where McLaws was supposed to be, had been exposed to merciless enfilade fire. At their climactic moment on the southern end of Little Round Top, when they were minutes and yards away from taking the crest, no other troops had exerted pressure on the Union troops to the north. Their own left brigade, G. T. Anderson's Georgians, clung to a foothold on the northwestern wall of Little Round Top, making their own ragged line intact on the ground from which they had driven Birney's wrecked division. That was as far as Hood's division could go.

Evander Law, who did not have that day the luck of the brave, recognized that the troops could do no more than hold on. After sending his "compliments" to Major Rogers, the acting division commander rode across the frightful field, his horse picking its way among the corpses and the wounded, to discover what had happened to McLaws on the left.

14

Longstreet had happened to McLaws. Having pressed McLaws to the point of committing his troops to an assault that all general officers on the field regarded as impractical, Old Pete joined the division commander only to order him to wait until Hood went in. Then, when Hood's men plunged forward, Longstreet gave no orders for supporting Hood.

Instead, in irrational anger, he pointed to a spot where the narrow back road by which they had approached the front emerged from the woods. "Why is not a battery placed there?" he demanded.

"General," McLaws replied, "if a battery is placed there it will draw the enemy's fire right among my lines formed for the charge . . . and will tend to demoralize my men."

Longstreet's reply was a peremptory order to place a battery there. As soon as the four guns opened, the heavy Union cannon began throwing shells, "cutting the limbs of the trees in abundance," McLaws reported, "which fell around among my men, and the bursting shells and shot wounded and killed a number whilst in line formed for advance, producing a natural feeling of uneasiness among them."

On Kershaw's left, facing the peach orchard, white-haired William Barksdale, who looked more the "elder statesman" than the impetuous fighter, grew excited at all this maiming among his brigade and began to petition McLaws to let him go in. Badgered McLaws, forced to prepare the assault and then to hold his assaulting line idle under enemy fire, could only tell him that Longstreet's orders were to wait. For what, McLaws did not know. Hood's men were already heavily engaged as far as Little Round Top.

Barksdale was only forty-two, despite his snowy locks, and one of the few generals who had been violently pro-slavery and secessionist—both as a newspaper editor and Mississippi

Congressman in Washington. A little out of hand that afternoon, like most of the others, the ante-bellum "fire-eater" approached the corps commander directly. "I wish you would let me go in, general," said the Mississipian. "I will take that battery in five minutes."

Longstreet told him to wait. "We are all going in presently," he said.

With the battle joined, Old Pete had lost his outward surliness. To his A.A.G., Longstreet looked "a martial figure" as he rode back and forth with fine horsemanship, "most inspiring." The fighting had stimulated the aggressive man out of his mechanical state, but his actions showed that he was not in full control of himself.

In holding back McLaw's division, he may have been motivated by no more than his natural deliberateness. It was obvious to everyone else that action was demanded immediately and was, indeed, long overdue. But Longstreet may well have been unconsciously trying for another Second Manassas.

There he had thrown a counterstroke designed by Lee's great battle plan. At the peach orchard, however, the withheld attack was no part of a counterstroke and only vaguely related to any battle plan. One half of his corps having on their own gone straight ahead, McLaw's division could now only make a frontal assault in order to come up on Hood's left. With the northward-angled attack simply abandoned, all that was left for McLaws was to drive the enemy from the rough country of the ridge north of Little Round Top. A successful thrust could still win the Union flank by power, instead of by the originally planned enveloping movement, but it is axiomatic that a power thrust should come with the full weight of the attacking force. (McClellan, with overwhelming numerical superiority, had failed at Sharpsburg the summer before by throwing his attacking units in piecemeal.)

If Longstreet was thinking at all, he may have decided to let Hood's division completely entangle the Union left, drawing off reinforcements, in the hope that the heavy firepower of McLaw's division could then break through. Hood's Texas Brigade at Gaines' Mill in the Seven Days had made the same sort of breakthrough by a direct thrust at a stretched line.

The difference at Gaines' Mill was that the whole Confederate line attacked simultaneously and kept up the pressure until something had to give. At the peach orchard, one division was wearing itself out while the other waited, and Anderson, farther north, was in turn waiting on McLaws. The result was piecemeal attacks that nullified the combined weight of the three divisions. When McLaws at last was sent in, Evander Law had already turned his men to throwing up rockpiles in order to hold their comfortless ground.

Longstreet left no record of the reasoning processes that led him to restrain McLaws until Evander Law came back from Little Round Top and asked Kershaw for support even to hold his position. Determined to shift the blame to Lee in his post-war self-defense, Longstreet limited his report to glowing descriptions of his men's fighting. "The attack was made in splendid style by both divisions," he said in one place, with no mention of the fact that they attacked separately.

Yet it was not even true that "the attack was made in splendid style" if that implied co-ordinated troop action. Certainly no troops ever fought more valiantly, with less regard for life, and seldom have troops been given less chance to make their valor count. In McLaws's attack, a confusion in command separated the two lead brigades before they even started out.

As the brigade that delayed belonged to impetuous Barksdale, it must be assumed that the orders from division head-

219

quarters reached Barksdale later than the attack order reached Kershaw. The slackness in the army's control that hot afternoon reached from general command down to every level. After many hours of Longstreet's erratic assertions of authority and changes of plan, McLaws retained little sense of control over his own troops and little certainty about their purpose.

He perceived that Longstreet, who had held them all to the letter of Lee's orders, was now himself belatedly violating the order for an oblique attack. He was committing them to a frontal assault when the divisions, McLaws said, "were not strong enough to cover the front of attack, much less envelop the flank." McLaws believed that Longstreet should either have arranged for this second wave to go in with Anderson's division or, preferably, conferred with Lee. But it was now too late for that.

Even McLaws's operational control of his division was undermined by Longstreet's periodically assuming personal command of Kershaw's brigade. Kershaw said of his numerous orders: "These instructions I received in sundry messages from General Longstreet and General McLaws. . . ."

The final message to Kershaw directed him to move out, in conjunction with Barksdale, at the firing of signal guns. Longstreet himself was there to start out with the brigade. Because of the rough ground, all generals and staff officers moved out on foot, burly Longstreet among them.

That a corps commander should walk out with a brigade, while ignoring McLaws, its division commander, shows the extent to which Longstreet's disturbance had broken down his command of himself and of his troops. As a corps commander, he was no longer responsible for his actions, and no one was responsible for the assault.

Waving his hat and urging on the men, the lieutenant general left Kershaw's brigade at the Emmitsburg road. Beyond the road, heavy contact would be made with the enemy. Even as Longstreet shouted encouragement, Kershaw, with sinking heart, heard Barksdale's drums beat the assembly. He said: "I knew *then* [his italics] that I should have no immediate support on my left."

It would appear that Barksdale, impatient to go in, had received no instructions about the signal guns. McLaws reported that when the order to advance "was signified to me, I sent my aide-de-camp, Captain G. B. Lamar, Jr., to carry out the order to General Barksdale." Lamar reported that "when I carried him [Barksdale] the order to advance, his face was radiant with joy. He was in front of his brigade, his hat off, and his long white hair reminded me of 'the white plume of Navarre.' I saw him as far as the eye could follow, still ahead of his men. . . ." So strong was their impetus that when they reached a picket fence, "the fence disappeared as if by magic. . . ."

Barksdale filed no report. He fell, mortally wounded, soon after passing beyond Lamar's field of vision. But certainly that eager fighter who had chafed at the waiting was not responsible for the delay.

The delay, reflecting the absence of a controlling hand, caused further failures in concerted action among the units. Like overlapping repercussions from a single event, each crisis that an isolated group met as best it could created another crisis for another unit, until the men were fighting as at Little Round Top, only for survival.

With no one certain of the objective and no central control over the details, the unco-ordinated movement forward was directed by no more than the instinct of veteran soldiers to reach the commanding crest. From there guns were spreading death and mutilation among their ranks, and where those guns stood was the enemy's heart.

15

As Kershaw's men moved in their lonely assault "with the steadiness of troops on parade," a still unexplained blunder shook his units before they were properly started. Crossing the Emmitsburg road, the four South Carolina regiments moved beside the lane that led to and beyond the house and building of Rose's farm. They were on the southern edge of the peach orchard, passing over fields of corn and rye and heading for a wooded stony hill directly in their front. On the opposite side of the low hill was the large wheatfield, and beyond it and the marshes of Plum Run Valley was their objective—the slopes of Cemetery Ridge north of Little Round Top. Birney's broken division was scattered in there, mostly in retreat except for one brigade, but three other brigades from other Union corps (II and V) were to come in. Humphrey's division was on Kershaw's left, where Barksdale's brigade was headed.

As Barksdale had not attacked with him, Kershaw divided his regiments. With two going straight on toward the stony hill, he sent two to their left to take the Union batteries in the back of the peach orchard. The 2nd and 8th South Carolina had moved close enough to the Federals to drive off the gunners when some person whose identity is unknown to this day ordered the two regiments to shift their front and move by the right flank—or away from the guns.

The Federal cannoneers, overcoming what must have been a vast surprise, hurried back to their pieces. Not looking a gift horse in the mouth, they opened with grape and canister at close range on the flanks of what Kershaw called "these doomed regiments. . . . Hundreds of the bravest and best men of South Carolina fell, victims to this fatal blunder."

With the usefulness of these regiments temporarily destroyed, Kershaw made his move toward the left of Hood's division with his remaining two regiments. Emerging from the woods of the stony hill, they met a Federal brigade coming at them from the wheatfield. In that exchange of shots, where the veteran troops of both sides fired with cruel accuracy, the second wave of the unco-ordinated Confederate attack began to disintegrate into another soldiers' battle. From Kershaw's right, bordering on the scene of Law's earlier fight for Little Round Top, the break in order spread steadily northward.

In a curious way the confusion was made more general by the frenzied, fragmentary supports thrown in by the Federals. For one mile between the Emmitsburg road and Cemetery Ridge regiments fought regiments and brigades fought brigades in countless fluid fights, shifting eastward and westward without a defensive line or an attacking front.

The Union defensive line, foolishly extended by Sickles to the peach orchard, broke wide open when its projection was hit on three sides. Good soldier Humphreys, commanding the division among the trees, never lost his poise, but his division was swept backward, as Birney's had been, and Sickles's III Corps was a wreck. A division of Hancock's II Corps was thrown in, the division of Sykes's regulars went in, two other brigades from Sykes's fine V Corps, and finally any regiments that came to hand.

Paul Semmes brought up his brigade in support of Kershaw. Looking like a grand seigneur with his curly beard, walking in front of his troops with sword in hand, Semmes, brother of the captain of the raider *Alabama* and a solid brigadier since the Seven Days, fell at the moment of contact. He died of his wound a few days later. Leaderless, his brigade bent back. Wofford's, the next brigade, came on along the edge of the abandoned peach orchard. Again segments of the Confederate line lunged forward and again they were checked. Although unable to advance consistently, the three brigades of McLaws's division were keeping a lot of Federal troops busy. Some of the deadliest personal fighting of the war created a touch-and-go situation north of Little Round Top resembling the simultaneous fighting around that hill.

Kershaw said that "amid rocks and trees, within a few feet of each other, these brave men, Confederates and Federals, maintained a desperate conflict." He lost more than 600 killed and wounded, about half of his brigade strength, and in one company of the 2nd South Carolina only four men of the forty who marched out across Emmitsburg road "remained unhurt to bury their fallen comrades."

In taking their heavy losses, McLaws's three brigades—those of Kershaw, Semmes, and Wofford—used up so many Federal reinforcements and exerted such a continuing threat to the Little Round Top flank area that the late-starting brigade of Barksdale's Mississippians had relatively easy going through Sickles's peach orchard. They got guns of their own across the Emmitsburg road and among the peach trees and began to spray the retreating Federals, driving them all the way up onto Cemetery Ridge.

With the Union left pinned down and no reinforcements coming against them from the center, the Mississippians were driving for the wildly rugged and untillable hillside near George Weikert's house, between the Little Round Top area and the open stretches of Cemetery Ridge. The only element that could possibly have stopped them was the reserve artillery that had survived all reorganizations of the Federal army. They undertook the job.

One six-gun battery came down to the choppy floor of the valley and unlimbered near the Trostle house, a large two-story affair with a rear gallery on the upper floor—one Dutch house that was not smaller than its barn. Barksdale's men moved in against the point-blank firing of the cannon and got among the gunners, killing half of them and taking four of the guns. They had been delayed just long enough for other reserve batteries to open on them from the crest. The Mississippi brigade went after those too.

They were losing heavily from the grape, canister, and shell exploding in their faces, and when they got among the guns the Federal cannoneers fought with pistols and sabers and whatever came to hand. In what was like a dock brawl among armed men, the Mississippians took the first line of guns.

But the rear line of artillery kept flinging the close-range charges among them, and enemy infantry began to arrive from the Federal right. Like the other successive waves of isolated brigades, Barksdale's fragmented units fell back, their grasp falling short of the object of assault.

16

Before the Union forces could draw breath, still another isolated Confederate attack struck farther north, directed toward the open plateau of Cemetery Ridge. This attack, by a brigade of Dick Anderson's division, was made with even less co-ordination than the other two. Anderson, accustomed to Longstreet's close supervision, was apparently unsettled by Lee's orders. Placed between his former and new corps commanders, the usually steady soldier employed his troops tentatively, as if waiting for direct orders from either Hill or Longstreet.

Lee's report said: "General Hill was ordered to threaten the center, to prevent reinforcements being drawn to either wing, and to co-operate with his right division [Anderson's] in Longstreet's attack. . . ."

Ordinarily, this divided assignment would have been routine for Hill. However, three factors operated against him at Gettysburg. In the first place, the surface civilities established between Hill and Longstreet did not include trust on either side, and no communications passed between them on the use of Anderson's division. Hill reported: "I was ordered to co-operate with him [Longstreet] with such of my brigades from the right as could join with his troops in the attack." Apparently A. P. Hill then turned over the execution of the order to Anderson.

At the other end of the line, around Cemetery Hill, Ewell asked for co-operation from Pender's division in an assault he suddenly decided to make on Culp's Hill. This drew Hill's attention from the portion of his assignment dealing with the demonstration in the center at a time when a third factor affected him: the shocking loss of his best division commander, Dorsey Pender.

The twenty-nine-year-old North Carolinian with the ingrained sense of duty was struck in the leg by a large stray piece of cannon shot while riding casually along the lines. He died two weeks later after intense suffering. He showed no more fear of death than had the great Stonewall in whose Second Corps he had matured. Completely conscious, he said: "Tell my wife I do not fear to die. I can confidently resign my soul to God, trusting in the atonement of our Lord Jesus Christ. My only regret is to leave her and our children." Then, summing up his journey on earth, the twenty-nine-year-old father said: "I have always tried to do my duty in every sphere of life in which Providence has placed me."

These were words Lee understood, and he recognized the magnitude of Pender's loss to the South's struggle for independence. To Powell Hill, the loss of Pender meant both emotional distress for a friend and an upheaval in his newly formed corps. Following the wounding of Heth on the day before, Pender's removal took from the new corps commander the second of the two familiar division commanders on whom he had built his corps. With Hood down, Lee had lost three of his nine division commanders in two days.

Hill temporarily assigned Pender's division to James Lane, a capable brigadier not considered for division command during the reorganization. Heth's division was commanded by Johnston Pettigrew, who, despite the "gallantry" that had won praise for this untrained leader, was scarcely ready for division command.

Only a man less sensitive than Powell Hill could have suffered blows to his emotions and to his new command with equanimity. Unsettled by them and given orders whose vagueness was unsuited to his nature, Hill, besides putting Anderson on his own, directed only a weak demonstration. The presence of his one division in line, sporadically firing, retained Federal troops in his front. But with aggressive Pender gone and his successor distracted by Ewell, the division never mounted any action so threatening as to cause the Federals to divert reinforcements away from the Little Round Top area and Cemetery Hill.

As for Longstreet's relations with his friend Anderson, Old Pete's report referred only to "the brigades of General Anderson's division, which were co-operating upon my left. . . ."

The whole responsibility for this co-operation thus rested on Anderson, and the unassertive South Carolinian said that he was ordered "to put the troops of my division into action *by brigades* as soon as those of General Longstreet's corps had progressed so far in their assault as to be connected with my right flank."

"By brigades" is italicized to indicate that Anderson was still operating on Lee's original order to attack in echelon across the Emmitsburg road. When that order, proved on the scene to be impractical, was first abandoned by Evander Law in defiance of Longstreet, the results caused Longstreet, without announcement, also to abandon the order. But, though he sent Lafayette McLaws forward in violation of the letter of the order, Longstreet did not so notify Anderson.

Anderson, adhering to the original order of Lee, sent in his troops, as he said, with "the advance of McLaws's division . . . immediately followed by the brigades of mine *in the manner directed.*" The italics, not his, stress that he sent in his brigades in echelon on what had become a frontal attack.

Whether or not the illogical order of advance caused further breakdown in concerted action, Anderson's tough veterans were the third body of attacking Confederates who just failed to achieve a big breakthrough. Profiting by the bloody work being done by Hood's and McLaws's men on the Federal left, one of Anderson's units—again a single brigade—made it all the way to the crest of Cemetery Ridge. For one eventful fall of time Wright's Georgians held the middle of the Union position.

The way had been prepared by Wilcox's Alabama brigade and Perry's small Florida brigade, both attacking, as had the Confederates all day, by themselves. These two brigades, the first of Anderson's to go in, drove to the foot of Cemetery Ridge on the left of, but not connecting with, McLaws. There, against massing Federal reinforcements, the brigades held on against counterattacks. To their left, northward, Brigadier General Ambrose R. Wright led his Georgians nearly a mile across the broken ground of the valley and stormed up the slope. He was directly opposite Lee's command post and under the eye of the Old Man.

Lee saw Wright's Georgians drive a Federal line from a stone wall at the crest of Cemetery Ridge and, all alone, try to hold their position in the enemy's center. From where "Rans" Wright had pierced the defense to Law's brigade south of Little Round Top, the Confederate attacking line was thinned by its spread across a two-mile front. Yet, unused brigades of Anderson's were available to support Wright, and Wright's men seemed to be solidifying their hold.

Using the stone wall themselves, his riflemen silenced the enemy's cannon by picking off the gunners, and then the excited Georgians ran forward to take the guns.

Even as they rushed forward, Perry's little brigade on their right fell back under the pressure of counterattacks. Wright could have faced a regiment about in order to protect that flank, but simultaneously on his left another body of Federal reinforcements appeared out of the dusk.

A fourth brigade of Anderson's, under Carnot Posey, had been ordered up on Wright's left to cover his flank, but Posey was nowhere in sight. Threatened with encirclement in the center of the enemy's position, Wright, very bitter, could only order his Georgians to withdraw.

Posey, for his failure to come up, gave the lame excuse that he was waiting for the fifth brigade, under Mahone, to support him. Fortunately for Posey's people, his discovery that he was not going to be supported occurred before, like Wright, he was all alone on Cemetery Ridge.

For Billy Mahone, a little man with a large ego who had enjoyed previous big moments and was to know more of them, there was no excuse at all. A V.M.I. graduate, prewar railroad-builder and executive, Mahone simply refused to accept the orders delivered by Anderson's staff officers. Claiming he had been given contrary orders, Mahone kept his men rooted to their safe ground while their companions in Wright's brigade were left dead and dying on the slopes of Cemetery Ridge in a somber withdrawal from the crest of the hill.

The three divisions had fought (with Hood attacking at 4:00 p.m., McLaws after 5:00, and Anderson around 6:00) five enemy divisions from three different corps, brigades and regiments from other corps (troops from six corps altogether), and a heavy concentration of artillery. Yet the game had seemed within the hand of any of the three.

Beginning with Warren on the column of Little Round Top and ending with combative Hancock, who sent in reinforcements near the center, there had invariably been an energetic Federal general to rush some of the steadily arriving troops to a threatened point at the very last moment. The Confederates had first Evander Law, a young brigadier acting on his own; then Longstreet, overriding McLaws and mishandling what turned out to be the middle attack; and, finally, the previously competent Dick Anderson exercising no control whatsoever over what should have been the climactic thrust.

So supine was Anderson that Cadmus Marcellus Wilcox related his A.A.G's account of the division commander when Wilcox's staff officer rode back across the Emmitsburg road to ask for support to hold the brigade's advanced position. "He found General Anderson back in the woods which were in the rear of the Emmitsburg road several hundred yards in a ravine, his horse tied and all his staff lying on the ground [indifferent] as tho' nothing was going on. . . . [General] Wright never liked him afterwards. I really thought that I should have made some report or complaint against him, but I did not, lest my motives might have been misunderstood. . . ."

This was Wilcox, who, like Wright, felt that he had sacrificed his men in vain. It is true that no report mentions a staff officer of Anderson's carrying a single message.

At some point this competent subordinate, left floundering between familiar Longstreet and strange Hill, had, like Ewell in a different test of decision, quit under an unfamiliar responsibility. As an animal does in an insoluble maze, Dick Anderson, the self-effacing gentleman with the Pennsylvania wife, simply sat down and eschewed resolutions.

Nor does this grim parlay complete the record of command failure on that hot Thursday in July. The overlong

Confederate line spread on northward and northeast, embracing the bastions of Cemetery Hill and Culp's Hill. There Ewell was to exert a pressure that would at least prevent reinforcements from moving southward. At best, he would deliver, in the tradition of Stonewall Jackson's corps, the assault that had been withheld the day before.

17

Ewell's action, coming at the end of the afternoon and as inconclusive as all the rest, seemed something of an anticlimax after Longstreet's attack, for which the army had waited all day; yet this unco-ordinated assault came closer than any other Confederate thrust to winning a commanding position in the Union defenses.

Law's "fight for Little Round Top" was more dramatic, but Hays's unsung attack in the dark actually carried Cemetery Hill. Had he been supported, the Battle of Gettysburg might have ended there—where it should have ended the night before. It was another story of three divisions working independently, with no general control over the corps.

Essentially, Dick Ewell, though showing more outward composure than the preceding day, lacked the self-command to control the destinies of three separated divisions in a movement in vague conjunction with Longstreet's distant operations. The paralysis of his will having worn off, he was acutely aware of his earlier failure. After the indirect proddings of General Lee during the morning, Ewell suffered between fear of another failure and an inner goad to commit his troops to action. His unsettled state could not have been helped by the long wait for the sound of Longstreet's guns, which frayed everyone's nerves.

These tense hours Ewell apparently passed in solitary fretting. He had advised his three division commanders—Allegheny Johnson, Jubal Early, and Robert Rodes—that they should begin their demonstration when they heard Longstreet's guns. He left to their discretion whether or not they should change the threat into actual assault.

The three divisions were well situated to deliver a three-pronged attack, if the attacks were made in concert. Rodes would strike from the northwest, where the Federals on Cemetery Hill faced across the valley toward Seminary Ridge; Early would come in from almost due north, where the Federal flank turned at a right angle on East Cemetery Hill; and Johnson would storm the difficult terrain of Culp's Hill, on the northeast, almost in the rear of the Union flank.

As if sensitive about their exposed flank south of Culp's Hill, the Federals had been giving Johnson's division trouble all afternoon, particularly with heavy sharpshooting. Some of his troops were engaged in limited actions when at four o'clock the sonorous roll from down the valley told Johnson that Longstreet had opened at last. To Benner's Hill, east of Gettysburg, Johnson dispatched Andrews's sixteen-gun Maryland battalion with the support of the Rockbridge battery.

Andrews was out of action because of wounds, and his four batteries were commanded by twenty-year-old Major Joseph Latimer, who looked, according to one of the Rockbridge gunners, "a mere youth." Latimer was cool in action, very skillful in directing his guns while under the enemy's fire, and he was much admired in the Second Corps. That afternoon his cannoneers had no chance. Heavy Federal artillery immediately answered him and soon found the range. Within five minutes one of his caissons exploded. Twenty-seven men went down in the Allegheny Roughs. Gunners in other batteries began dropping, and it became evident that the open hill was too hot a place to stay.

Major Latimer advised Johnson of the hopelessness of the duel, and Old Allegheny immediately ordered him to get out.

While the guns were being withdrawn, the "Boy Major" suffered a wound from which he later died.

This depressing business happened around sundown.

At that point Ewell's compulsion to deliver an attack finally overcame his fear of failure, and he ordered a general attack. In so doing, he made virtually no artillery preparations. Only four batteries were scattered in support of Early and Rodes, and two battalions remained inactive while the gunners grazed the horses. Unaware of this demonstration of their superior officer's temporary unfitness, Johnson and Early rushed their men into action as if relieved that the tension of the long wait was over.

Johnson, waving his hickory club, sent in three yelling brigades from Stonewall's old division at the rock formations of Culp's Hill. The tumbling hillside, cluttered with woods and thickets and low boulders, was almost a duplication of Little Round Top, though not so precipitous. As at Little Round Top, the attackers breached the first defense line, established a foothold around the base of the hill, and, at darkness, settled down to a savage, formless fight that streaked the smoky blackness with flashes of rifle fire. Also, as the Confederate units at the other end of the line had done, Johnson's brigades were containing Federal troops, posing a threat, and opening other sectors of the defense arc to attack.

In the middle, Jubal Early's troops made the most of the opening, though with only two brigades. The brigade of Extra Billy Smith was kept back on the York road, where the political general was still waiting for the phantoms of the evening before to materialize into an enemy. Early, normally an aggressive fighter, for some reason decided to go by the book, and held Gordon's hard-striking brigade in reserve.

By now Jeb Stuart's troopers had arrived. Exhausted though they were, his men could have relieved Smith from his anxious guard duty instead of merely supporting him—

as they did—against nothing. With Smith moved up in reserve, Gordon could have thrown in the weight of his brigade, which had turned the tide in the previous day's battle.

But Early made no use of Smith and cautiously conserved Gordon to be advanced where he would be most effective after Rodes went in on the right and the battle had developed its form. Jubal Early would probably have sent Gordon in anyway had he seen the position taken by his two active brigades. But the attack was delivered so late in the day that dusk had fallen when the two brigades reached the foot of East Cemetery Hill, and as they fought their way to the top they were lost in the heavy battle smoke. Gordon remained idle while the two brigades actually took the heights and were abandoned there.

Hoke's North Carolinians were taken in by Colonel Avery, who fell with a mortal wound, and brought out by Colonel Archibald Godwin. Hays commanded the fierce Louisiana brigade.

Harry Hays was the brigadier who, in the Gettysburg square the day before, had demanded directly of Ewell that he be allowed to continue the pursuit and take the hill. Another of the non-West-Pointers who shone that day, Hays was a forty-three-year-old Tennessean with a law practice in New Orleans. With only the usual Mexican War experience with volunteers, he had come into the Confederate armies as colonel of the 7th Louisiana, and had inherited the sometime unruly brigade of President Taylor's son.

This brigade comprised an odd collection of plantation scions, New Orleans plug-uglies, an Irish regiment replete with its own flag bearing a harp, a regiment of Acadians who danced the polka around campfires, and sundry rough characters from the bayous. Before they lost their colorful leader, Richard Taylor, the Louisiana Tigers had rivaled the Texans in their imperviousness to discipline, and they boasted a

Creole cook who became the colored Casanova of Virginia. Although somewhat subdued in their extravagant assertions by casualties and time, they were still very tough fellows.

Harry Hays had come along after their early gaudy flare had dimmed, and the men had conformed to army standards according to their natures. It was a happy meeting of troops and leader. Always a good man, in the dusk of July 2 Hays just missed becoming militarily immortalized in a niche above any other officer in either army on that field.

Hays's men moved straight up the hill, taking three successive positions. The first was a fence by a ravine at the bottom of the hill, the second was a stone wall, the third was a fixed line of rifle pits behind an abatis of fallen trees. Hays's Louisianians drove the enemy with more finality and consistency, and with fewer losses to themselves, than any other Confederate troops who attacked that day.

Hays attributed his comparatively light losses during the climb through three lines to "the darkness of the evening, now verging into night, and the deep obscurity afforded by the smoke of the firing. . . ." Except for that, he said, the massed guns on the crest would have produced "slaughter."

The men's partial concealment also caused the Federal infantrymen, firing downhill, to shoot over the heads of the climbing Confederates. Finally, the Federal defenders belonged to Howard's corps, those victims of Chancellorsville who had caught it again in the fighting the day before. They gave up in droves. Hays reported that he "found many of the enemy who had not fled hiding in the [rifle] pits for protection."

All at once the Louisiana troops were on top of the hill with not a hostile enemy in sight except for the gunners. The four regiments swooped down on them before a blast was fired, and with a right good will joined the hand-to-hand fighting for the pieces.

Farther to the east, Hoke's North Carolinians had encountered harder going. They had three stone fences to get. Nearing the top, the brigade came under punishing enfilade fire from the guns and from one immovable line of infantry behind a last stone wall at a right angle to their advance. With a steadiness that the officers admired, the Tarheels changed front under the hail of fire and advanced straight toward the stone wall and the guns. The enemy infantry dissolved, the gunners were dispersed, and the North Carolinians joined with Hays's Louisianians in silencing the Union artillery.

For one incredible moment, as Hays reported, "every piece of artillery which had been firing upon us was silenced," and two Confederate brigades possessed the enemy stronghold.

Then, from their right, a blurred body of troops advanced in the darkness. At that time Hoke's brigade was scattered from the climb and change of front, but Hays's was fairly compact. Harry Hays had been "cautioned to expect friends" from the position where the indistinguishable mass was moving toward him, and he withheld fire.

The silent line was advancing from the direction where Rodes's division was expected to come out in their attack from the northwest. With desperate hope influencing his judgment, Hays waited to see if the new troops were friends.

Even when fire spurted from the advancing line, Harry Hays clung to his hope. Then the flashes of a second and a third volley "disclosed the still-advancing line to be one of the enemy." Not at all shaken, the veteran Louisiana troops poured answering volleys into the blurred mass, and the advance was halted. Then Hays saw vaguely the movement of other troops. He ceased to hope for Rodes. Abandoning the guns, the disappointed troops of both brigades retired down the hill, unpursued. The great chance had come and gone.

236

18

On that day big Robert Rodes, with a fiercely swirling mustache to emphasize the resolute mouth in his bony face, was not, as a Second Corps staff officer called him, "the best division-commander in the army." The undoubted effect on some individuals of the uncertainty characterizing the total command situation seems particularly apparent in this thirty-four-year-old Virginian. Perhaps still shaken from the near-disaster the day before, Rodes displayed a lack of diligence and energy which was untypical of his career, as civilian or as soldier.

His troops had been resting around stacked arms all during the day of July 2 in the main street that crossed Gettysburg from the Chambersburg pike to the Hanover road. That was the point they had reached in their pursuit of Howard's corps in the late afternoon of the 1st. Rodes knew that he was to attack simultaneously with Early, striking toward Cemetery Hill from southwest of the town. Yet, instead of getting his brigades out of the cramped quarters of a city street, he spent the time dickering with Pender's division for support on his right when he went in.

Brigadier General Lane, who had only just succeeded the fallen Pender in division command, had no feeling of certainty in his new post. He spent much time trying to clear plans through A. P. Hill. By the dusk hour when Lane finally assured Rodes of support for his right, Early's attack order had been given. Thus, while Early's two brigades were approaching the ravine at the bottom of East Cemetery Hill, Rodes was getting his men out of the town.

The long line of marching men in columns of four had to clear the town to the west before swinging south, and then bend back to their angle of attack as they deployed. It was a dispiriting sort of movement. When the assaulting fronts were established, they had three quarters of a mile to advance across open fields and cornfields, with the usual fences, before reaching the enemy.

The two leading brigades, George Doles's and Dodson Ramseur's, had covered about half a mile toward the enemy's lines when, in the dusk, the two young brigadiers got a good and very sobering look at the Federal position. These two, among the heroes of the preceding day's fighting and naturally offensive-minded, studied the lines of enemy infantry behind stone walls and breastworks in front of massed guns, and went into a little conference. Before advancing farther, they agreed, as twenty-six-year Ramseur put it, "to make representation of the character of the enemy's position" to the division commander.

When their query on instructions reached Rodes, the big blond had just been notified that Hays's and Hoke's brigades were falling back from East Cemetery Hill. It was then dark. As the time was past when Rodes's assault could support Early's, he decided that "it would be useless sacrifice of life to go on."

Recalling the advance, Rodes evidently felt a sense of his own remissness, and Early's division forever after blamed him. In his report Rodes sought to make the movement seem less futile than it had been. He said: "But instead of falling back to the original line, I caused the front to assume a strong position in the plain to the right of the town, along the hollow of an old roadbed. [Actually, this was a little-used private road called Long Lane.] This position was much nearer the enemy, was clear of the town, and one from which I could readily attack without confusion. . . . Everything was gotten ready to attack at daylight. . . ."

At the end of that day there were no plans for an attack at daylight of the next, and Rodes was claiming credit for an alertness he had not displayed. His troops should have been approximately in that fine position, "clear of the town," for the attack he had been ordered to make that day. Had his division been ready when Hays and Hoke moved out, his assaulting troops would have diverted reinforcements from going in strength against the two brigades that had taken the hill. Conceivably Rodes's fresh brigades could have created real havoc in the darkness, because the Federals' attention, from privates up to and including Meade, was frantically directed at the Rebels who were up on the hill with them.

Unknown to Hays, he was only a quarter of a mile from the rear of the Union guns massed on the hill facing Doles and Ramseur. This was not unknown to the Federals. And Hoke's scattered troops were within sprinting distance of Meade's headquarters, so close that Lee's old friend was himself excitedly sending in reinforcements.

If Rodes had struck at that time *and* then Gordon had come on up in support of Hays and Hoke, possibly it would have been all over. Shaken as the Union army was from losses of the day before and successive assaults all during the late afternoon, a confusion beginning around Cemetery Hill might well have spread extensively enough to give Lee the needed victory of tremendous proportions.

But Ewell had no control over his corps. Three division commanders were co-ordinating without a central control—and one failed.

Although post-war arguments made Longstreet a controversial figure for years after the battle, he was only one of several who made of the chain of command something like a vacuum of command. Honest Ewell later said that "Gettysburg was lost by our mistakes and I committed dozens of them myself." Because he was involved in no after-the-fact controversies, his failures were largely forgotten. At Gettysburg, however, Ewell was far more condemned in the army than was Longstreet. He actually had been given the chance on the first day, and his men had won it again on the second.

The worst said of Longstreet was that he had fought a poor battle tactically. But who at his level had not?

19

General Lee, alone in the center of the vacuum, could not have been less aware of the total collapse of co-ordination than were his staff officers, who commented bitterly upon it. He was also aware, however, of the thrusting power of his veteran brigades and their near misses despite lack of co-ordination.

At three points in the three-mile Union line the Confederate soldiers had barely missed carrying a position whose capture would cause the collapse of the whole line. Importantly, one of those irresistible assaults, Wright's, had been seen by the general through his field glasses. He had watched his men storm the crest, silence the Union guns, and then fall back from want of support.

All through the frustrating day it had been the nonprofessionals who looked good. Unaffected by the collapse in the chain of command, the patriots had fought at the peak of their potential. At one end of the line twenty-seven-year-old Law, who determined the day's action, was an educator; at the other end Hays, who barely missed winning the day, was a lawyer. Where the men had been directed to fight, there had been no failures. Lee's soldiers seemed, as he said, "invincible."

When uneasy silence descended on the field after nine o'clock, General Lee evidently retained the image of those troops sweeping across the rough fields and storming the enemy's hill, and he could envision his men holding that high ground—*when* the army had restored co-ordination among its units. Nothing that he recorded indicated any apprehension about the army's ability to achieve co-ordination. As the failures that spread successively from right to left had come from usually dependable men, Lee knew that the potential for co-ordination existed; and he believed that, by exploitation of the advantages won during the day, the potential could be realized. This, in effect, he wrote in his report.

If there was one moment when he made the conscious decision to renew the attack the third day, the general took no one into his confidence. Across the dark valley, General Meade held a council of war, and his general officers agreed to hold the ground against one more thrust. As the enemy assumed that Lee would try to exploit his gains, it is probable that he felt this to be the inevitable, if the obvious, course. His army was now too far entangled with the enemy's position to permit any other maneuver except withdrawal, and that alternative seems not to have occurred to him. He had come North for a decision.

At full night, when the reports on another day of might-have-beens came in, Robert E. Lee was not put in possession of the details of the failures. Longstreet, with no one knows what feelings, stayed away from general headquarters that night. He established corps headquarters at a little schoolhouse, hardly larger than a corn crib, in the area from which his troops had launched their assault. There he remained, sending in a verbal report but not asking for orders for the next morning.

Sometime during the night he began plotting new maneuvers for persuading Lee to adopt his obsessive plan of swinging around Meade's left. As when he appeared on the field the first day, Longstreet still could not relate himself to the battle that was going on. His conviction about succeeding to Jackson's status may have been fading, but he had not resigned himself to the role of a subordinate, and he was as determined to fight another Fredericksburg as he had been before the army left Virginia.

None of this was known to Lee, two miles away, where headquarters tents were pitched in a clearing south of the road from Cashtown. Even more significantly, he did not know the details of Longstreet's mismanaged battle, and it was in these—not in the much-discussed delaying tactics— that the "warhorse" displayed his unreliableness at Gettysburg.

Despite all the controversies over Longstreet's dragging of his heels and the dramas built on its consequences, his delay in moving into action had not, of itself, ruined the second day for the Confederates. Only by moving with an unaccustomed urgency could methodical Longstreet have launched Hood and McLaws at the Little Round Top end of the line appreciably before nine o'clock in the morning. By then the ridge where Lee designed the attack was defended in about the same strength that the Confederates encountered at four.

Not until approximately eight thirty did Lee tell Longstreet: "You had better move on." Longstreet's delay of nearly eight hours before sending troops into action unquestionably affected the resistance his assaulting columns met, for in the interim Union reinforcements reached the field to contain the breaks accomplished by independent deviations from the Confederate battle plan. Yet, even in the absence of the reinforcements of the late afternoon, Lee's original order could not have been executed as he planned it. On the other hand, the Union left could conceivably have been taken if Longstreet had fought a sound tactical battle.

Lee's ignorance of Longstreet's unsound battle and the reasons for it was an element in his conviction that "proper concert of action" could be achieved after two days of unprecedented lapses. Another element in his clinging to this

242

conviction was unquestionably the toll taken on Lee's faculties by the cumulative nerve strain of the campaign.

Staff officers observed that he showed more tension than on any former campaign. The combination of the crucial nature of the invasion and the unremitting frustrations from subordinates' failures would explain such tension—and its effects. Lieutenant Colonel Blackford, Stuart's staff officer and a reliable witness, reported that on the second night the General was "in weakness and pain" from a severe attack of diarrhea. It seems unlikely that a man of his vigorous health, inured to changes of food and water by more than thirty years of army life, would suffer from dietary causes an ailment that afflicted none of the staff officers who reported his. Whatever the cause of the diarrhea, its severity was exhausting and, added to a general lowering of energy, would tend to impair judgment.

This is not to say that General Lee's belief that his soldiers could win the Federal ridge *with* co-ordinated action was evidence of impaired judgment. Major Scheibert, the observer from the Prussian Royal Engineers, and many of Lee's officers believed that the enemy's position could be won by, as Major Scheibert said, "one concentrated and combined attack." But, in his condition, Lee was influenced by the desperate need of the elusive victory into believing that the failures in his command system were remediable at Gettysburg.

Lee defied the maxim "A good general knows when to retreat" because in his heart he knew that the next retreat he began could have only one end. He had defied many maxims —"Never divide an inferior force in the presence of a superior force" was one—but in those decisions he had been, as on the first two days at Gettysburg, "coolly calculating." On the night of the 2nd, in the midst of the restlessness of his camp, he was not.

Ultimately, General Lee's decision to renew the attack on

243

the third day was based on the knowledge that the soldiers sleeping in the darkness around him represented the last gathering of his army capable of delivering an assault for a decision. All of his far-flung forces were on or near the field, except some oddments of cavalry; and they, finally accounted for, were due the next day.

It is impossible to arrive at an acurate number for the Army of Northern Virginia, or for the Federal army. No one agrees with anyone else, and critics dismiss even Meade's own estimate that his army aggregated something over 100,-000 of all arms. A composite of most figures approximates 60,-000 Confederate infantry who reached the Gettysburg area. Losses on the first two days had been extremely heavy (the second was the heaviest of the campaign), and Lee would not have more than three fourths of his original number for the final effort.

By a similar composite approximation, Meade began with 80,000 infantry. His losses had been somewhat heavier, though proportionately the same, and Lee would renew the attack with the same ratio of strength as when the armies collided.

Federal artillery outnumbered Confederate in a ratio of four to three, and Meade's gunners had the advantage of weapons superior in weight, range, and accuracy. But Lee's cannoneers had some good Federal guns too, scattered among their batteries, and two long-range British rifled guns that had recently come in through the blockade.

Some estimates swell the number of Lee's "total effectives" by counting the 12,000-plus troopers to get whom Lee had stripped Virginia of mounted forces. As the battle was fought, these numbers on the muster rolls had no practical effect on the relative strength of the opposing armies. Aside from Buford's alert aggressiveness on the first day, the cavalry of neither side figured to any decisive extent. It would have been another story if Jeb Stuart had been present, with his command fit, even as late as June 30. The story might have had the same ending, but it would have been different.

On the night of the 2nd, Stuart and his three brigades were present to operate on the left flank that had so plagued Ewell. With Pickett's division only a few miles away and having rested since their arrival in late afternoon, at last all of Lee's men were "present or accounted for."

While General Lee planned the fresh dispositions for the next day's assault, there was about his tent little of the flurry that had characterized the first night. Neither A. P. Hill nor Ewell came. Various staff officers visited friends, but they did not approach the general. His own staff officers were kept working, writing out orders and delivering them. Perhaps because of their fatigue from the long day that had begun before daylight, none of the men left a personal report of those last waking hours of July 2.

The reasons for Lee's decision to renew the attack were known only to him until he delivered his report in January of the following year. Based on the troops' performance during the second day and with a possession of the high ground won along Emmitsburg road to provide advanced artillery support, he wrote that "with the proper concert of action . . . we should ultimately succeed."

He made no reference to any of the alternatives that must have presented themselves nor to any of the intangible considerations that must have influenced him. Reduced to the bare, impersonal realities of tactics, he concluded his report of that night with: "Longstreet . . . was ordered to attack the next morning, and General Ewell was ordered to assail the enemy's right at the same time."

Orders were also sent to artillery officers to have their guns in the new positions by sunrise, ready to open in the early light. At midnight the cluster of Lee's headquarters tents were dark. In the moonlight, picketed horses moved slowly, foraging for grass. By one o'clock the last soldier was rolled in his blanket on the ground. Beyond the rows of sleeping men, at the hospital tents in the valley on the western slope of Seminary Ridge and in barns and houses, doctors and orderlies worked on through the morning hours on the wounded who had come in. On the silent field the only men stirring were the personal servants who, wandering about since dark, could not find their masters.

8

"Pickett's Charge"

THE FIRST light of Friday, July 3, showed a clear sky and promised another hot day. The night air had lifted the closeness of the day before, and the warm morning felt fresh, though little breeze stirred. The men awakening to reveille first heard birds singing, "the chirp and motion of winged insects," and those west of Seminary Ridge heard a stream rippling. Sitting up under the trees, the men looked at the wild flowers and the fields of ripening grain, and, as one said, "never was sky or earth more serene—more harmonious— more aglow with light and life."

Then, as they stood and stretched out the cramps from sleeping on the ground, the men looked at the ground of the fighting of the day before. All thoughts of the tranquillity that a summer morning suggested were jarred from their consciousness. From Devil's Den north along Plum Run Valley, across the peach orchard they had captured, and on the slopes of the enemy-held Cemetery Ridge where Wright's brigade had reached the top, the line of battle was marked by corpses. From this grisly outline to their bivouacs the ground was littered with exploded caissons, dismounted guns, scattered rifles, and dead artillery horses that looked, curiously, at once flat and bloated in their grotesque positions. Closer still, all among them, they saw and then heard the wounded of both sides who had not yet been moved to field hospitals or tents.

The survivors had been too tired to bury their dead or to help much with the wounded, and there had been too many wounded for the small medical corps and the stretcher-bearers attached to each regiment to handle. Many of the stretcher-bearers themselves had gone down, and wounded men had kept crawling in from the field all night, begging for water.

The unwounded had slept through it all. The fighting had gone on so late the day before, until full darkness, that many of the troops had not reached the lines where they formed for the night until ten o'clock or later. In their exhaustion and disappointment at having failed to carry the enemy positions, they grouped in messes and built their fires. The fine food confiscated on the march was all gone, and the men cooked "sloosh"—cornmeal in bacon fat fried into loose, meat-flavored cornpone. Some messes had the peculiarly distasteful Nassau bacon (a blockade-run import), a fat pork they called either "Nausea" bacon or "salt horse."

Artillerists had worked still later under bright moonlight, feeding and watering their horses, bringing up replacements from the wagon teams for disabled animals, and changing harness to the new horses. Past midnight the officers continued to examine the ground in the eerie light and arrange battery positions for the morning.

By three o'clock the artillery officers and other officers were up again, an hour and a half before the drums rolled. By first light, when the soldiers were stirring, General Lee and sleepy-looking staff officers rode out on Seminary Ridge.

248

Dressed neatly as always, and inspiring, as Pickett said, "a reverential adoration" by his presence, Robert E. Lee showed care-worn fatigue. His whitening beard and hair, fluffy below the gray planters' hat, added a suggestion of age as well as dignity to the composure that seemed impervious to all collapses of the flesh.

For the second successive morning he silently surveyed the ramparts of Cemetery Ridge nearly a mile distant. No sounds came to him from the enemy's lines. North of the border of yesterday's battle, the hill and the farmland under the early morning sun presented a pleasing scene of country life. Probably he did not reflect on the contrasts. He studied instead the ground his men had won along the rise of the Emmitsburg road northward from the peach orchard.

Colonel Alexander had the First Corps batteries posted along the road when Lee viewed the ground at first light. Where the road bent east in front of the Spangler farm, the guns were posted back from the road, on the edge of a cornfield and northward in an orchard. At the end of the line the sixteen guns of Cabell's battalion were almost directly in front of General Lee's command post on Seminary Ridge and less than half a mile away.

Cabell's batteries stood in the line of march taken by Wright's Georgians late in the afternoon of the 2nd, when Lee had watched this unsupported brigade of Anderson's division reach the crest of Cemetery Ridge. The approximate mile covered by Alexander's batteries represented the front of the attack Lee designed for Longstreet's corps. According to Lee's plan at this early hour, the area of the objective would run from the point of Wright's breach in the center to the northern edge of the Federal flank of the day before.

In the locale of Sickles's break on the second day's flank, from the wheatfield east of the Emmitsburg road southward to the Devil's Den terrain, the front was as irregular as the

ground. Both armies had bivouacked where their fierce and
fragmentary action broke off in the dusk, and a regular line
of front had not been formed. Lee was inclined to dismiss the
possibility of counterthrusts from the Federal units bent
back in that rough country, and to mass his men and artillery
for one concentrated assault at what might be called the
enemy's left-center.

The commanding general's post, in the clearing at the top
of the gentle rise from the road to Seminary Ridge, was
alongside Spangler's Woods. This heavy growth covered the
ridge for about a quarter of a mile southward from Lee. From
those woods the Third Corps batteries, except Poague's, were
posted northward along Seminary Ridge to the Cashtown
road. In that mile covered by Hill's guns, the men of Pender's
division, brooding over the loss of their major general, and
Heth's troops, with their leader still incapacitated by his first
day's head wound, lounged in groups around mess fires and
stacked arms. They lay well back on the ridge, beyond the
range of any enemy battery that might be seized by an urge
for target practice. Only their skirmishers were advanced—
ragged, hungry-looking fellows, alert of posture and spry of
movement, cradling rifles that glinted in the sun's rays.

In the town there was more movement. Citizens in bold
curiosity hovered around the mess fires in the streets, record-
ing in their minds the carelessly spoken words of the Alabama
troops in Rodes's division. There was to be no more fighting
in this town.

East of the town, beyond Lee's view, at the back door to
the Federals' position, Allegheny Johnson's division held
enemy lines on the slopes of Culp's Hill. Even if unable to
carry the crest, these stout troops could exert enough pressure to divert troops from the main attack. If the enemy was
not sharp, the men could carry that hill which commanded
the Union rear. To strengthen their attack, Lee moved over

two brigades of Rodes's division which had been idle the day before. Also, Extra Billy Smith, the political general of Early's division, was finally freed from his vigil against the phantom enemy on the York road and moved up to the front.

For guarding the flank, the army had Jeb Stuart and his three favorite brigades. They had arrived during the afternoon and early evening of July 2, with men and beasts exhausted from Stuart's futile ride for fame. However, their mere presence brought reassurance, and they could move enough to threaten the Federals' line of communication on the Baltimore pike. The other missing cavalry was also up— Imboden's raiders and the two regular brigades that had spent the idle summer days gazing through the empty passes of the Blue Ridge after the Union army had moved out of Virginia.

To complete the army's concentration and to spearhead the attack, the division of George Pickett was expected momentarily. Because of Jefferson Davis's manipulation of Lee's troops for the invasion, the division was at 4,700 effectives instead of 8,000. However, the all-Virginia division was composed entirely of tested veterans, and in the past six months Pickett's men had fought less and marched more than any of the other troops with Lee. They were the only units that had not seen heavy action since Fredericksburg, and, from Pickett to privates, the soldiers were eager to have at the enemy again.

But as the sun rose over the stirring camps around Lee, there was neither sign nor word of Pickett's three brigades. On the day before, Lee had ordered Pickett to halt his troops a few miles from the field around three in the afternoon, so that the army's one unused division might be rested for any action required on the third day. On the night of the 2nd, Lee had sent Longstreet orders for early action involving those fresh troops.

251

There was nothing discretionary about the orders. Lee's relatively simple and untypical battle plan required no waiting for reconnaissance reports nor shifting of units. The troops were all in position, except Pickett's, who by five in the morning had had fourteen hours to move from three to five miles. Yet not even their van was reported in sight, and Pickett had sent no report to the commanding general. If Pickett had reported to his corps commander, Lee did not know it.

Longstreet still remained at the temporary headquarters he had established the night before at the shack in a meadow a mile or more southwest of Lee's post on Seminary Ridge. Except for the generalized verbal report Longstreet sent during the evening, Lee had heard nothing from him since they parted sometime after one o'clock the previous afternoon.

For what every soldier in both armies recognized would be the climactic assault of the three-day battle, the commanding general did not send officers from his staff to discover where Pickett was and what Longstreet was doing. He went himself.

Mounting his gray horse, Lee rode down the western slope of the ridge, along the valley where hospital tents were pitched, through the woods jutting east from Pitzer's Run, and out onto the meadow. There he saw Longstreet and his staff gathered in an idle group.

2

The early-morning encounter between Lee and Longstreet was a decisive event of the third day at Gettysburg, but very little is known about it. The only full reports were written by Longstreet years after the war. His later versions, published after Lee's death, not only contradict his official report (written one month after the battle and subject to Lee's review) but contain some improbable speeches of the sort one wishes one had made at the time. As these successive speeches increasingly rounded out the military rationale he developed after the war, in support of his opposition to Lee during the battle, it can be presumed that his various accounts reflected more his state of mind than what transpired. The one certainty is that Longstreet had not executed the orders Lee sent him the night before.

According to Longstreet, he spoke first, before Lee asked him anything. He opened the conversation with fresh arguments for changing Lee's battle plan, and it was in the arguments that Longstreet revealed he had never intended to execute the orders received earlier. At this point he was neither would-be collaborator nor resentful subordinate; indeed, his attitude reflected no accountable military relationship with Lee. He announced, in effect, that he had organized a movement of his own—a movement that would have been unrelated to what the rest of the army was doing or to what Lee expected of him.

It has been said that Stonewall Jackson would have placed him under arrest on the spot and that Napoleon would have had him shot, and many have been the reasons advanced for Lee's putting up with the insubordination. The simplest explanation is that Lee had no one with whom to replace him. Hood was wounded, Pickett not on the field, McLaws manifestly inadequate for corps command. The effect of Longstreet's dismissal at the hour of his corps's assault would have been disastrous to the morale of his troops.

Lee's mistake was not in retaining Longstreet in command; for that he had no alternative. It was in entrusting, for the second successive day, an unsupervised offensive movement to a normally defensive fighter whose opposition made it apparent that he had placed himself outside the control of the command system. In making this mistake, Lee, distracted

253

and in an exhausted condition, failed to appraise the extent of Longstreet's intransigence and agitation. Yet it was not that simple.

This failure of judgment was not influenced by any such high-blown dramatic scene as Longstreet later described. Nor did Longstreet then propose to Lee the larger strategy that he later attributed to himself in what has usually been accepted as an accurate version of the morning meeting.

No officer of either staff mentioned any exchange at all between the two generals, and Lee dismissed Longstreet's reasons for delay in executing his orders with: "General Longstreet's dispositions were not completed as early as expected." Although Longstreet had not executed his orders and did offer a counterplan, Lee, after three days of Longstreet's countersuggestions and delays, thought of nothing beyond getting his one trusted corps commander into action as soon as possible.

What Longstreet proposed to Lee, as an explanation for not having put his troops in movement, was undoubtedly what he wrote in the official report that Lee approved. "Our arrangements," he said, meaning those of his staff, "were made for renewing the attack by my right, with a view to pass around the hill [Little Round Top] occupied by the enemy on his left, and to gain it by a flank and reverse attack. This would have been a slow process, probably, but I think not very difficult."

In a post-war account, however, Longstreet wrote: "I sent to our extreme right to make a little reconnaissance in that direction, thinking that General Lee might yet conclude to *move around* the Federal left [and] I stated to General Lee that I . . . was much inclined to think that the best thing was to *move to* the Federal left."

"*Move around*" and "*move to*" have been italicized to stress the difference in meaning between these words and "*gain it*

254

[the enemy's flank] *by . . . attack*" in the report submitted through Lee.

In another version he went further and wrote: "Fearing that he [Lee] was still in his disposition to attack"—Longstreet had *orders* to attack—"I tried to anticipate him by saying, 'General, I have had my scouts out all night, and I find that you will have an excellent opportunity to move around to the right of Meade's army and *maneuver him into attacking us.*'" (Not his italics.)

Thus, with slight changes in wording, Longstreet progressively altered his account of what he had said from a suggestion for attacking Meade to a suggestion that Meade attack them. This fundamental difference between his official report, which Lee approved, and the version later developed has usually been ignored.

His suggested move, as recorded in his official report, would have been a tactical change in the battle, a reversion to the urgently offered plan of Hood and Law which he had overruled the day before. But the move outlined in the often quoted version of the reminiscences would have broken off the battle; reverting to the plan he had introduced to Lee the first day, it would have been a continuation of his purpose to fight a defensive battle elsewhere.

Even without this basic contradiction between the memories and the official report, it would seem unlikely that Longstreet would have proposed that the Confederate army, poised for attack with 140-odd guns in position—half of them far advanced—should disengage itself, cross the enemy's front, and, presumably at its leisure, select a new position that Meade would be forced to attack. There was nothing to reduce energetic Meade to the role of spectator while this cumbersome withdrawal took place in front of him. Ewell alone, five miles away from Longstreet and without a good road between them, had some fifteen miles of wagons; and

Buford, then refitting his hard-worked Federal cavalry, would be ready again to take up the pressing work he had abandoned after the first day. In every respect the proposal is too illogical to have been advanced by an experienced soldier at that stage of the army's commitment.

It is probable that somewhere back in Longstreet's mind lurked a hopeful, unarticulated scheme that would have enlarged his corps's movement to the Federal flank into a total movement of the army away from Gettysburg. When he said in his official report that "our arrangements were made" for, in effect, evading Lee's battle plan, he was motivated by the same determination to shift to the defensive which had caused his procrastination on the 2nd. But, though all that was a part of his immovable opposition to attack, it was not a part of what he said to Lee.

Other references in Longstreet's writings indicate distortions of what happened there in the morning. Years after the war he composed a declamation in which he supposedly told Lee that "no 15,000 men" could carry "that position." At the time of their scene in the meadow no one knew that only 15,000 were going to make the assault, and the position finally assailed was not Lee's point of objective when he talked to Longstreet.

Aside from the apparent lapses in Longstreet's reconstruction of the morning encounter, the probability is against Lee standing there as an audience to Shakespearean speeches and suggestions of grand strategy when he was so anxious to begin an early action that he had ridden from general headquarters in person. Longstreet reported that Lee "was impatient of listening and tired of talking." The commanding general very likely showed his impatience as soon as Longstreet revealed that, instead of following orders, he was trying to change them.

In ignoring the exchange in his reports, Lee showed that

the discovery of Longstreet's inaction immediately diverted his thoughts to Culp's Hill, where Ewell had orders to attack at early light in conjunction with Longstreet's move. He had to send a message advising General Ewell that Longstreet would not open the action until ten o'clock.

Longstreet, magnifying his status in retrospect, saw the point of the exchange to be that Lee "knew I did not believe success was possible."

Lee was not even thinking of what his subordinate believed.

The real significance of the disparity between the reactions of the two men was that Lee failed to recognize the balky defeatism implicit in Longstreet's behavior and attitude.

On the ragged edge of his own self-control, Lee completely missed the disturbed state that rendered his senior corps commander unfit to direct the assault. In some excitement, General Lee brushed aside the arguments and told Longstreet that the attack was going to be made where he wanted it and that the First Corps was going to make it.

Impatient and distracted, expecting every man to do his duty, Lee attached no such importance to the encounter as Longstreet did. As a commanding general who expected his orders to be carried out, there was no reason why he should —*if* the exchange had ended there.

As all the to-do about Longstreet's delays on the second day missed the fundamental reasons for the failure of the assault, so all the analyses of the supposed clash of opinions on the third morning missed the point of why the battle was fought as it was. Whether or not Lee should have dismissed Longstreet for offering counterplans instead of following orders was not the decisive element. The nature of the attack was determined *after* Longstreet was overruled, and it was then that Lee showed himself to be no longer in possession of his full faculties as a military commander.

When Lee gave Longstreet the flat orders to prepare for action, the corps commander suggested a change in the details of the battle plan.

He pointed out that McLaws's and Hood's divisions, in the irregular battle line from the peach orchard to the boulders of the Round Top area, would be exposed to enfilade fire from their right flank. That was the same objection that McLaws, Hood, and Evander Law had advanced to Longstreet the day before. It was not that he had come around to the reasoning he had rejected on the 2nd. He was seeking a means of shifting the responsibility for the assault from his unit of command. As a countersuggestion, he proposed that McLaws and Hood remain where they were to immobilize the Federal flank, and that the assault force be formed of Pickett's fresh troops and brigades from A. P. Hill's corps.

The decisive element in the Lee-Longstreet meeting was the commanding general's agreement to this change in his battle plan.

For not only was the complement of the assault force changed from a single corps into a loose collection of units, but the objective of the attack was shifted from the Federal left-center to the exact center. The point of Wright's breech of the day before would more nearly represent the southern end of the attacking front than, as Lee had planned when he studied the terrain, approximately the northern end.

In the strange, undeclared conflict of wills that had begun thirty-six hours before, neither general was thinking clearly. As Longstreet would by now do anything to avoid assuming responsibility for a full-scale attack, Lee would do anything to get him to move out.

Facing each other in the early morning sunlight, neither read the outward evidences of the other's state of mind. Erect and massive, fifty-six-year-old, half-sick Lee showed the strain by what Longstreet called the loss of "his matchless equipoise." Powerful Longstreet at forty-two, his face reflecting the vigorous health that, despite heavy wounds, was to extend his span of life into the eighty-third year, showed his inner turmoil by a surliness unwonted in a naturally hearty man. He was never reconciled to delivering an attack even after Lee agreed to his conditions; but General Lee made the mistaken assumption that the recalcitrant subordinate had been brought into line by the compromise plan.

The compromise they reached was as fateful for the final action as the compromise with Jefferson Davis was for the whole campaign.

By the arrangement Lee and Longstreet made for the attacking force, the eleven brigades selected were like men who drew the short straw where the losers were picked to die.

3

Lee had ridden back to his clearing beside Spangler's Woods when Pickett's van was reported approaching Seminary Ridge sometime before seven in the morning. As the other divisions of the First Corps were not going in with Pickett, his three brigades were ordered to the western side of Seminary Ridge behind Dick Anderson's division, immediately to the south of Lee's command post.

Pickett had not moved his men out early or hurried them on their march across country lanes because he had received no orders to do so. As far as officers and men knew, they came up with the army when they were expected. Between seven and nine on a morning already uncomfortably warm, the regiments broke ranks in a valley below the western slope of the ridge. Arms were inspected, men who had not already thrown away their blankets dropped them on the grass, and the more prudent wandered about in search of water for their canteens.

Unknown at that time to the commanding general, the first part of his two-pronged attack was collapsing even as his army was completed. Ewell had been ordered to deliver his attack on Culp's Hill at dawn, in conjunction with the attack Longstreet had been ordered to make on the Federal left-center. Old Baldhead, as if resolved to make amends for his failures, was very alert during the early morning hours of July 3. Daniel's and O'Neal's brigades, shifted from Rodes's division to support Allegheny Johnson, were up at one thirty and moved eastward through the streets of the sleeping town. In the moonlight they approached the ghostly figures of Johnson's men stirring in their camp around Culp's Hill.

Brigadier General Steuart's Virginia brigade had won an advanced position on the rocky slope at the end of the second day, and the assault was to be launched from there. Their line was only a quarter of a mile from the Baltimore pike, which served Meade's army, and one mile in the rear of the Federal center on Cemetery Ridge, where Longstreet was supposed to strike from the front.

Although the darkness prevented Ewell from recognizing the full extent of his threat to the enemy's position, he knew that gaining the crest of Culp's Hill could, combined with Longstreet's attack, open the way to the victory that had been hanging for two days. Also, impressed by his troops' attacking power despite lack of co-ordination the day before, General Ewell made dispositions for realizing their striking potential which were sounder than any he had made since arriving on the field. He could not get guns up the craggy slopes, but the high spirit of Johnson's infantry and Rodes's two brigades showed their willingness to go in without artillery support.

By first light Allegheny Johnson, brandishing his club, had his men ready to open the action. But the Federals, uneasy about that half-open door at their backs, had Slocum's corps ready at the same time, and fresh batteries had been brought into position on the pike by indefatigable General Hunt.

The guns opened first, and there was nothing that Ewell's people could do except huddle close to their boulders and wait. When the cannonade ended, the men sprang ahead up the rocks, their bayonets glistening through the thickets in the early morning light.

The use of quickly erected breastworks had been developed by this stage of the war, and Slocum's men were well dug in. Within a few minutes the desperately engaged men were repeating the pattern of the dusk fighting of the day before. The Rebels, with their familiar high screams, overran lines of works and clambered on, firing, toward the top. The Federals, holding steady when they fell back, counterattacked with shouts echoing over the hillside. All through the rise and fall of the action the Federal guns sprayed the Confederate troops, sometimes firing so closely over the defensive lines that shots burst among their own troops.

With heavy casualties and short breathing-spells, Johnson's men, powerfully supported by Daniel's North Carolinians, kept reforming and trying again. Each new effort promised to carry them all the way to the crest. At the hour when Lee, with Longstreet about three air-miles away, was thinking that he must send Ewell an order to hold off his attack until Longstreet was ready at ten o'clock, the issue at the Federals' back door was being decided. Hour after hour, to seven, to eight, to nine o'clock, Ewell's men and Slocum's gave the best they had and took the best the other had, and neither attack nor defense could change the pattern. Nothing could sweep the Federals from the crest, and nothing could prevent the reforming gray waves from rolling uphill—as long as the men's energy lasted.

By the time the last of Pickett's division came up back of Seminary Ridge, barely two miles away, the energy was fad-

261

ing and casualties were taking the weight from Johnson's blows. A North Carolina battalion with Junius Daniel lost 200 of 240 men. When Ewell received Lee's order to hold his attack off until ten o'clock, all attacking power had been drained from Old Allegheny's division and its supporting brigades. This division, originally formed by Stonewall Jackson, was never the same again. Its glories were in the past.

After about nine o'clock, though rifle fire crackled on through the morning, men died, and groups maneuvered for new position, the issue was no longer in doubt. The Federal back door was shut, their rear was safe, and there was no threat to divert their attention from the center.

Historically, the fierce fighting on Culp's Hill seems almost a peripheral action, which it was never intended to be. Seven of Lee's brigades were allotted to that small field of action, only two less than were to form the charge at the center of Cemetery Ridge.

In ordering that dual attack Lee seems to have reverted to the goaded, slugging tactics of Malvern Hill, his poorest battle. As at Malvern Hill, feeling that a frontal assault should be accompanied by a flank thrust to divert the enemy, he attempted a combination movement with an army not capable of the co-ordination necessary for such an action. The difference was that at Gettysburg he had not acknowledged the breakdown of the methods of operation perfected after Malvern Hill. Believing that a proper concert of action was still possible, General Lee weakened each movement by dividing his total strength.

When Daniel's and O'Neal's brigades were removed from support of Rodes's other brigades south from Gettysburg along Long Lane, Ramseur's and Doles's strong offensive units were relegated to an idle defensiveness on the flank of the assault that came at the Federal center. Although those two handsomely led brigades would have strengthened the center attack, they were wasted on both the second and the third days. In turn, Daniel and O'Neal, not providing sufficient weight to Johnson's attack, were used up in what became the first of two separate battles. In so far as a combined dual movement affected the enemy, Ewell's flank attack and Longstreet's center attack might as well have been different battles on different days.

At ten o'clock, when Ewell's action was beginning to dwindle into sporadic, personal fighting, Longstreet was no more ready to attack than he had been when Lee left him at six. As is true of Old Pete's inanition during the forenoon of the second day, no one knows what he did during those hours. He said that until noon the time "was consumed" in readying Pickett's three brigades for the assault, but Pickett's division needed no readying. On the contrary, from their arrival on the field until twelve o'clock, the waiting in the rising heat wore at their nerves.

None of the men knew anything about the two-pronged attack, one half of which had already been broken off. In his official report Longstreet never mentioned Ewell or in any way referred to the Second Corps's assault that was to have coincided with his in the early morning. (Ewell, however, made a somewhat heated reference to Longstreet's part in the joint action.) In Pickett's division the troops knew only that they were going in, and, from general officers to privates, they wanted to get it over with.

The inspector general of the division spoke for them all. "It is said, that to the condemned, in going to execution, the moments fly. To the good soldier, about to go into action, I am sure the moments linger. Let us not dare say, that with him, either individually or collectively, it is that 'mythical love of fighting,' poetical but fabulous; but rather, that it is nervous anxiety to solve the great issue as speedily as possible, without stopping to count the cost. The Macbeth principle—'Twere well it were done quickly'—holds quite as good in heroic action as in crime."

4

When Pickett left his troops in the little valley and went to report to Lee, the thirty-eight-year-old major general looked confident and eager. To British military observer Fremantle, he appeared to be a "desperate-looking character." The swashbuckling appearance was given by a dark mustache drooping and curled at the ends, a thin goatee, and hair worn long and curled in ringlets. His hair was brown, and in the morning sunlight it reflected auburn tints. George E. Pickett stood slender and graceful at the middle height, and carried himself with an air. Dandified in his dress, he was the most romantic-looking of all Confederates, the physical image of that gallantry implicit in the South's self-concept.

Pickett was also of a romantic turn of mind. A widower, he was then engaged to young Sallie Corbell, a girl who had loved him since her childhood and to whom he was the embodiment of military glamour. She always called him "My Soldier." Pickett was in the throes of a middle-life resurgence of passion, and he could think of nothing but his agonizingly postponed marriage to Sallie and the glory he wanted to win for her. Gettysburg offered him his first real opportunity for a big moment since he had volunteered for the Confederate army.

In the old army he had shown a flair for the spectacular. As a young lieutenant in the Mexican War, he had been the first American to scale the ramparts at Chapultepec, where he had planted the flag before the admiring gaze of his friend Longstreet. But in the Confederate army, fame had eluded him.

Arriving late in Virginia after secession, coming a roundabout way from Oregon, he went in at the customary rank of colonel and did not make brigadier until February 1862. He fought his brigade in the action around Richmond preceding the Seven Days, and in the savage battle at Gaines' Mill he was wounded just before his troops went in with the final charge that won the day. His brigade, led by its senior colonel, Eppa Hunton, performed well, but the hero of the day was John Hood leading his Texas Brigade.

Although invalided out during the summer fighting that evicted the Federals from Virginia, Pickett was promoted to major general in October 1862 and returned to duty wearing two stars that Sallie embroidered in a wreath for his collar. It is probable that his advancement was helped along by the influence of Longstreet, who had long regarded Pickett almost as a younger brother. Their friendship was an example of the attraction of opposites, and stolid Old Pete was particularly proud of what he called Pickett's "pulchritude." Placed in Longstreet's newly formed corps, Pickett was given five first-line brigades of 9,000 veterans to form one of the largest and best divisions in the army.

Yet, again he was passed over by opportunity. His division saw little action at Fredericksburg (December 1862), and he spent the following winter and spring in Davis-inspired guard duty and sieges, interspersed with pointless marches and defensive stances in southeastern Virginia and North Carolina. He was relieving the tedium of camp by stolen rendezvous with Sallie when the army opened the spring campaign, and missed the great day at Chancellorsville when Pender and Rodes won glory.

Then, for the Gettysburg campaign, he was deprived of his two largest brigades and, as the army's smallest division, was held at Chambersburg during the convergence on Gettysburg. When Pickett marched his men to Seminary Ridge on the morning of the 3rd, he was the only division commander on the field who had seen no action with the army during the

265

entire year. Having missed all opportunities for distinguishing himself, General Pickett was on that morning only another division commander, with no legends about him or record of proved performance.

Even without Sallie, this would have been hard on Pickett, a born soldier. Growing up in the James River plantation country in the environs of Richmond, he had never wanted to be anything else.

Pickett's grandfather, a vastly wealthy Richmonder, had left a working plantation to each of his three sons. But Pickett's father, like many another of his generation, enjoyed the idyll of plantation life without the talents for sustaining it. Although George Pickett grew up in an aura of baronial privilege, the strong man in the family was his mother's brother, Andrew Johnston, a successful attorney. Johnston had been associated in law with Abraham Lincoln, and the Pickett boy, visiting his uncle in Quincy, became Lincoln's intimate friend. When Johnston showed a lack of enthusiasm about an army career for George at a time when Virginia appointments were going to his cousin Harry Heth and to Powell Hill, it was Mr. Lincoln who was instrumental in obtaining for the Richmond boy an appointment to West Point from Illinois.

According to Sallie, who became Mrs. Pickett, Lincoln wrote the seventeen-year-old that "I should like to have a perfect soldier credited to dear old Illinois." Mrs. Pickett also stated that Mr. Lincoln gave the boy advice to follow "the old maxim that 'one drop of honey catches more flies than half-a-gallon of gall.'" Wherever the advice came from, George Pickett had a pleasing personality. Genial, informal, and considerate, with a turn of humor, he made many friends. Perhaps because of his quick temper and the theatrical element in his character, he was—like other colorful personalities—abidingly disliked by a few.

This dislike, inflamed by jealousy of the post-Gettysburg glory that came to him, was an element in a subsequent denigration of Pickett's personal conduct at Gettysburg. The ancient canard should be disposed of here. A South Carolinian named Haskell started a rumor that Pickett and his staff huddled in the Spangler barn during the assault, and Kirk Otey, a Virginian from Pickett's division, published in a Richmond newspaper a charge that two of Pickett's staff officers were waiting their turn at the "whisky wagon" in the rear of the lines during the attack. In time the two slanders merged to form the single story that Pickett and his staff were drunk in the stone barn.

Every conceivable form of evidence was published in refutation of the slander, including the indisputable fact that the Spangler barn had been burned before the charge. Longstreet and Wilcox, in official reports uninvolved with the scandal, substantiated the staff officers' accounts of their performance of hazardous duty. The truth is that the calumny made a better story than the facts.

An element in Pickett's actual behavior that offended some brother officers before and after Gettysburg was the emotionality brought to the surface by his autumnal romance; at times he behaved more like a mooning schoolboy than was considered seemly by contemporaries in the army. But, whatever personal reservations his fellow officers may have had about him, the open enmities and the "controversy" were in the future when General Pickett joined the group with Lee on the crest of Seminary Ridge.

During the prolonged period of waiting, while others clearly showed their tension, Colonel Alexander observed that Pickett seemed cheerfully composed and "sanguine of success." Moving back and forth from the command post to his troops, General Pickett passed the time by writing a letter to Sallie. He was acutely aware of the diminished strength

267

of his division, reduced to 4,500 men from 8,000, but he was even more aware that his hour of destiny had come at last.

5

As the sun climbed toward noon and the day grew unbearably hot, the officers and men did not share General Pickett's cheerful composure. While the soldiers were kept from seeing the field across which they were to attack, the brigade leaders strolled up to the crest for a good, sobering look, and it would be difficult to say whether the waiting bore harder on the officers who saw the field or the men kept from seeing it. The longer they waited, the more they began to think.

There was a close relationship in the personnel of the three brigades, composed of intimates and kinsmen from the old Tidewater and the beguiling Piedmont regions of Virginia. The division's assistant inspector general was Major Charles Pickett, the general's only brother, and, curiously, the major's mustache drooped in precisely the same shape as his older brother's, though without the curling ends. One regiment from Jefferson's Albemarle County was known as the "Berkeley Regiment" because the colonel, lieutenant colonel, major, and senior captain were brothers, all from civilian life.

One of the brigadiers, James Lawson Kemper, had been for ten years a state legislator from the Piedmont plantation country and twice speaker of the House. Then thirty-nine, General Kemper was another of those civilian leaders who, accustomed to authority, translated their native gifts to command in the field. Although his only previous military experience had been as a young captain of volunteers in the Mexican War, thin-faced Kemper looked impressively military in his uniform.

His brigade had been successively commanded, and molded, by Longstreet, Ewell, and A. P. Hill, and his veterans included the 1st Virginia Regiment. Composed of a cross-section of Richmond militia and volunteer companies, the "Old First" was a descendant of the first command of George Washington, on whose staff Kemper's grandfather had served as colonel. Not a particularly warm man, Kemper was very determined and was respected by brother officers for "solid qualities and sound judgment." Before and after battles, the peacetime politician was given to high-flown oratory that was vastly appreciated by his troops, who took great pride in their brigadier.

The two old pro's at brigade command, Garnett and Armistead, were no speechmakers. The only public speech ever made by Dick Garnett was a strong appeal for the Union and against secession. On the morning of the 3rd he was in no condition for speeches. Physically ill, he was wrapped in a blue overcoat on that hot day. Friends had urged him to remain in the ambulance, but General Garnett had personal reasons for joining in the division's action.

Of a distinguished family in the Rappahannock River country, Garnett had cousins and brothers-in-law who had brought honor to the family by their Confederate service, while his war career had been overshadowed by a single event that he could not forget.

Garnett, of the West Point class of '41, had resigned his regular-army commission after long frontier service in the West on the grounds that he "felt it an imperative duty to sacrifice everything in support of his native state in her time of trial." Thoroughly competent and highly courageous, he advanced to command of the famous Stonewall Brigade when Jackson was promoted to major general.

At the Battle of Kernstown, prelude to Jackson's Valley Campaign, he ran afoul of Stonewall's displeasure. Feeling that the situation of his brigade was hopeless, and with ammunition running out, Garnett ordered a retreat without consulting his commanding general. Stonewall *might* have for-

269

given this in any other brigade, but not in the one that his own stern demands had transformed from the Valley bumpkins of their early days into the unshakable line that at First Manassas won Jackson his sobriquet. He placed Garnett under arrest for ordering a retreat without orders.

Garnett demanded a court-martial, and the case dragged on for months, made into something of a cause by Garnett's friends, who felt that he had been treated unjustly. The case represented only an extreme example of Jackson's customarily cold justice that took no heed of extenuating circumstances, but he was particularly implacable toward Garnett. After battles had broken up several attempts to hold a court-martial, Lee finally resolved the situation by transferring Garnett to Pickett's division.

Richard Garnett, a kindly, courteous, and generous man, was no grudge-holder, but he was a sensitive man with a deep awareness of personal honor and family honor and a justifiable pride in his career. His friends said that after his arrest he unnecessarily exposed himself to danger in order to expunge the black mark from his record. Gettysburg offered Garnett his first real opportunity with Pickett's division to clear his honor as a gentleman and a soldier.

A sloping black mustache and pointed beard and a proud expression gave the forty-four-year-old man the look of a warrior out of the heroic past. Yet, despite his personal resolve to lead his men in the charge, Garnett was awed by a survey of the field to be crossed. Turning to Brigadier General Armistead, he said: "This is a desperate thing to attempt."

"It is," Armistead agreed, "but the issue is with the Almighty, and we must leave it in His hands."

Brother officers always referred to Lewis Armistead as "Old Lewis" or "Brave Old Lewis." There was something indomitable in this warm-hearted man, a sort of "bravest of the brave," which aroused affectionate respect in all who knew him. Then forty-six, Armistead wore a close-cropped graying beard, and his gray hair was balding in front. His gaze was steady, his manner casual and friendly. A widower, he had one son, Keith Armistead, who served as his aide-de-camp. A sentimental turn in Armistead caused one of his colonels, John Bowie Magruder (not to be confused with "Prince John" Magruder), to call him "Lo" as an abbreviation of "Lothario."

Armistead was the only general officer with Lee who had been born in a regular-army family: his father, General Walker Armistead, a member of the second graduating class at West Point, had been second-in-command of the U.S. army. Despite this background, Lewis Armistead left West Point before graduation—some said it was because he had hit his classmate Jubal Early over the head with a mess plate. He received his commission from civilian life, and in the Mexican War was breveted captain and then major for gallantry in action.

At secession, he was a captain in the garrison at Los Angeles, and the decision to leave the old army was painful to a man who had grown up in its traditions. Although he came of a powerfully connected seventeenth-century Virginia family, most of Armistead's friends were in the army. The closest was General Winfield Scott Hancock, the thirty-nine-year-old Pennsylvanian who was defending the Federal center at Gettysburg precisely where Armistead's brigade would be pointed. On Armistead's last night in Los Angeles, Hancock had given a dinner party for the Virginian and other Southerners who were going home to defend their land. They had not met since.

Reaching Richmond after First Manassas, Armistead did not make brigadier until April 1862, but he distinguished himself for "extreme gallantry" the first time he took his brigade into action, at Seven Pines, June 1, 1862. At the mismanaged and poorly fought Battle of Malvern Hill, where his brigade was part of the division of pompous and ineffectual Huger, Armistead was one of the few leaders who enjoyed an outstandingly good day. Despite the ineptness of Huger and the miserable liaison between the attacking units, Armistead showed initiative and brilliant judgment of the military situation. He fought to an advanced position on the bloody hill and, almost isolated, held the ground as a rallying-point that, because of failures in command, was never rallied on.

Armistead never performed so conspicuously again, though Lee mentioned his "devotion" and "courage" in reports, and his soldiers were devoted to him. His men came from the area around Suffolk in Tidewater Virginia, a town distinguished for the quality of its social life, and the troops, mostly planters and farmers, were sturdy, self reliant, and mannerly. The regiments, like those in the other brigades, were fortunate in the uniformity of proved competence and bravery in their field officers. In a division characterized by happy personal relations, Armistead and his men were particularly close.

While the brigade was waiting on the western slope of Seminary Ridge for orders to move up, Armistead, probably feeling the tension mount in the sweating men around him, strolled over to join George Pickett and his staff.

After losing his own wife, Armistead had apparently felt sentimentally toward the young girl to whom George Pickett was betrothed. On reaching his friend, Armistead removed a ring from his little finger.

"Give this little token, George, please, to her of the sunset eyes, and tell her 'the old man' says since he could not be the lucky dog, he's mighty glad you are." Pickett was still writing Sallie his piecemeal letter in snatches, and he added:

272

"I'll keep the ring for you, and some day I'll take it to John Tyler's in Richmond and have it made into a breastpin, and set around with rubies and diamonds and emeralds. You will be the pearl."

Sometime before noon the orders came for the division to move up into the positions from which the attack would be made.

6

According to Major Walter Harrison, A.A.G. and inspector general, 4,481 men plus officers were present to fall in at "assembly." From the unseen side of Seminary Ridge, the men heard only the light scattered fire of sharpshooters as the three brigades started climbing through the hot woods of the hillside toward the crest.

At the top, where an old trace ran from north to south, the men on the left of Garnett's brigade came alongside the right of Heth's division of Hill's corps. Archer's brigade of Alabama and Tennessee troops, that day commanded by Colonel Fry, were already formed in line. Garnett's brigade formed to the right of them, their double lines stretching several hundred yards southward through the woods.

Kemper's brigade came up on Garnett's right, below the woods in an open field. Seminary Ridge sloped off to the south there (where, technically, it became Warfield Ridge), and the men took shelter in a swale, or "hollow," according to Captain Dooley of the 1st Virginia. Kemper's men felt exposed under the full glare of the noon sun. The woods had been hot enough, but the soldiers glanced back a little wistfully at the shadowed places where Garnett's men stretched out under branches and behind tree trunks.

Armistead's men came up last, and found no room between Garnett's left and Fry's right. Armistead was ordered to deploy his men in the rear of Garnett's brigade, in close support.

Old Lewis did not like the position at all. As soon as his men had made themselves as comfortable as possible in the smothering woods, he sought Major Harrison.

With a little hemming and hawing, Armistead asked the inspector general to ask Pickett if maybe he would not prefer Armistead's brigade to push out in *front* of Heth's right. Walter Harrison accepted this request with amused tolerance. As he said, "Brave old Armistead was very tenacious of place to the front."

Major Harrison passed among Hill's artillery pieces posted on the crest and approached the groups of officers gathered in the clearing around General Lee, but did not find Pickett. Eager to get a personal look at the field, he made "a little trespass on military etiquette" and accosted General Longstreet. He asked Old Pete about Armistead's position.

Longstreet revealed to Harrison "anything but a pleasant humor at the prospect 'over the hill.' He snorted out, rather sharply," the staff major reported, and said: "General Pickett will attend to that, sir."

Harrison turned away. Longstreet, recovering what the major regarded as "his usual kind-heartedness," called after him in a different tone: "Never mind, colonel, you can tell General Armistead to remain where he is for the present. He can make up the distance when the advance is made."

Major Harrison, knowing nothing of the lieutenant general's agitation, dismissed the episode. In exchange for the passing rebuke, the A.A.G. got his look at the sloping land between their crest and the enemy's ridge. On the enemy's side of the Emmitsburg road, his eyes followed the ascent from the post-and-rail fences at the bottom, over a line of skirmishers, "almost as heavy as a single line of battle," up the steeper climb to the loose stone fence or wall, back of which were two lines of blue infantry and two tiers of artillery. On the plateau beyond were dark masses of reserves.

To the solitary major, standing outside the groups with stars on their collars, the approach to the Federal position looked like "a passage to the valley of death."

Subdued, he walked back to the temporary safety of the woods and found the men getting restless in their "ardor-cooling inactivity." No one knew why they were waiting again.

The only action on their front was a local affair over a barn between Hill's sharpshooters and some Connecticut troops of Hancock's corps. The Bliss house and barn were about midway between Seminary Ridge and the Emmitsburg road, where the road bore close to Cemetery Ridge, and provided a fine "nest" for the sharpshooters. A Federal brigade came up to root them out, Hill's guns became engaged, the Federal cannoneers answered, and Colonel Lindsay Walker let the Third Corps artillery waste a lot of ammunition. Finally, some of Hancock's people burned both house and barn, and an uneasy silence settled over the field.

Among Hill's guns, Poague's artillery battalion was the most advanced, posted to the north of Cabell's batteries at the end of the arc of Longstreet's guns, and directly below Lee's command post. At intervals General Lee moved close to young Poague's guns, as if to study the field from a different vantage point. Lee showed none of the nervousness of the day before. As on his early morning trip to Longstreet, the Old Man seemed anxiously intent on investigating every detail.

Once, while standing back of Poague's guns, he even delivered one of his customarily involved rebukes to a young officer.

Major Dearing, commander of the artillery battalion attached to Pickett's division, followed the fashion set by his general and dressed in high Confederate style. Although an able cannoneer, Dearing was on the showy side, and during the morning preparations he went galloping along the line of batteries about seventy-five yards in front of them. He made a handsome figure out there alone, and also a handsome target for sharpshooters.

General Lee, pretending he did not know who the rider was, called: "My friend! This way, if you please."

Major Dearing swung his horse around, guided him between the guns, and saluted smartly.

"Ah, major, excuse me," Lee said. "I thought you might be some countryman who had lost his way. Let me say this to you and to these young officers, that I am an old reconnoitering officer and have always found it best to go afoot, and not expose oneself needlessly."

Yet, despite his personal attention and the dragging hours of preparation, the formation of the assault force was the weakest arrangement for battle in the history of the Army of Northern Virginia. The details of arranging the assault Lee had turned over to Longstreet and A. P. Hill, and neither of these old enemies assumed responsibility for the combined force. Longstreet would not, and Hill, accepting Longstreet as commander of the attack, could not. As no one knew that Longstreet was not assuming responsibility, the assault force was formed without controlling supervision.

The sequence of orders involving the arrangement of the attack is not known. When Longstreet rode from his headquarters to Lee's command post, the divisions of Hood and McLaws, who had been removed from the attack on Longstreet's suggestion, were left with orders to remain alertly in their positions. Their irregular lines from the peach orchard to the southern base of Little Round Top projected at something like a forty-five-degree angle from the troops on Seminary Ridge and those extending southward from it. No plans were made for employing those divisions. They were to protect the attacking flank from counterattack from the Federal left and, of course, repel any thrusts at themselves. For the purposes of the assault, they were no more involved than Rodes's two brigades at the other end of the line, southward from the town.

When Longstreet arrived at the informal general headquarters, he conferred first with Lee, then with Lee and Hill, and then with Hill alone. During these exchanges Longstreet made no further importunities, but his downcast gaze reflected an apathetic state. He himself said: "I was never so depressed as on that day."

However, his mood went unnoticed, as everyone was absorbed in his own problem. Powell Hill was a shadowy figure on the second and third days. He was presumably not recovered from his illness of the first day, and the assignments he received were unsuited to his nature and training.

On the second day, on Hill's right, Anderson's division was partially detached from him, partially attached to Longstreet, by Lee's most ambiguous order. On the left, Pender's division was ordered to demonstrate, with discretion to exploit any opportunities. After Pender fell, the temporary commander became involved with Rodes's proposed late attack on Cemetery Hill and did nothing. By the time Brigadier General Lane assured Rodes of support, the attack had been called off, and Ramseur and Doles went into bivouac a few hundred yards ahead of where Pender's division had waited all day.

Following the futility of the second day and the loss of the two major generals who were his personal friends and military dependables, for the third day Hill was ordered to lend eight brigades to go in with and to support Pickett's division in Longstreet's attack. Two brigades from Pender's division and all of Heth's division, now under Pettigrew, were to join Pickett in the attack, and two brigades from Anderson's division were to act in support.

Lee selected the units from the Third Corps according to

their positions in the line. Pender's came from the left of Seminary Ridge, leaving two brigades there in loose juncture with Ewell's right, which curved from south of town to Culp's Hill. Anderson's brigades came from the right of Seminary Ridge, where his other three made juncture with McLaws. Heth's division, which had been held in reserve since its rough time on the first day, went in as a unit from the center. The selection of brigades was eminently sound in relation to the disposition of troops over the whole line; but as the complement of an assault column the selection formed the basic weakness in the arrangement of the attack.

The six attacking and two supporting brigades were drawn from three separate divisions, a fact which, because of Longstreet's tacit refusal to assume supervision, caused eight of the eleven brigades to be without a directing leader. The one division that went in as a unit, Heth's, was then the weakest in the army.

Heth's division had two good brigades, Archer's and Pettigrew's. They could be depended upon even though colonels would take them in and though Archer's was very low in numbers. But by the chance of their position in camp, these two brigades joined Garnett's crack brigade at the center, and two undependable brigades were placed on the flank. In Field's frequently orphaned Virginia brigade there was some unexplained dissatisfaction with its senior colonel, John Brockenbrough, who had twice assumed temporary command, and twice was passed over. Brigade morale was poor. The new Mississippi brigade that had been palmed off on Lee, combining green troops with the inexperienced leadership of Joe Davis, had not been improved by its disastrous Wednesday morning in the railroad cut.

Heth's division was led by a brigadier new to the army. Despite the often mentioned "gallantry" of the scholarly and imposing Pettigrew, this thirty-five-year-old North Carolinian with limited experience and no formal military training needed more background to control the offensive movement of four such brigades in a severely taxing action.

All six of the brigades going in with Pickett had been badly cut up on the first day, and their numbers were less than Lee estimated. They would not count 10,000 rifles. With Pickett's approximately 4,500 men, the combined force would muster something like 14,000 muskets—or roughly 15,000 officers and men, as usually estimated.

The responsibility for conveying this information to Lee was A. P. Hill's. It is probable that no "present for duty" reports had been given Hill for July 3. With two division commanders and a brigadier lost in two days, attention was centered on the shifting around of field and general officer personnel. It is also probable, however, that Hill was aware in general of the reduced numbers in the six brigades, for he suggested to Lee that he be allowed to throw in his whole corps.

Lee replied that the Third Corps constituted his only reserve, and added: "It will be needed if General Longstreet's attack should fail."

There is no evidence that Hill said anything more about the attacking force, and the likelihood is that he never told Lee—certainly he did not stress—the condition of his troops, in quantity and quality.

Of what passed between Hill and Longstreet, nothing at all is known. Hill wrote sparse, undetailed reports, and Longstreet in all his voluminous writings never mentioned his part in arranging the attacking force with A. P. Hill. In fact, Longstreet was always extremely reticent about the deployment of the combined force that was formed at his suggestion.

After he and Hill had received general orders from Lee on the merger of the corps, the lieutenant generals strolled away together for a short distance and sat on a fallen log. They were seen talking for a while, and it must be presumed that they agreed on the positions where the brigades would form and the direction the men would follow on moving out. Hill conveyed the instructions to his men, with orders to get their specific assignments from Longstreet. The heavy cannonade of the two corps' artillery, which was to precede the infantry advance, had been arranged by Lee, and presumably Longstreet informed Hill that he would give the order for the two signal guns that would mean "commence firing." No arrangement at all was made for liaison with Longstreet, and again Dick Anderson was left dangling between his corps commander and the general commanding the attack.

Hill and Longstreet arose from the log, parted without shaking hands, and evidently communicated with each other no more that day. From what followed, it is evident that Hill assumed he had turned his brigades over to Longstreet, and that Longstreet did not accept responsibility for them. Old Pete acted as if some of Hill's troops were employed in conjunction with some of his, but not under him.

Pickett and other First Corps officers had the impression, both before and after the battle, that Hill's men were either independently employed or in support, or both. Pickett clearly regarded his division as the main force of the attack. When he heard the heavy firing in the fight over the barn, he wrote in his letter to Sallie that it "brought a wail of regret" that "went up from my very soul that the two brigades of my division had been left behind. Oh, God, if only I had them . . . a surety for the honor of Virginia, for I can depend on them."

This undefined command situation was not suspected by General Lee. Believing that Longstreet was supervising the charge, he assumed that the passing hours were being spent in preparation. Other instances of neglect in the arrangements—the most crucial were in the artillery—were also unknown to Lee. As the hour passed noon, however, and there had been no activity since Pickett's men had moved up onto the ridge, he began to show anxiety.

Lee rarely gave field orders to his subordinates once they had expressed understanding of his battle plan, and the order to commit the troops to the attack must come from Longstreet. But the suspense bore as heavily on the commanding general as on the men, and he kept moving from one place to another, as if seeking reassurance that all was ready. Finally he turned Traveler into the woods along the old trace and walked his horse past the lines where Pickett's men were enduring the long wait. The silent ride seemed a sort of informal farewell inspection. The men, ordered not to cheer, raised their tattered hats as he passed.

7

From the time of Lee's ride, the nervous impatience for Longstreet to open the attack began to mount, and toward one o'clock tension became acute. The waiting men were sweating heavily, as the woods became an oven, and Pickett wrote in his running letter: "The suffering and waiting are almost unbearable."

No one had then, or has had since, any explanation for this second wait after the troops were in position. Pickett's men have held the center of interest, but the suspense was equally hard on Hill's men.

Below the wooded ridge where Garnett's brigade waited, Wilcox's brigade of Anderson's division was deployed in an advanced position about two hundred yards west of the Emmitsburg road, immediately behind the First Corps batteries. Wilcox had the dual assignment of supporting the guns when they opened and then supporting Pickett's movement after his division cleared the guns on their way in.

General Wilcox had established temporary headquarters by the Spangler house and barn, near a small orchard. As no immediate orders had come to Wilcox and nothing seemed to be happening, the old army hand thought of some cold mutton he had on hand and generously invited his friend Dick Garnett to share a lunch with him.

Cadmus Marcellus Wilcox, thirty-nine, was another professional soldier, having graduated in the same West Point class as George Pickett and Stonewall Jackson. Commissioned brigadier of Alabama troops in October 1861, he was among the earliest leaders to build high morale in his troops; during the Seven Days his brigade sustained fifty-seven-per-cent casualties without breaking. Sound in tactics and judgment rather than spectacular, he was a brigadier marked by Lee for future division command.

Punctilious in military matters, very old-army in his manner of speaking, Cadmus Wilcox was affable and unaffected and extremely well liked. His closest friend was Harry Heth, and Grant, at whose wedding he had served as groomsman, was one of his friends from the U.S. army. When relaxed, Wilcox did not present a very warlike figure. His broad, plain face was decorated by bushy sidelocks of the Burnside variety, and on that hot Friday at Gettysburg he wore an old, floppy straw hat.

On July 2 it had been Wilcox whose advance toward Cemetery Ridge, in support of Wright on the crest, was halted by the failure of Anderson's other brigades to move out, and he had sent back the staff officer who had found Dick Anderson lolling with his division staff in apparent indifference to the urgent need for reinforcements. Regular soldier Wilcox resented this behavior of his division commander, and during the long wait on Friday morning there seemed to be scant communication between the two men. From Longstreet, Wilcox had heard nothing for hours.

282

His good Alabama brigade, unsupported in a critical movement the day before, seemed in a fair way to be totally forgotten in its assignment to cover Pickett's right in the most
crucial movement of the campaign.

After waiting until noon for specific orders, when Garnett
hobbled over to share his cold mutton Wilcox was past worrying about what might happen later. The lunching officers
were distressed by the immediate problem of the hardness
and coldness of some Gettysburg well water that seemed to
shrivel their insides. Fortunately, a staff officer still had some
of the whisky confiscated in Chambersburg on the Sunday
before, and the men used the whisky as a chaser for the
water. They were discussing such matters as the Confederates' difficulties in victualing when they noticed activities
that, to their experienced eyes, foretold the beginning of the
long-awaited action.

The officer who was the center of the preliminary stirrings
was a twenty-eight-year-old colonel of an artillery battalion,
E. Porter Alexander. Born in Washington, Georgia, in a plantation town house, Colonel Alexander was a highly gifted and
literate young aristocrat whose range of talents extended far
beyond his chosen profession of arms. As a soldier, his energy,
confidence, and flexible intelligence had earned him a more
varied career in his six years out of West Point (class of '57)
than many competent professionals in both armies achieved
in a lifetime.

After some frontier service and a period as instructor at
West Point, the impressive-looking young Georgian was selected to study the newfangled system of signaling by flags.
At First Manassas, attached to Beauregard's staff as engineering and signal officer, Alexander made important use of his
flags and introduced the "wig-wag" method of signaling into
warfare. Transferred to field ordnance, he rose to chief ordnance officer before, in November 1862, he was drafted into

the artillery. As he first commanded a gun battalion in action at Fredericksburg, during the Gettysburg campaign Colonel Alexander had little more than six months' artillery experience behind him.

Because of the brevity of his service, in the May reorganization Colonel Walton, of the famed Washington Artillery from New Orleans, was appointed chief of corps artillery, and Porter Alexander was *not* (as is usually stated) chief of Longstreet's artillery at Gettysburg. What happened was that General Longstreet, perceiving Alexander's unusual talents, used Walton's temporary absence from the field on administrative duties as an excuse for placing the young Georgian unofficially in field command for that battle. Later Colonel Walton showed a bitter resentment at the assumption that Alexander was chief of First Corps artillery at Gettysburg. Without belittling Walton, it is nonetheless true that Longstreet's pragmatic shift in his artillery command placed at the head of his guns the most brilliant cannoneer ever in the Army of Northern Virginia and one of the instinctive soldiers in the war.

Yet Alexander's role further muddled the already confused situation in army artillery command. The source of the confusion was the abolition of the reserve artillery corps in the pre-invasion reorganization. The Federal army made the same experiments with abolishing the artillery reserve, and the wisdom of retaining it was never more forcefully illustrated than at Gettysburg. If, as is probable, Lee was influenced in his decision by the ineffectualness of the Reverend General Pendleton as chief of reserve artillery, he was betrayed by his personal loyalties in upping the well-meaning bumbler to the official, if nominal, status of chief of artillery.

The clergyman, whose only military training lay mistily among memories of his youth, was not an instinctive soldier, and the absorption with details that made him an able ad-

284

ministrator gave him the type of vision that sees the trees instead of the woods. In battle, he fussed over pieces of artillery rather than viewing the effect of fire on the enemy. In
giving him a higher title while placing more authority with
the artillery corps commanders, Lee evidently expected his
friend to content himself with the administrative duties of
the artillery corps. This was a not inconsiderable task, and
its proper performance would have been highly useful.

The Confederate caissons and ordnance wagons carried
from 130 to 150 rounds per gun into Pennsylvania, and the
practice was for the cannoneers to supply the caissons with
ammunition from wagons "parked" (as they said) near by.
The reserve supply of ammunition was carried in other wagons with the wagon trains, and the wagoneers near the guns
replaced their ammunition from these reserve wagons.
Ideally, the reserve ordnance wagons carried about 100
rounds for each of the 240 guns with the army, though Alexander believed that on the invasion they carried no more
than 60 rounds. To maintain the flow of ammunition from the
reserve wagons through the ordnance wagons to the caissons
was an assignment that Pendleton was ideally equipped to
fulfill.

But, a dedicated Confederate and too obtuse to perceive
the nuances of his promotion, this "Granny" (as a First Corps
captain called him) took his title literally. With the best intent in the world, he sought to "supervise" the whole artillery
operation. The result was that he parked the reserve wagons
too far from the field to be of any use. Then, although he
placed the lighter ordnance wagons near by in a protected
hollow, some unauthorized person (unknown to this day)
moved the ordnance wagons without telling anyone. Vital
time was lost while frantic caisson-drivers searched for the
wagons. On finding them, they discovered that the wagons
had not been re-supplied from reserve ordnance for shot

spent the day before. By trying to supervise everywhere, conscientious Pendleton had failed to exercise control where he was most needed.

This contribution of Pendleton, costly as it was to the assaulting forces, merely illustrated the effects of his anomalous status. Not doing that which he should have done, the chief of artillery lurked around the artillery corps commanders and gave them the impression that he was exercising the supervisory control implied by his title. He was not.

Alexander did not know what Lindsay Walker was doing with Hill's artillery, and Walker apparently was not even sure of what he was doing himself. A fundamentally capable man who improved steadily in command of the Third Corps artillery, the personable and well-connected Virginian showed at Gettysburg the effects of his inexperience at the post, of the uncertainty in army command, and of the long wait.

Walker had allowed his men to waste ammunition during the late morning in the pointless fight over a barn, while Alexander forbade his gunners to fire a shot. Then, because his corps commander, A. P. Hill, had tacitly turned over his attacking troops to Longstreet, Walker's artillery was left somewhere between the authority of Hill, Longstreet, and Pendleton.

Pendleton's supervision of Walker's guns consisted in removing nine howitzers, whose range was too short for the bombardment, and transferring them to Alexander. They were the guns Alexander planned to use in immediate support of the infantry in the charge. When he turned to send them in, Pendleton had moved them elsewhere. Pendleton's reason was sound—their placement exposed them to the enemy's counter artillery fire—but he neglected to inform Alexander.

With his attention thus occupied by moving nine guns around, when the great cannonade opened Pendleton took

286

no notice of the number of Walker's batteries which were silent. Even more fundamental, he permitted the traditional parallel alignment of Walker's guns which ignored the opportunity to direct crossfire on the enemy. It is more than possible that earnest Pendleton did not himself recognize this missed opportunity. The same opening was offered to Ewell's corps artillery and was equally ignored. Those guns actually needed supervision, as Stapleton Crutchfield, corps artillery commander, was out wounded.

For whatever reasons, two thirds of Lee's artillery was idle or improperly employed. The guns achieved little beyond adding to the terrifying noise and, overshooting, scaring the men in Meade's noncombatant services who had hitherto opperated safely in the rear.

Colonel Long, of Lee's staff, in the old army had received gunnery instruction from General Henry Hunt, now commanding the Federal artillery. When the fire became scattered, Long wondered what his old instructor would think of it. General Hunt thought very little of it. After the war he told his former gunnery student that "he had not been satisfied with the conduct of the cannonade"—which he had believed was under Long's direction—"insomuch as he [Long] had not done justice to his instruction."

Pendleton cannot be said to have been responsible for all the errors, but his fussy presence made nobody responsible.

Alexander's attention was directed away from the details of ammunition toward the larger sphere of a decision involving the whole attack. This decision was placed upon the young Georgian by Longstreet.

With every foot soldier and every gunner in position, ready and waiting, Longstreet could not bring himself to commit the troops.

Between twelve and one o'clock, wherever he had been earlier, Longstreet was in the clearing north of the Spangler's

Woods which served as general headquarters. There Lee's staff officers moved restlessly in the glaring heat, other staff officers came and went, military observers from other countries, field glasses in hand, sought points of vantage to view the charge that must eventually be delivered. No newspapermen were present. Longstreet may or may not have conferred with Lee during this final hour of the wait. No record shows any exchange between them—or, indeed, that Longstreet consulted anyone.

He wrote a rather garbled note to Alexander, the burden of which was to give the twenty-eight-year-old cannoneer the responsibility for ordering the attack. After sending the message off by a courier, Longstreet settled down on the grass with his back against the snake fence that, running east to west, marked the northern boundary of Spangler's Woods. There he was completely alone. The day before, Longstreet had shown his ability to immobilize himself in a state of complete inanition. Propped against Spangler's fence the stolid general went further: he fell asleep.

Thus it was that an obscure artillery colonel, placed temporarily in charge of one corps's batteries, was given the responsibility of opening the decisive action of the Battle of Gettysburg.

It was Alexander's first large assignment with the army that, in his experience, had always performed with heroic adroitness. Out in front of the infantry with his guns along the road, away from all general officers, Porter Alexander had no reason to suspect that the assault forming behind him was collapsing in detail before it started. Had he known this, the charge would probably never have been made.

The artillery colonel, who all day had done those things that should have been done, grappled with the immediate problem presented to him by Longstreet's note.

8

Colonel Alexander was among those officers who began their day at three in the morning. In the moonlight he was placing gun batteries for the morning attack, following orders that Longstreet later claimed had not been given the night before. By daylight Alexander had seventy-five guns in proper position except for one battery that he observed was exposed; to his relief, he was able to shift it without drawing enemy fire. From then on, his biggest job, like that of his companions, was to do nothing in the face of a powerful enemy. But he was not a nervous man, and, probably more than any other Confederate on the field, he perceived precisely what was expected of him.

Under some negligent provocations from the enemy and uneasy bustlings around him, Alexander succeeded in doing nothing while waiting until Longstreet's curious note reached him around noon. The note said:

> If the artillery fire does not have the effect to drive off the enemy or greatly demoralize him, so as to make our effort pretty certain, I should prefer that you not advise Pickett to make the charge. I shall rely a great deal upon your judgment to determine the matter and shall expect you to let General Pickett know when the moment offers.

This note made a profound impression on the young artillerist. Alexander wrote about that moment three times after the war—around the ages of forty, fifty, and nearly seventy —and his accounts never varied. A composite of his reports of receiving Longstreet's message reads:

"The note rather startled me . . . [It] suggested at once that there was some alternative to the attack, and placed me on the responsibility of deciding the question. . . . If that assault was to be made on General Lee's judgment it was all right, but I did not want it on mine. . . . Until that moment, though I fully recognized the strength of the enemy's position, I had not doubted that we would carry it, in my confidence that Lee was ordering it. But here was a proposition that *I* should decide the question. Overwhelming reasons against the assault at once seemed to stare me in the face."

Alexander here revealed the tremendous expansion required of mind and character in passing from the subordinate's responsibility, limited to tactical performance, into the sphere of making decisions that affected the whole army. The depth of Longstreet's disturbance was indicated by his willingness to shift such a responsibility onto a young gunner; Alexander's contrasting soundness was indicated both by his declining to accept this responsibility and by his manner of so doing.

He hurriedly wrote on a piece of foolscap paper an answer which, if not (because of excitement) illustrative of his literacy, showed his comprehension of the total military situation and went to the heart of Longstreet's proposition.

> General: I will only be able to judge the affect of our fire on the enemy by this return fire, as his infantry is little exposed to view and the smoke will obscure the field. If, as I infer from your note, there is any alternative to this attack, it should be carefully considered before opening our fire, for it will take all the ammunition we have left to test this one, and if result is unfavorable we will have none left for another effort. And even if this is entirely successful, it can only be so at a very bloody cost.

A courier rode off from Alexander's post at the peach orchard with this reply that, giving clearly the artillerist's military opinion, declined to act for the corps commander. The courier aroused the stocky general who never admitted he had been asleep. He said he had retired to think.

Years later, in trying to show that he had acted despite his opposition to Lee's plan, Longstreet said he had replied to Alexander that, according to Lee's orders, "there was no alternative; that I could find no way out of it; that General Lee had considered and would listen to nothing else; that orders had gone for the guns to give signal for the batteries [to open fire]; that he should call the troops [forward] at the first opportunity or lull in the enemy's fire."

That is the way Longstreet wanted to remember. What he actually wrote Alexander, who published the note, was:

> Colonel: The intention is to advance the infantry if the artillery has the desired effect of driving the enemy's off, or having other effect such as to warrant us in making the attack. When that moment arrives advise Gen. Pickett and of course advance such artillery as you can in aiding the attack.

The letter assured Alexander that the cannonade was to open as scheduled, but, as he wrote, "The responsibility would be upon me to decide whether or not Pickett should charge. . . . I felt it very deeply, for the day was rapidly advancing . . . and whatever was to be done was to be done soon."

He anxiously questioned General Wright, who had breached the crest on the day before. "It is not so hard to get there," Wright said. "The trouble is to stay there."

Then Alexander left his guns to search for Pickett. He found the division commander standing with his staff, Garnett, and Armistead in front of the troops. All were obviously waiting to go in. The guns of Dearing's artillery battalion, which was to be moved out in immediate support of Pickett, were limbered up and ready to roll, though Dearing was frantically sending gunners back to look for the ordnance wagons in order to replenish his caissons.

In approaching men of an older generation with awesome

reputations earned in the old army and in Lee's, young Alexander retained his clear-headed coolness. With native discretion, he did not tell Pickett of the question in his mind. Instead, he sounded out the general.

Pickett stood gracefully, with the sun bringing out the auburn lights in his flowing dark hair. His answers to Alexander's questions showed that he was entirely confident of the success of the charge, "and was only congratulating himself on the opportunity."

Partially reassured, Alexander returned to his post at the peach orchard. Still not believing that the enemy's guns would be driven off even by his massed batteries—75 pieces stretching for nearly a mile, with 60-odd more of Hill's continuing the line northward—the Georgian then wrote Longstreet a very guarded and carefully phrased note.

> General, when our fire is at its best, I will advise General Pickett to advance.

This note was not answered. Instead, Longstreet *then* wrote Colonel Walton (and not earlier, as he claimed afterward) to fire the signal guns from his own battalion. Commanded by Major Eshleman, the Washington battalion was posted about midway in the First Corps batteries.

There is no record of the time the message was at last, reluctantly, sent by Longstreet. After Walton received the message and gave the order to Eshleman, it was between 1:00 and 1:11 p.m. when the first gun from Miller's battery boomed out in the silence hanging over the field. A moment later the second gun fired. The battle was to begin.

9

Porter Alexander believed that "any halfway effort would insure the failure of the campaign." He said: "After all the time consumed in preparation for the attack, the only hope of success was to follow it up promptly with one supreme effort. . . . My mind was fully made up that *if the artillery once opened Pickett must charge."*

The italics are his. In his whole-souled commitment to the assault, Alexander intended that Pickett should start not later than fifteen minutes after the fire opened. Pickett's men had about 400 yards to move from the brow of the wooded hill and the concealing swale before starting down the slope in view of the enemy. They would then move over half a mile, 1,000 yards or better, in the open, all downhill and up, with several fences to cross.

As soon as Alexander ordered his batteries to fire, he turned to arrange for the nine guns to follow behind the infantry. But the guns had been moved elsewhere. It seemed a portent of the nature the "one supreme effort" was to assume.

As the two miles of batteries commenced firing, blasting by salvos that shook their world, the enemy's powerful guns replied. With revealing association of ideas, Alexander said: "As suddenly as an organ strikes up in church, the grand roar followed from all the guns of both armies."

Soldiers in both armies could liken it to nothing they had ever heard. One of Pickett's men said: "Such a tornado of projectiles it has seldom been the fortune or misfortune of any one to see." Though the cannonade lasted barely two hours, to the most hardened and experienced veterans it seemed to go on indefinitely. The sky became "lurid with flame and murky with smoke." The sun was obscured by sulphurous clouds, eclipsing the light "and shadowing the earth as with a funeral pall."

Each side was shooting at the other's guns. In Alexander's own twenty-six-gun battalion, nearly 100 horses and over 100 men went down. A Union battery, coming into line, lost 27 of 36 horses in ten minutes. From that side the concentrated blast of an exploding caisson penetrated the roar, heartening the Confederates momentarily.

Alexander was peering through the thickening smoke, trying to discover whether any enemy batteries were affected by his fire. He could observe no slackening at all when his allotted fifteen minutes had passed. On the hill behind and north of the stout Codori barn he counted eighteen guns jammed into a projection of the stone wall where a grove of chestnut trees (shaped like "umbrellas," according to a resident) stood out along the barren crest rolling southward from the cemetery. This "little clump of trees" was the guiding-point for the attack, a landmark for the eyes of brigadiers and colonels, captains and guide sergeants.

In the units that were to go in, officers and men were suffering their final ordeal of waiting. The shells from the Union batteries, frequently overshooting, whined over the swale and along Seminary Ridge to burst among the huddled troops.

A young soldier in Kemper's brigade said: "The atmosphere was rent and broken by the rush and crash of projectiles. . . . The sun, but a few minutes before so brilliant, was now darkened. Through this smoky darkness came the missiles of death. . . . The scene of carnage beggars description . . . The men remained steadfast at their posts . . . [but] it must not be supposed that men were not alarmed. . . . Many a poor fellow thought his time had come. . . . Great big, stout-hearted men prayed, loudly too. . . . They were in earnest, for if men ever had need of the care and protection of our Heavenly Father, it was now."

Near the young soldier a solid shot burrowed under a man, lifting him three feet into the air. He fell back dead, without having been actually struck. In another company in Kemper's brigade, a whole squad—eight men— were killed or wounded under one burst. Then the young soldier started to lift his head to get some fresh air, and his lieutenant said: "You'd better put your head down or you may get it knocked off."

Young David Johnston replied: "A man had about as well die that way as suffocate for want of air."

At that moment a shell burst over them, carrying off the heads of two men above the ears, and a downbreaking piece struck his side. He was knocked insensible for several moments and came to "lying off from the position I was in when struck, gasping for breath."

His colonel ran up, gave him water, and made a cursory examination. Johnston's ribs on the left side were fractured, his left side and leg were paralyzed, and later a contusion of a lung was discovered. Two friends from the company moved him out of range and placed him on a blanket at the base of an apple tree.

The casualties while the men waited were never computed. Soldiers believed that a minimum of three hundred were killed or wounded before they ever moved out. Some men fainted from the heat and the strain of waiting.

Chaplains moved up and down the lines of tense-faced men. For once, only one joke was recorded among Confederate troops, and that one rather wan. A soldier, seeing a rabbit dart out from some bushes and head for the rear, called out: "Run, old hare. If I was an old hare, I'd run too."

But nobody moved to the rear. Nobody moved at all, except to squeeze closer to the brushy earth. Describing the waiting under the shellbursts, a soldier in the 1st Virginia Regiment from Richmond contented himself with saying: "It was simply awful."

Lewis Armistead and Dick Garnett, friends whose families were friends, stood together in somber silence. A shot struck a tree near by, shaving a splinter that stuck out toward them.

Armistead picked the wood off and turned to the troops. "Boys, do you think you can go up under that? It is pretty hot out there."

Most nodded, some spoke in assurance, but there was no swell of voices. That would come as an expression of relief when they moved out—if they ever did.

Pickett finished his running letter: "Oh, may God in His mercy help me as He has never helped before . . . remember always that I love you with all my heart and soul . . . that now and forever I am yours." Then he sealed "the scraps of pencilled paper" and walked out to join Garnett and Armistead.

A courier came riding through the woods. He dismounted before their group and thrust a paper at General Pickett, who read: "If you are coming at all you must come immediately or I can not give you proper support; but the enemy's fire has not slackened materially, and at least 18 guns are still firing . . ." from the angle containing the clump of trees. It was signed "Alexander."

This was the nearest thing to an order that Pickett received. In his eagerness to relieve his men of the horror of waiting, he seized on the discretionary words as a command subject only to Longstreet's approval.

The hour had come. Pickett shook hands with Garnett and Armistead. The three men murmured "Good luck" and parted.

The brigadiers went to their commands. A horse was brought up for Dick Garnett, too weak to walk. Except for staff officers, no officers below brigade rank were to ride, though Colonel Eppa Hunton and Colonel Lewis Williams, on account of physical illness, were allowed mounts. Colonel Hunton was suffering from a painful fistula.

Pickett, riding a black horse, joined Longstreet at the snake fence from which he was glumly watching the field.

Alexander had continued his fire additional periods of fifteen minutes each, and, he wrote, "the enemy's fire was so severe that . . . I could not make up my mind to order the infantry out into a fire which I did not believe they could face. . . ." But the decision had been left to the twenty-eight-year-old cannoneer. Although "I could not bring myself to give a peremptory order to Pickett to advance," he nevertheless, "feeling that the critical moment would soon pass," had dispatched the discretionary note that sent Pickett riding to Longstreet.

The powerfully built lieutenant general was dismounted, and Pickett, swinging down, handed him the note. Longstreet read it through without a word or a change in his heavy expression.

Even so close a friend as Pickett had no inkling that his corps commander was immovably opposed to the charge. Evidently thinking only that his stolid friend was slow to speak, Pickett asked cheerfully: "General, shall I advance?"

In his reluctance to give the order, Longstreet could do no more than lower his head.

Pickett was too excited to study Longstreet's mood. He said confidently: "I am going to move forward, sir." He saluted, swept lightly into the saddle, and galloped back to his lines.

10

The general commanding the attack had actually made no decision about sending the men in and had given no order. Yet, as soon as Pickett rode out of sight, the finality of the moment seemed to overcome him.

Just as on the preceding day the action had stirred him to erratic impulsiveness, so, while orders were being shouted in the near-by woods, Longstreet was again seized with an impulse to movement that bore no relation to assuming control of the eleven brigades. Unaccountably, he rode down to the peach orchard, where he found young Alexander in a state of high excitement. Disturbed because Pickett had not responded immediately to his note, he had been suddenly heartened when through his glasses he saw the eighteen guns in the clump of trees limber up and move out of range. He reasoned: "As the enemy had such abundance of ammunition and so much better guns than ours that they were not compelled to reserve their ammunition for critical moments (as we almost always had to do), I knew that they must have felt the punishment a good deal, and I was elated by the sight."

His hopes betrayed him. The enemy guns *had* moved to reserve ammunition. Under the stimulation of his false impression, and carried away by the magnitude of his assignment, Alexander quickly scrawled another note to Pickett: "For God's sake come quick; the 18 guns are gone." As his rank of colonel commanding a gun battalion entitled him to no couriers except the one he had sent off earlier, he urged a lieutenant and a sergeant away from their guns, gave one the note and the other the oral order.

Then, turning from his role of extemporized commander to his temporary assignment of artillery corps commander, the Georgian asked captains and lieutenants about the ordnance wagons that had been moved. He had just learned that the men had located the missing wagons and found them perilously low in ammunition when General Longstreet appeared alone. He had ridden away from his staff—his later explanation was that he had gone forward to a vantage point for watching the assault column move out. The troops were now behind him.

Apparently Longstreet asked no question of Alexander. He was always very vague about the encounter. The accounts of both men agree that Alexander volunteered the information about the nine supporting howitzers having vanished and about the scant supply of ammunition. Alexander mentioned the ammunition because of his anxiety to get Pickett moving forward while support could still be given.

Longstreet, in his turmoil, missed the point the cannoneer was trying to make, and seized on the scarcity of ammunition as an excuse for calling off the attack.

According to both their versions, he shouted: "Go and stop Pickett right where he is, and replenish your ammunition."

Alexander must have looked with astonishment into the general's small blue eyes. It was Longstreet's responsibility to stop Pickett if he wanted to. As the troops had not then emerged from their shelter, Pickett's division of Longstreet's corps was behind him. Longstreet could at least halt Pickett until he had advised General Lee of the ammunition problem.

It was Alexander's impression that Longstreet waited for him to agree, but in his "youth and inexperience" he felt unqualified to assume still more responsibility for General Lee's plans. As he had throughout the long, baffling morning, Alexander kept his answers to the point at hand. He explained that the ordnance wagons were down to 20 rounds a gun, "too little to accomplish much." While the cannoneers broke off fire to bring up that twenty rounds, "the enemy would recover from the effect of the fire we were now giving him."

Longstreet looked at Alexander and said: "I don't want to make this charge; I don't believe it can succeed. I would stop Pickett now, but that General Lee has ordered it and expects it."

Longstreet, in later accepting this version of Alexander's, perceived no fault in his attitude. Rather, he used the quote to buttress the soundness of his judgment, and expatiated on the point that people had suggested he *should* have used his discretion and halted the attack. This was part of his later life's distortion of his status in Lee's army. He was given no discretion to halt an attack ordered by the commanding general, except for the purpose of conferring with him, as on the ammunition. Lee's one criticism in his official report was of the failure to notify him of the lack of ammunition to support the charge; had he known, he would have called it off.

Even where Longstreet was not ordering events to fit his post-war rationale, time and self-defensiveness increasingly clouded his memory of Gettysburg. Sometime during the hot afternoon he took a couple of swigs from Colonel Fremantle's flask of rum, and it is possible that he was more confused on the field than has ever been recognized.

After his demoralized outburst at Alexander, he just stood there, with no apparent awareness, then or later, that Lee's desired "concert of action" depended on him. Alexander understandably made no reply to these strange words from a corps commander at what the gunner considered a crisis for their country.

At that moment Garnett's troops came out of the woods behind the guns, then Kemper's men appeared over the brow of their hollow, and the exchange was ended.

Forgetting Longstreet in his meticulous attention to his duties, Alexander gave orders to cease fire so that the damp-faced troops could pass between the guns. As the artillerist stood back, he saw Dick Garnett, the older man who had befriended him during his first days of service on the plains. As there was no firing to be supervised for the moment, he ran over to Garnett, who, wrapped in his blue overcoat, was unsteadily holding his saddle, determined to live down the stigma placed on him by Jackson. Alexander walked alongside Garnett's horse until they reached the slope that faced the enemy.

"Good-by," Alexander said. "Good luck."

11

The assault whose delivery Lee entrusted to Longstreet was called "Pickett's Charge" primarily because George Pickett led the crack division from the corps designated as the attacking force. The other troops filled out the complement of the force and, as the attack was designed, essentially served as substitutes for the First Corps. It was part of the tragedy of Hill's men that, in a way, they were the orphans of the assault force. Because of Longstreet's state and the confusion of command between him and Hill, the soldiers from Heth's and Pender's divisions were left to tag along.

Despite all his uncontrollable shirking of duty, Longstreet was responsible for the attack, and it was from him, through Alexander, that the orders came for Pickett to move out. The movement into action of Pickett's three brigades began the charge.

They were the first attacking troops seen by the enemy and by their own comrades. The attention of both armies was fixed on them from their first appearance, and they held it to the end. It was as if both sides felt that as went Pickett's fresh, compact division, so went the charge. But Pickett commanded only those three brigades, and was given no responsibility beyond them.

If Longstreet had been in condition to perform his duties as a capable subordinate, he might have been immortalized as the leader of "Longstreet's Charge" instead of being a subject of controversy, and history might have been different.

The charge as it became immortalized was the quintessence of Southern myth and aspiration. It was dramatically, if not tactically, sound that the doomed assault should be associated with an elite division of troops descended from the somewhat fabled founders of Virginia, who preferred the land they founded to the nation that grew around it.

Pickett, though aware of supports he would supposedly be able to call on, nevertheless felt that his immediate responsibility was to his own division. This is shown in the words he addressed only to them: "Up, men, and to your posts! Don't forget today that you are from Old Virginia."

Johnston Pettigrew, leading Harry Heth's division, addressed his troops in the same localized sense of responsibility. Indeed, the recently appointed and temporary commander of the division forgot the veterans from Alabama, Tennessee, and Virginia in his inherited division and spoke only to the North Carolina brigade with which he had joined the Army of Northern Virginia. Turning to Colonel Marshall, who had temporarily succeeded him in command of the brigade, Pettigrew called: "Now, colonel, for the honor of the good old North State, forward!"

One hundred or more yards behind Pettigrew's two lines, General Trimble could make no regional appeals to the two brigades from Pender's division placed in support. General Lee, apparently uncertain of Lane's capacities, had placed sixty-year-old Isaac Trimble in command of the two North Carolina brigades barely an hour before, shortly before the cannonade began.

As Trimble said, "these troops were entire strangers to me." Nonetheless, he tried to "inspire them with confidence" by a short speech, which he concluded by saying that "I should advance with them to the farthest point." There was no doubt that this major general without a permanent command would certainly try.

In his anxiety to establish a quick accord between himself and the strange Tarheels, General Trimble accepted the disposition of his supporting line as he found it. The alignment was faulty, and nothing more revealed the attacking force's lack of responsible command than this weakness in the rudiments of offensive warfare.

Jim Lane, commanding one of the two brigades, had retained temporary command of Pender's division until replaced by Trimble, and it was Lane who had made the disposition under the divided authority of Hill and Longstreet.

Acting on Lee's orders, Powell Hill had directed Lane to assume command of the two brigades in support of Pettigrew and told him to report to Longstreet for specific directions for troop alignment. Obviously the punctilious Hill felt it proper for the general commanding the troops in the attack to assume authority for their alignment. And Longstreet appeared to think it proper that he should exercise this control, for Lane's official report stated: "General Longstreet ordered me to form in the rear of the right of Heth's division. . . ."

When Lane formed his troops according to Longstreet's orders, he observed that Pettigrew's line of four brigades was "much longer" than the line of his own brigade and Scales's commanded by Colonel Lowrance. In his official report he stated: "There was consequently no second line in rear of its [Pettigrew's] left." Shortly after Lane noticed this, he was relieved of command. But he said nothing to Trimble, nor to Hill or Longstreet, about the faulty alignment that Longstreet's orders had caused. The silence of James Lane is something of a mystery.

A college professor in civilian life, he was a consistently able brigadier whose North Carolina regiments boasted a record of steady achievement. On the first day their attack had been part of the wave that rolled the enemy back to Cemetery Hill. Perhaps his dutiful acceptance of the weakly disposed attacking line indicated no more than a limitation that had caused Lee, in evaluating Lane, to place Trimble in command of the supporting line. Lane remained a brigadier until the end of the war, a good man at that rank.

This further illustration of the breakdown in command completed the arrangement for disaster. While the two good

North Carolina brigades were placed behind Pettigrew's line at the point where it was to join Pickett's, the two least dependable brigades in the attacking force Davis's and Brockenbrough's, were left unsupported on an exposed flank.

Johnston Pettigrew, on assuming command of Heth's division the day before, had found the brigades aligned from right to left as they had arrived on the field after the first day's fighting. As the division remained in reserve on the second day, there was no reason to rearrange their position. The thirty-five-year-old lawyer directed his attention to the colonels, Marshall and Fry, who were placed at command of his own brigade and Archer's, and neglected to acquaint himself with the personnel of Davis's and Brockenbrough's brigades. As in the excitement of ordering the attack he addressed only the North Carolinians in his own brigade (the troops who had first heard of the shoes in Gettysburg), he would seem to have relegated the unfamiliar troops to the care of their immediate commanders. With all his civilian accomplishments and qualities of leadership, Pettigrew was a modest and deeply courteous man, and perhaps he did not presume to supervise brigades in a division to which he was new.

Also, by the order of command, Pettigrew could exercise no supervision on the two brigades under Trimble which were placed in support of his division. As no one supervised the left wing of six brigades, Joe Davis's new brigade of Mississippians formed part of the unsupported flank, and the brigade farthest to the left, actually alone on the flank, were those Virginians, temporarily under Colonel Brockenbrough, whose morale was shaken by continued lack of a permanent commander. (There is evidence that Brockenbrough was replaced on the third day by Colonel Robert Mayo, but, as Mayo himself later stated that he was not in command, Brockenbrough—who was replaced after Gettysburg when a permanent brigadier was appointed—is presumed to have led.) With Pettigrew responsible only for his attacking lines and Trimble only for the two supporting brigades the only "concert of action" possible between the units of the assault was their common objective of attack.

On the right wing of the attacking line the only co-ordination was in Pickett's division. In Anderson's division, no orders for advance went to Wilcox, who was to support on Pickett's right, or to Perry, whose small Florida brigade (three regiments) was to come up as support. Without orders, these two brigades remained stationary even after Pickett's men began the first stage of the march out with their own flank completely open.

General Pickett and his brigadiers and colonels had no attention to spare for forces other than their own. Each officer concentrated on the group of men entrusted to his immediate care. The last words addressed to troops before the division advanced were probably those of Lewis Armistead. It was his custom before an attack to walk up and down in front of his line. He said: "Remember, men, what you are fighting for. Remember your homes and your firesides, your mothers and wives and sisters, your sweethearts." Then he halted in front of Blackburn, color sergeant of the 53rd Virginia.

"Sergeant, are you going to plant those colors on the enemy's works over yonder?"

"Yes, general, if mortal man can do it, I will."

Armistead shouted a command to follow the colors of the guide battalion and stepped out twenty paces in front of the 53rd, the regiment of direction. In front of him the lines of Garnett and Kemper started forward at regular time. Those generals, both mounted, rode up and down behind the lines of the marching men. Garnett was on a black horse, Kemper on a little sorrel.

Armistead, a foot soldier all his life, led in the cavalry tradition of "Follow me." He unsheathed his sword and, uncovering his gray head, placed his black hat on the sword point. Thrusting it out, he boomed: "Forward, guide center, march!"

Leaving their woods, the men looked back at the wounded left behind. "Good-by, boys. Good-by."

12

The prevailing impression of the charge is a panoramic picture of one long battle line emerging from the woods of Seminary Ridge and marching straight forward to their doom. That is not the way it was. The two wings of the assault started separately, and it was Hill's six brigades who emerged from the wooded crest of Seminary Ridge and marched out across the open country north of Lee's command post.

Pickett's three brigades came out of the woods and the hollow and moved down into a ravine, or swale, that coursed in a northeast direction. A ten-foot rise there ran in front of Spangler's Woods from about the center to the northern end of the timber. At the beginning of their advance, though they had been seen by the enemy, Pickett's division had this cover.

When the troops of both wings began their march, Alexander and Walker, commanding Hill's guns, broke off fire. The gunners stood by to allow the infantry to pass between the pieces. When the Confederate guns ceased firing, the Federal artillery fire also faded off. The enemy gunners were preparing their pieces for the infantry.

There was thus an eerie silence over the field when Pickett's troops began to emerge on a rise of ground about four hundred yards east of General Lee's command post and directly opposite the Federal center. The hush, as if the gathered forces were spectators at a pageant, ended abruptly as the heavy Federal guns commenced firing at the gray lines of the separated wings. The eighteen guns in the copse of trees reopened, then twenty more, then twice that number, until more than eighty guns were hurling explosives into the two ranks of foot soldiers.

Pickett's men began to fall as the ranks cleared the ravine. By the time the whole division was in view, gaps were appearing in the lines. On the open high ground the regiments made a wheeling movement to face obliquely toward the point of attack. To a soldier in the 1st Virginia the enemy's fortified hill looked like a semicircle of guns and blue masses, and his own regiment seemed aimed at the exact center.

The smoke from the cannonade had spread a dark pall over the field, and as the three brigades wheeled to the front, geysers of exploding shells opened holes in their ranks. Under this fire, before starting ahead, the men dressed the line.

As if they were on parade, their left arms shot out and their heads turned right to form a straight alignment. The man one soldier was dressing on would fall before the alignment was completed, and the men kept closing up, eying the guide flags that dipped and rose, while the metal burst over and among them.

Even the waiting infantry of the enemy was awed by the spectacle. "My God, they're dressing the line!"

Then, under their red battle flags, the men began the forward movement down the slope. They were carrying their rifles, with fixed bayonets, at right-shoulder-arms. There was no cheering among them, not even any talk. The men were getting a good look at where they were going. At their oblique line of march, they had about eight hundred yards to go to the road, and something over two hundred yards from the road up the hill to the enemy's lines.

No troops on either side had ever attacked over so long a distance without cover. At Fredericksburg, where Burnside's men had come up a long hill, only the last quarter of a mile was open. There not one man in the repeated waves of assault had reached the Confederate crest.

Here, the fences ahead provided no cover, but only presented obstacles. At the fences along the road the strong Federal skirmish line waited as if no attack were coming at them. The thinner Confederate skirmish line, under orders not to fire until close, moved ahead like figures in a dream.

Through the smoke the watchers around Lee's command post could see their men going down steadily under cannon fire. Some doubled over and sank to the ground, some rocked back as if pushed, some stumbled and slowly sprawled on the farmed earth. Others staggered, then halted to inspect what had happened to them; some of these hurried to take their places in the line again.

While Private Robert Morgan was examining the damage a Minié ball had done to his right instep, another bullet entered the front of his left foot and plowed through the flesh to the heel. He decided to call it a day and, using his own musket and another belonging to a fallen comrade as crutches, hobbled to the rear. He was part of a small trickle of individuals flowing backward.

A soldier named Byrd was spun around by a shot that tore into his right arm, and asked his captain if he could go back, as he could not hold a rifle. The captain did not want anyone retreating from his company, but Byrd's corporal said: "Our bird has been winged." They let him start back. He never made it. A shell caught him from behind.

Colors began to plunge down, to reappear instantly. A color guard walked four paces in front of the line, holding up the ragged flag with the battle names stitched on in white letters by ladies in the soldiers' families. Colonel Rawley Martin said that the soldiers kept "constantly in view the little emblem which was their beacon light to guide them to glory and to death."

Many colors were carried successively by six or even eight members of the guard, as one after another went down, and finally were picked up by anyone near. In the 1st Virginia, all five members were killed or wounded, including sixteen-year-old Willie Mitchel, the son of the Irish patriot and Confederate sympathizer. Armistead's Sergeant Blackburn went down early, but the colors of the 53rd Virginia went on.

By the time the three brigades neared the Emmitsburg road, the first large gaps appeared in the line. They were quickly closed, but still and tortured figures were left where the gaps had been. On Kemper's right flank the men began to fall as if the line were being gnawed at. A battery on Little Round Top had them in its range and, like a hunter holding a slowly moving object in his sights, followed them with an enfilade fire that almost kept pace with the rhythm of march.

The Confederate gunners had, after the infantry passed below their gun muzzles, opened a scattered fire to try to silence the Union batteries. It was without effect on the deadly work.

The Federal artillerists had stood up under the worst that Alexander could direct against them. Caissons had burst, horses and men been killed or wounded, and scenes of disorder created in what a Union general called the "pandemonium." But the destructive, demoralizing effect that General Lee had hoped for had not been achieved. The gun crews manned their pieces and directed them at the advancing gray line in—that most cold-blooded of military phrases—"anti-personnel fire." They were firing bursting shells, some solid shots, and much canister.

Tireless Alexander (he had had two hours' sleep and no food except his breakfast cracker with unsweetened potato-coffee) turned to arranging guns to follow Pickett. Ammunition was so low that he could load the caisson of only one gun in each battery. By the time the troops were reaching the foot of Cemetery Ridge, he had limbered up between fifteen and twenty guns to move out behind them—less than one artillery battalion to give the support that General Lee had planned for the infantry.

By then, though the smoke was thickening again over the field, the artillerist could see George Pickett and his staff riding close behind the advancing lines. His staff officers were his only brother, twenty-three-year-old Major Charles Pickett, and Captains Stuart Symington, Ed Baird, and Robert Bright. Their party had moved out last, "as closely in rear of the line of battle as it was possible to do," one of them reported, "and, at the same time, be able to observe the advance" of the whole action.

Starting down the hill, Pickett, looking very jaunty on his black horse, had waved once. He was wearing a small blue cap and buff-colored gauntlets that covered the blue cuffs of his sleeves; above the gauntlets the swirls of cloth-of-gold *galons* glinted briefly against the light-gray cloth. Once he faced forward, none of them looked back.

13

Farther north on Seminary Ridge, Pettigrew's line emerged from the cover and started down the slope, the ranks well dressed. Behind them came Pender's two brigades, with General Trimble riding between the first line and his supports. When he appeared, he was adjusting his seat and his reins with, wrote one observer, "an air and grace as if setting out on a pleasant afternoon."

The curious calmness characterized almost all of the attacking force. They were trained soldiers and dedicated patriots, but that was not the whole explanation. There was a fatalism about the movement out. The men's identities had become submerged in that of the regiment, the brigade, the division, the corps, the army. They did not talk or think of their rights or even of the Confederacy. They said "the army"

—meaning Lee's army—and that distilled all their reasons for walking across that field and probably not walking back.

Only where the unit spirit had not been developed or sustained did the individual's consciousness of self assert itself. That happened in the two brigades fatefully placed on Pettigrew's left flank—the sporadically led Virginians under their senior colonel, and the green troops among the Mississippians led by President Davis's well-meaning nephew.

Sometimes in a steeplechase a horse and rider are seen early to fall behind the field. The abused Virginia brigade, commanded by Brockenbrough, was like that. They wavered when the fire struck them, paused irresolutely when it grew heavy, and then, as the rest of the line swept on, the group became isolated, no longer part of the attack. Many openly went back to where it was safe. Others stayed where they were. Some individuals and small units—squads and companies, segments of regiments who remembered the great days when Field was their brigadier—tried to press on.

Their only chance for even an illusory sense of security against the volume of destruction coming at them lay in seeking their fellows. They veered to their right, toward Davis's brigade, and found his units in similar disorder.

The early volunteers in that brigade, including the Mississippi regiments built on the nucleus of students from the university, went on in a group spirit evolved by time and pride. But with nearly all their field officers lost in the first day's disaster, they lacked leadership at the unit level and went on blindly.

The green troops, remembering the railroad-cut massacre, simply broke out and got out of there before it could happen again. Inexperienced Joe Davis was helpless to control them. As military units, the two flank brigades disintegrated—to the shocked amazement of Rodes's idle veterans, who had

311

watched them in confidence that any Confederate would go all the way.

Pettigrew's attacking line was reduced, with the disorganized survivors of Brockenbrough and Davis, to his own North Carolina brigade under Marshall and Archer's Tennesseans under Fry. In spite of incredible casualties, remnants of those two brigades came on. Trimble, following with the tough brigades from Pender's division, said his supporting line walked through blood.

With their left flank composed of nothing more than corpses and fleeing and moaning men, the compressed brigades began their climb up the slope to the enemy. Their right flank had been separated from Pickett's left when the two sections first started down Seminary Ridge, and the attacking front covered about three quarters of a mile. As Pickett's brigades drifted northeast, when the lines neared the road the gap between the wings slowly closed.

When the two forces started up the hill there was some jamming between units. It could have been here that the classic Confederate line was spoken: "Cousins, move on, you are drawing the fire our way."

Although Pickett's men and Hill's were directed toward the same objective, there was no accord between them. When the men thought it over later, there was considerable discord. Pickett's men seemed generally to regard the Pettigrew-Trimble soldiers as supports who had not supported; the Pettigrew-Trimble forces of Hill's corps seemed to regard Pickett's division from Longstreet's corps as another assault group who had done no better than they themselves had done. The crux of the argument, which went on for decades, was command. There was none.

It is true that Pickett had no weak brigades to fade from his flank; expecting Wilcox, he had no flank to begin with. It is also true that his troops came under the cannonade first because they were the first out and closer to the enemy's guns. Finally, he had no troops who faltered, because the only change President Davis had made in his division was to take away its two largest brigades. All those who marched down the hill beyond Alexander's guns could say "the army" and mean what Alexander had said: "I had no doubt that we would carry the position, in my confidence that Lee was ordering the attack."

14

No officer reflected the men's confidence more than George Pickett. There was no fatalism in him. Believing that his hour of destiny had come and expecting to take fortune at its flood, he rode down the slope like a knight in a tournament.

The smoke hanging over the field formed a "glowering darkness," he said, but so high were his spirits that he made a joke with Captain Bright. Observing a shell fragment strike the staff officer's spur, forcing the shank around and pointing the rowel to the front, Pickett said: "Captain, you have lost your spurs today instead of gaining them."

Going down the hill, Pickett on his black horse could view the foggy field over the heads of the men. His confidence was heightened when he saw the battle lines of Hill's troops emerge from the woods and sweep down the slope to his left. On his open right Wilcox's brigade lay ready to move into action. Perry's Florida brigade, under Colonel Lang, was deployed for support. The details of assault had been made no clearer to Pickett than to anyone else, and he seems not to have expected Wilcox and Perry to move out with or immediately after him.

General Lee evidently planned that Wilcox and Perry should form part of an attacking force comprised of eleven brigades, with Hill's five remaining brigades acting in reserve. Officers close to Lee always maintained that he never planned the attack for only nine brigades, and the positions in which Perry and Wilcox were deployed indicate that their brigades were to be "in support" of Pickett's wing much as Scales and Lane were in support of Pettigrew.

As Longstreet had not ordered the Alabama and Florida brigades forward with him, Pickett evidently assumed "support" to mean an active reserve on which to call. His actions immediately following suggest that such was his understanding.

When his first line, the troops of Kemper and Garnett, neared the fences that lined the Emmitsburg road, Pickett observed the confident belligerence of the enemy's heavy skirmish line. They did not fall back until the battle line approached within one hundred yards of them. Then they withdrew up the hillside in good order, still firing.

After that, the Federal skirmish line maintained a greater distance, as their batteries behind them poured metal on the advancing Confederates. Pickett saw with pride that his lines went steadily on under the carnage, closing up well. He also watched professionally for the effects of the artillery on the foot troops who themselves had no one to shoot at.

At the road, the line paused to allow the men to break down the fence, cross the road, and break down the other. The bursting shell and rain of canister tore great gaps in the ranks then, and there was some crowding among the regiments. Parts of the first fence had not gone down, as men fell along those sections. But there was no need for officers to steady the soldiers, though some talked to them. The men began to talk too, and their irrepressible humor began to be heard here and there.

Where the lines of Garnett and Kemper crossed the road, the brigades divided around the house and large barn of N. Codori on the enemy side of the road, known thereafter as "the Codori barn." Garnett passed on the northern side of the farm buildings and headed straight up the slope toward the projecting angle of stone fence. Armistead followed. Kemper passed the buildings on the southern side and swung sharply northeastward to come up on Garnett's right.

When the three brigades started up the rough incline, they were only two hundred yards from the stone fence. Low on the Union side, it loomed about breast-high to the attackers. The crest of the ridge, the heart of the enemy's defense, was no more than fifty yards beyond the wall.

At that final stage of their march out, the officers and men expected to go all the way to the crest, and they advanced as men who did not believe they could be stopped. Commanding General Meade said: "The assault was made with great firmness," and Major General Hancock, whose II Corps bore the brunt, said: "I've never seen a more formidable attack."

Climbing, the men felt the intense heat burning through the swirls of smoke, and they still had the infantry fire to face. Their discipline was such that the men acted as if controlled by a single mind. No one was firing nervously. They moved up the hill in grim silence. One of the foreign observers said: "They seemed impelled by some irresistible force."

Armistead's second line pushed close up behind the first line going up the hill, and the three decimated brigades were so bunched as to seem almost a single unit.

From Pettigrew's line, Archer's Tennesseans under Fry and Garnett's left companies began to press against one another. A captain, in the lackadaisical voice of a gatekeeper at a fair, said: "Don't crowd, boys."

Then, directly ahead of them, rifle fire blazed out in a solid spray from tall grass where the last enemy line outside the works had waited for them.

At this stage of the advance, through the dark smoke Pickett could see the left flank of Pettigrew's brigades melting

315

away. A heavy flank fire from the Union guns on Cemetery Hill was cutting into the ranks of the compressed survivors. A few steps farther on, his own line would encounter the concentrated rifle fire of the infantry behind the stone fence.

It was clear to Pickett that his men would not be stopped. It was also clear that there would not be enough of them left to hold the crest. Pickett and his staff were then on the enemy side of the road, north of the Codori farm buildings. The general turned to Captain Bright.

"Go to General Longstreet," he said, "and tell him that the position will be taken, but we cannot hold it unless reinforcements be sent."

Captain Bright whirled his horse around with his single spur and started back over the littered field. He had to check his horse to avoid running down a group of stragglers from Pettigrew's division. Although he had no authority over those troops, he halted them and commanded them to go back and support the troops moving up the hill. In his excitement, he yelled: "What are you running for?"

One of the soldiers, seeing Bright's horse pointed toward the rear, said: "Why, good gracious, captain, ain't you running yourself?"

Too flurried to think of an explanation, Bright rode off feeling baffled by the encounter.

Pickett sent Captain Symington and Captain Baird to try to rally the broken units from Pettigrew's division. He was growing excited now as he witnessed the slow wreckage of his division, marching on with no support on the right and the left falling away on its flank. While he was desperately dispatching his staff officers, the advancing lines moved within range of the Federal muskets behind the stone fence, and the men were finally relieved of the strain of marching into fire without fighting back.

The shouts of Garnett and Kemper released them. The

316

men brought the rifles down from their shoulders, holding them straight out with bayonets glinting ahead, and, breaking into double-time, opened their throats in the spontaneous, indescribable, high-pitched scream called the Rebel Yell.

They were little more than one hundred yards from the stone fence, their thinned ranks still loosely holding regimental order, when Garnett shouted: "Fire!"

Hardly more than half his men were left to slow their steps, aim, and pull triggers. They made their bullets count. There was no wild shooting. Blue-covered heads disappeared from behind the stone fence.

Biting off the cartridge from the powder load, each man jammed a charge down his long rifle barrel with his ramrod and trotted on. As they prepared to fire, the foremost troops were no more than twenty-five yards from the faces behind the stone wall. The blue infantry was growing unsteady. Beyond them, Garnett's men saw some of the guns that had poured shells among them. They broke into a run, yelling, firing at the gunners.

Dick Garnett, muffled in his dark overcoat, cheered his men on, waving a black hat with a silver cord. His sword was in its scabbard. Suddenly he rocked back in the saddle. The screaming horse bolted, and Garnett fell heavily to the trampled ground. He never moved again.

Just before Garnett went down, one of his soldiers was struck by a shell fragment on the head. Stumbling, blinded by blood, he fell among rocks and injured his knee. Lying there, he wiped the blood from his eyes and saw that he was in a small clump of rocks with a wounded captain who had crawled there for shelter. A moment later two Federal soldiers squeezed into the rocky shelter. They had been in the line that fired from the grass. Caught between the shooting from their own people and the advancing Confederates, they had had enough for the day.

As they joined the Confederates, a riderless black horse, out of control, galloped past them with blood streaming from a shoulder gash. The two enemy soldiers told the Confederates that it was their general's horse. They had seen Garnett fall. Then they offered to help the two Confederates back to Seminary Ridge. Without considering motives, the wounded men gratefully accepted the offer.

Kemper's men had opened fire almost simultaneously with Garnett's. When his brigade hurried on, preparatory to making the final rush, Kemper spun his horse around and called to Armistead.

"Armistead, hurry up!" he shouted. "I am going to charge these heights and carry them, and I want you to support me."

"I'll do it," Armistead called back. His men were already hurrying, closing in on the heels of the advance line. As yet, with the two other brigades in front, they had been given no chance to fire. Just before ordering the men to double-time, Lewis Armistead could not repress his pride in them. "Look at my line," he yelled to Kemper. "It never looked better on dress parade."

Then he gave the order for double-time to the colonel of the regiment of direction and adjusted his hat on the sword point. A bullet going through the hat had caused it to slide down to the hilt, and Armistead was determined to keep the black hat waving.

When his brigade ran forward, the advance lines were so rent that his men moved into the gaps and the three brigades began to merge. Their front was spared the direct fire from the heavy guns now, but from the left the firing from Cemetery Hill plunged through and over Pettigrew's survivors to tear at Garnett's men. On the right, Kemper's men, punished for half a mile by the batteries on Little Round Top, had also been ripped in the flank by some Vermont troops who had

318

rushed out from an advanced clump of trees at the side of the battle line. Through it all, Kemper's men, like Garnett's and then Armistead's, shot deliberately. Taking aim, the soldiers brought surprisingly heavy firepower to the point of contact. In front the rifle fire burning out from the stone wall lost its solidity, becoming scattered as Federal soldiers dropped and others fell back toward their second line.

Lewis Armistead, leading his own men on foot, was the only general in view when, with the three intermingled brigades, he ran the last few yards toward the stone fence. While Armistead was bringing his troops up and into the advance line, Kemper had gone down, shot in the groin.

Two of Kemper's staff officers had been killed, and no others were near by. A Union officer, rushing about with three privates in the confusion, saw the star-in-a-wreath on Kemper's collar and placed a blanket under him. The Federal told the wounded general that he would move him back to one of their field hospitals. Then a group of Confederates appeared out of the smoke, and the Federal party left. Several of the men lifted General Kemper and started back to their own lines.

The other two mounted officers who went up the hill with Pickett, Colonel Eppa Hunton and Colonel Lewis Williams, were both down. Colonel Hunton was wounded and Williams dying, his little bay mare standing quietly near by. Two other colonels who were killed, Patton and Allen, had been Williams's roommates at V.M.I.

Among Hill's men, Pettigrew was wounded in the hand and Trimble seriously in the leg, which later had to be amputated. Colonel Fry, who had taken in Archer's brigade, was down wounded, and Colonel Marshall, temporarily commanding Pettigrew's North Carolinians, had been killed outright. A shell burst had knocked him from his horse; shaken, he ordered his men to place him in the saddle and turn the horse to the front. He was shot dead from the horse near the crest of the hill.

The colonels and lieutenant colonels leading on foot had suffered almost total casualties. Of field officers in Pickett's division only one man, Colonel Henry C. Cabell, stayed on his feet, and he was slightly wounded. The others were not all dead—more than half recovered from their wounds—but none was in condition to exercise command. Colonel Hunton's regiment, which became the "Berkeley Regiment," was commanded by the youngest of the four brothers, whose only experience had been as lieutenant in a company commanded by an older brother.

By the time Lewis Armistead neared the stone fence, regimental order was going. With less than one fourth of the 4,500 men still pressing on, the foremost of the scattered survivors pressed together in no organized battle line. Those in front were merely the fastest. One of the first at the fence was John Bowie Magruder, twenty-four-year-old University of Virginia graduate and academy teacher, the colonel of the 57th Virginia who had given Armistead the nickname "Lo" for "Lothario." Climbing up on the stones, he pointed to the enemy guns and shouted: "They are ours!" As he uttered the words he fell back, dead when his body struck the earth.

Armistead reached the fence a moment later, his gray head rising above the men as he started to climb. "Give them the cold steel!" he yelled.

Men fired into one another's faces and then lunged. A Federal soldier was wounded in the shoulder by a gash made from an impromptu lance tied to a color standard. With cannon silent in this section and rifle fire now scattered, the struggling men, using bayonets and clubbed rifles, could hear the grunts and curses, the moans and panting breaths.

Somebody on the ground was praying. Wounded were begging for water.

The Federal line gave way. From the top of the fence, Lewis Armistead jumped down on the enemy side. The heights were won, as Pickett had prophesied, and the remnants of his men gave an exultant yell.

"Follow me!" Armistead shouted and pointed his hat.

Only 150 men climbed over the stone wall with him. They were a group now, without regiment or even company organization, though survivors from a single unit tried to keep together. The compression of the remaining force was shown by the twenty battle flags that fell in a hundred-square-yard space near the crest.

There were no more enemy soldiers at the fence. Clots of reserves were forming to the right and left of the Confederates, and a second line waited massed for them on the crest of the ridge. The men saw none of that. They saw immediately ahead of them the six guns of Cushing's battery, all except one silenced. Every horse in the battery was down, every officer killed or wounded. The surviving cannoneers were trying to haul their pieces away.

Lewis Armistead reached the first gun and in triumph placed his hand on it. He wanted his men to turn it on the enemy. As he touched the still warm metal, a bullet caught him. He arched back, hung for a moment, and wilted to the ground beside the gun.

Colonel Martin fell beside him, maimed for life, and forty-two Virginians from his regiment literally carpeted the ground around him and Armistead.

Leaderless, the huddled group then saw, emerging through the smoke, the solid blue lines of fresh units closing in on them from three sides.

Farther to the left, the survivors of Pettigrew's North Carolina and Tennessee brigades, with oddments of Mississippi

321

troops scattered among them, also halted. The projecting angle of stone wall did not cross their front, and they were fifty or more yards from the crest of the ridge. Probably none reached it.

With all leaders down, the men of both commands were on their own, and they reacted as individuals. Some fought on to the death—one Confederate fell twenty yards beyond Armistead's gun. Some surrendered. Some turned defiantly to withdraw.

There was no one to look after Lewis Armistead. He was taken to the Union rear by soldiers, through the corps of his old friend Winfield Scott Hancock, and died that night without fully regaining consciousness. Garnett's body was left on the field; his brigade was brought out by Major Peyton, a one-armed staff officer.

The 150 men who followed Armistead into the angle were not the only survivors of Pickett's division on the hill. Many who had reached the stone fence used it as a breastwork and fired over it. Many more in the confusion of the last hundred yards had not neared the fence until Armistead was down and his little knot of men was being engulfed. In the disorder, they stumbled over the dead and wounded. When the latecomers saw their unorganized remnants isolated at the enemy's stronghold, they knew that the charge was over for them.

In the 19th Virginia, twenty-four-year-old Lieutenant Wood of Company A (originally the Monticello Guard of Charlottesville) was one who reached the fence late after stopping to inspect a blow on the leg, which turned out to be a bruise from a spent ball. Reaching the stone-and-dirt wall, he "looked to the right and to the left and felt we were disgraced. Where were those who started the charge? With one exception I witnessed no cowardice, and yet we had not a skirmish line. Less than two hundred yards to the right the enemy was forming a line of battle on our side of the fence . . . rapidly being extended into the field to our rear. I watched them as they began to move in our direction. To remain was life in prison. To retreat was probably death in crossing the field, but possible safety within our lines, and without a moment's hesitation I turned my back to the fence . . . and . . . warm, tired and thirsty I limped down the hill. . . ."

The men had never questioned the work laid out for them. With their confidence in Lee, each man believed that, as in all their other battles, plans had been perfected to make their attack feasible. In their dazed state on the hillside, the men did not question the reasons for the failure of their assault, did not ask where the plan had gone wrong. They knew nothing about flanks melting away and no supports coming. They knew only that nothing more could be accomplished. They looked to the saving of their own lives and the lives of their wounded comrades.

Something over a thousand men who were unwounded or wounded so slightly as not to be incapacitated for long, or to be listed as battle casualties, made their way back down the hill as individuals. Five hundred or more wounded crawled or were taken back to their own lines. Several days later the division mustered 1,500, not all present for duty.

A. P. Hill's men with Pettigrew and Trimble fared about the same.

15

At the bottom of the hill George Pickett was slow to recognize the magnitude of the disaster. Expecting to carry the position, Pickett, from the moment his men started up the hill, had been alerted for the supports and intent on remedying the deteriorating situation on his left. It was his impression that the whole left column of the assault had collapsed.

Agitated at the time, he grew bitter later. His official report was so damning of Hill's troops that Lee refused to accept it on the grounds of avoiding inter-army conflicts. He asked Pickett to submit another, which was never done. Pickett's staff officers also blamed the troops on their left, and Longstreet in his official report mentioned "the wavering columns of Pettigrew and Trimble."

The four of Hill's brigades which started up the hill relatively intact as units did not collapse so completely as Pickett and his staff believed. But neither did the valor of those clusters of individuals who would not stop represent the unit achievement that their officers would have liked to claim. These troops had been shaken by the casualties sustained the first day, and on the third the leadership at brigade and division level was too new, the leaders too unacquainted with the personnel, and the over-all control too loose to ensure effective operations in the face of the murderous losses suffered during that unprotected journey of one mile. Also, none but the stoutest could remain unaffected by the dissolution of their flank brigade, followed by disintegration of the one next to it.

Pickett's staff was right in claiming that Federal units would not have marched out so boldly against the left flank if an even partially intact brigade had remained to face about and present a firing line. But by the time the men in Pettigrew's two right brigades found their flank completely gone, their own order had been lost. So the advancing men huddled together to press straight on as had Pickett's men. They knew nothing else to do.

However, Pickett and his staff could with equal justice have claimed that the Federal forces on their right, especially the Vermont regiments that slashed at them before they made contact, would not have come on unimpeded if Pickett's division had possessed a flank brigade to face about and protect the advancing line from harassment. But the brigade that should have been on their flank, Wilcox's, was directly under Longstreet's orders, and the men in Longstreet's corps entered no complaint against their corps commander.

When Captain Bright reached Longstreet with Pickett's call for his supports, he found the bulky lieutenant general seated on a snake fence whose direction ran toward the field. He was peering through the smoke with his glasses. Bright delivered the verbal message. Before Longstreet answered, they were joined by Colonel Fremantle of Her Majesty's Coldstream Guards.

The Britisher drew in his horse beside them and said breathlessly: "General Longstreet, General Lee sent me here, and said you would place me in a position to see this magnificent charge. I would not have missed it for the world."

Longstreet laughed. "The devil you wouldn't!" he said, in bluff heartiness. "I would like to have missed it very much. We've attacked and been repulsed. Look there."

While the foreign observer was staring at the field, Longstreet turned to Bright. Surprisingly, he said: "Captain Bright, ride to General Pickett and tell him what you have heard me say to Colonel Fremantle."

Shaken by this message of defeat—for the troops had been advancingly handsomely when he left them—Pickett's staff officer turned his horse for the ride back across the smoky field.

"Captain Bright!" Longstreet called after him. The captain turned in the saddle. Longstreet, pointing ahead, said: "Tell General Pickett that Wilcox's brigade is in that peach orchard, and he can order him to his assistance."

(Longstreet made no mention of Wilcox's long idleness in his official report.)

Bright, his horse leaping over motionless bodies and avoiding sightlessly stumbling men, returned unscathed across the field of fire and gave Longstreet's report to Pickett. In extreme excitement, Pickett ordered Captain Symington, then Captain Baird, and finally Captain Bright to ride to Wilcox and hurry him forward. Bright believed that Pickett sent all three staff officers because he feared that one or two might not make it.

According to Wilcox, all three made it to him. When Captain Bright galloped up, old-army Cadmus Wilcox had been himself infected by the urgency. He waved both hands at Bright and said: "I know, I know."

"But, general," Bright said, "I must deliver my message."

By the time Wilcox ordered his Alabamians out, there were no longer any lines to support. Alexander, with his assortment of guns firing off to Pickett's right, saw Wilcox's men march down the slope just after he had seen Pickett's men at the crest "swallowed up in smoke, and that was the last of them."

At Pickett's urging, Wilcox marched out twenty minutes after the Virginians—twenty minutes too late. To Alexander, Wilcox's men moving across a field empty except for the dead and suffering "looked bewildered, as if they wondered what they were expected to do, and why they were there." They suffered more than ten-per-cent casualties before the brigade reached the road. The men entered a small ravine east of the road and exchanged purposeless fire with Union infantrymen while Wilcox studied the field for the troops he was supposed to support.

By now Pickett's and Pettigrew's survivors were drifting out of the smoke, on the start of their journey back down the hill. Seeing no one to support, as he duly recorded in his official report, Wilcox sensibly kept his troops where they were. Later they retired, sustaining a loss of 204 out of 1,200 to no purpose whatsoever.

Colonel Lang, with the three Florida regiments that com-

posed Perry's brigade, started out bravely enough after Wilcox and got lost in the going. As his description of the woods
where his men floundered coincides with no known part of
the field in his area, Colonel Lang must have been as confused as his troops. The wreckage of that little brigade,
wandering about among heavy Federal reinforcements after
the attack was all over, represented the most hopeless waste
of all.

Even after that brigade disintegrated, Wright and Posey
started out as belated supports, but Longstreet stopped their
movement to save useless loss of life. It was when the attack
was over that Longstreet began thinking again as a soldier.
Aware of the possibility of the enemy opening a counterattack, he assumed an active supervision on his front for the
first time that day. With that appearance of stolid self-assurance which spread confidence around him, the corps commander looked to the immediate details of infantry and guns
which could be organized for a defensive stand. He was back
on his own ground now, working on tangible physical problems.

Things happened very fast from the time the charge began. Some estimated that scarcely more than twenty minutes
passed between the appearance of Pickett's men out of the
woods and Armistead's death beside Cushing's gun. The advance groups could have covered the distance in fifteen minutes, and they were probably no longer than five minutes at
the fence.

From the moment that the first half-stunned men reap-
peared out of the smoke along the stone fence until the last
started downhill, perhaps another twenty minutes elapsed.
Two captains from Kemper's division, John Holmes Smith
and Robert Douthat, remained that long in a small stand of
timber below the stone fence.

Smith and Douthat had reached that point in the charge

with a few men from their companies, and they estimated the time by watching the passage of a messenger, "Big Foot" Walker, sent back for reinforcements. When Walker's big figure disappeared beyond the opposite crest of Seminary Ridge, the two captains knew that no reinforcements were coming. The privates had known it long before, and had left. The captains, one with a badly bleeding leg wound, were left alone on the hill with enemies gathering all around them. When they started the run downhill, one helping the other to hobble on one foot, Captains Smith and Douthat were probably the last Confederates to leave the crest.

While Longstreet assumed responsibility for a defensive line and the thin streams of men began trickling down the slope from Cemetery Ridge, Pickett was fighting against the realization that his division was broken and the assault had failed. At no precise moment did he learn that supports were never coming on his right, or that the left could not be stabilized. He sent a staff officer with an order for Dearing's supporting battalion to open on the Federals advancing against his right flank, where Alexander was trying hopelessly to hold back the tide. A lieutenant of one of Dearing's batteries confessed that though the gun crews had come out as ordered, because of the moved ordnance wagons their caissons contained but three solid shot and no canister. Under the staff officer's urging, the cannoneers dutifully unlimbered one gun and opened with solid shot on advancing lines. The first shot missed; the second hit one man; the third missed. That was the close artillery support.

Knowledge that one flank was irretrievably gone and the other would not be supported came to Pickett through the visual evidence of the remnants of his command moving— walking, staggering with comrades, running—past him. He was restrained by his staff officers from a nearly hysterical effort to rally them. The captains forced on him the realization that it was over. Pickett's division, the first time it ever fought a major battle as a unit, was destroyed forever. He must turn his attention to the survival of his command.

In the midst of retreating groups as casually disorganized as strangers strolling in a park, Pickett turned his black horse around and recrossed the road. The dandified general was now almost completely out of self-control. In less than one hour his dreams of glory had reached what seemed their point of fruition and then collapsed in a rejection of his aspiration beyond any horror he could have imagined.

No Confederate force had ever before retired from a field in such a state of debris. All officers above the rank of major were gone save one, and gone were two thirds of the men who had lived, trained, and fought together for more than two years. Some among the fallen had been neighbors and friends since childhood, some had been kinsmen, most had been in the full flowering of their manhood. One father, Captain Spessard, had given water to his dying son, then fought his way in and out of the angle.

A representative company was one from Albermarle County, in Colonel Henry Gantt's 19th Virginia of Garnett's brigade. Of the 32 men listed by age, 21 were in their twenties, 3 under twenty, 7 between thirty and thirty-five, and one was older, a forty-four-year-old bricklayer. Four stood six feet or better and 3 under five feet four and one half inches. The rest measured from five feet five to five feet ten and one half, for a company average of about five feet eight —above the general average for their day.

A typical brigade was composed of farmers and planters, some artisans and storekeepers, lawyers, educators, a book collector, and college students and graduates who had had no chance yet to find a career.

Despite his craving for glory and his life's training in the hazards of soldiering, volatile Pickett felt very personally about his men. They had not chosen soldiering as a career. They were citizens on leave from their homes and families in defense of their land, and, as he saw it, the men had entrusted their lives to him.

In his shattering grief, Pickett possessed no inkling of the greater glory he had won for his name and his Virginians. It never occurred to him that the carnage he passed on his return over that field would immortalize his hour of anguish as the epic of "Pickett's Charge." He felt only shock at the death of a proud division and the failure of their charge to destiny.

Riding among haunted-eyed men with slack mouths grimed with powder, he was swept along by, rather than leading, the backwash of the assault.

Behind them the Federal guns were beginning to roar again, sending bursts of shells over the heads of men too spent to hurry or even acknowledge these blows at their backs. Great clods of earth spewed up among them, sending legs and arms into the air. One shell fragment sliced off the head of a lieutenant in a clean line above his mustache and goatee. Sightlessly the men trudged on toward their own lines, climbing the slope to Seminary Ridge. They were followed by Colonel Williams's little bay mare, walking quietly and carrying her empty saddle.

Formations of enemy infantry ventured out from their walls and breastworks, advancing tentatively down their slope. The scattered hundreds of retreating men, singly and in small groups, climbed on, unaware of new danger.

On either side of them—from McLaws's and Hood's divisions to the south, from brigades of Dick Anderson's division close by, and from Pender's division to the north—gray lines fired angrily at the advancing enemies. Guns from Longstreet's and Hill's batteries blasted out again. Alexander was herding back into lines the guns that had followed the infantry out, and the gun crews were aching to see the threatening Federals come on toward them. The Federals halted. Their "feeling-out" had discovered no break in the spirit of Lee's men.

To all of that the men stretched across the half-mile of hill from the road to the crest of Seminary Ridge were oblivious. They were not retracing the course of their charge. After falling back down the slope of Cemetery Ridge, they headed straight up the opposite hill. They were climbing in the vicinity of the plateau from which General Lee had watched the action.

When Pickett and his staff were part way up, General Lee on Traveler rode down alone to meet them. Sitting erect on his gray horse, the leader showed not a sign of emotion. The classic face was as still as a statue's.

"General Pickett," he said quietly, "place your division in the rear of this hill, and be ready to repel the advance of the enemy should they follow up their advantage."

Captain Bright was still sufficiently alert to note that it was the first time he had heard General Lee refer to "those people" as "the enemy."

Pickett, with his head down, salf sobbed: "General Lee, I have no division now! Armistead and Garnett and Kemper are all down, and—"

"Come, General Pickett," Lee said, "this has been my fight, and upon my shoulders rests the blame. The men and officers of your command have written the name of Virginia as high today as it has ever been written before."

Unable to answer, Pickett rode on.

General Lee, seeing four soldiers carrying a wounded officer in a blanket, then asked Captain Bright: "What officer is that they are bearing off?"

"General Kemper, sir."

"I must speak to him."

Feeling his bearers halt, Kemper opened his eyes and stared clearly at Lee.

The commanding general said: "General Kemper, I hope you are not very seriously wounded."

"I am struck in the groin and the ball has ranged upward. They tell me it is mortal."

"I hope it will not prove so bad as that."

The seriousness of Kemper's wound caused him to be left in a near-by house converted into a hospital for the critically wounded. He was later removed by Federal surgeons. After recovering in a Federal prison, he was exchanged and lived to be governor of Virginia, but he never regained his health.

General Lee asked: "Is there anything I can do for you, General Kemper?"

With apparently acute pain, Kemper raised himself up on one elbow. "Yes, General Lee," he said intensely, "do full justice to this division for its work today."

Lee bowed his head. "I will," he replied in a low voice. For him the ordeal was just beginning.

16

For General Lee, his officers, and his men, the Battle of Gettysburg did not end with the repulse of what came to be called Pickett's Charge. A decision had not been won: the failure of the offensive climax of their invasion was a certainty. But the army was still an invading force in the enemy's country, still in line of battle against the enemy's army and exposed to counterattack. While the army had not won, it could still lose.

The war was not over because an assault had failed to win a decision on an invasion. Lee himself had turned back four full-scale invasion forces in his own country. On three of the four repulses, Lee had attempted to destroy the invading army, and he feared that Meade might try to do the same to him.

General Meade has been unjustly criticized for not counterattacking. A North Carolina soldier summed it up more aptly than most of the critiques. He said: "Both sides got the worst of the fight at Gettysburg."

Strategically, Meade did not need a decision; time was on the Federal side. Tactically, his own army had been shaken and had suffered heavily (23,000 casualties to 20,000 Confederate), and Lee's army, in reacting to counterthreats, showed no demoralization at all.

It was not Lee's army that had been wrecked in the final assault, but only the nine of its thirty-seven brigades which had been involved in the charge. Besides the Confederate infantry, the cavalry was at hand, including Imboden's fresh troopers, and no batteries had been lost. The quantity of ammunition was unknown to General Meade, as indeed it was to Lee. Actually, the scurrying directed by Alexander brought rounds from the reserve wagons to the caissons and he found that the distributed ammunition was "enough for one day's fight."

The smaller Confederate forces had inflicted higher casualties than they received, even though attack is proverbially costlier than defense and though most of the positions they attacked were formidable ones. Meade assumed that (as Grant found out the following spring) on defense the firepower of the Confederate rifles would be tremendous.

What Meade would do was not known along the slope of Seminary Ridge during the backwash of the assault. The immediate knowns were the gaping center and the possibility of demoralization affecting the troops on the widely separated flanks.

Ewell's corps, extending in a long semicircle from Culp's

Hill to southwest of Gettysburg, contained something like 15,000 men left after casualties. Of the corps, only Johnson's division and Daniel's brigade from Rodes's division had been extensively engaged during the day, and three of Rodes's brigades had experienced no more than sharpshooting and some distant artillery fire since the first day. Robert Rodes, who had missed his chance on the second, never was given another in the campaign, though he kept hoping for it. In Early's division, Hays's and Hoke's brigades (the near-heroes of the dusk fight on Cemetery Hill at the end of the second day) were cut up; but Gordon's superb brigade had been inactive since he was halted by Ewell on the first day, and Extra Billy Smith's brigade were still unused. Gordon was so disgusted at his inaction that he wrote in his battle report: "The movements during . . . July 2nd and 3rd I do not consider of sufficient importance to mention."

At that end of the line, then, the attitude of the leaders and the condition of the troops indicated that they could take care of themselves at least temporarily. General Ewell would not be burdened with the necessity to make decisions in repelling a thrust, and the curved nature of the Federal defense position, where the troops were entrenched behind works, would make an attack by them physically difficult to mount. Whether or not he consciously considered these elements, General Lee diverted none of his attention to the left flank.

In terms of actual fighting, the Battle of Gettysburg was over for Ewell's corps. The officers and men, without this knowledge, remained tensely alert. The soldiers were unaware of the magnitude of the Confederate failure which history associated with the charge. As most of Ewell's men did not witness what they thought of as Longstreet's attack, for them the battle was still going on, though not, for the moment, on their front.

The sense of failure came to individuals in posts of command, especially to Richard Stoddert Ewell, who generously confessed his mistakes. Too well liked for the mistakes to be held against him, he aroused more sympathy than condemnation. But obviously he was no successor to Stonewall Jackson. Although he would never again experience such a harrowing afternoon as came when his power of decision became paralyzed under his first big test, he was physically and temperamentally unsuited for corps command. Gettysburg had proved what Lee apparently suspected from the first about a general whose devotion had to be considered in a personal army. Yet Lee, by leaving the unwieldy left flank in Ewell's care, showed that he retained respect for Ewell's fundamental qualities as a soldier in actions that demanded little initiative.

The commanding general also showed that his trust in James Longstreet had not been shaken. If, however, he had known what his old warhorse was doing on the right flank, Lee might well have been troubled by a few doubts.

17

When the disorganized men of Pickett's division and Hill's corps came limping up Seminary Ridge, Longstreet forgot all about his status with the commanding general and turned his distracted attention to his own corps. From the beginning of his essays at strategy, Longstreet's interest had revolved around the nature of the fighting that he and his own corps would do. When all questions of strategy had been settled by the debacle, Longstreet revealed his true status and his true condition.

As far as is known, no exchanges passed between him and Lee in the aftermath of the attack. Lee expected no consultations with Longstreet, any more than he had from the beginning. Suspecting nothing of Longstreet's agitation over his failure to establish a partnership, Lee accepted it as natural that a subordinate should look only to his own troops. Lee assumed personal responsibility for the broken center and, as he had turned over the left to Ewell, turned over the right to Longstreet.

It was against the Confederate right that the enemy directed their action after the assault, though for some while Longstreet ignored the divisions of Hood (now under Evander Law) and McLaws. Their unused brigades were dangerously projected in an angle to the southeast, with their own center in effect caved in below them. Law's brigade was still on the high ground in the rough country south of Little Round Top. But Longstreet was bustling about the batteries at Seminary Ridge as the gunners brought their pieces back to new positions, and for a time no orders went to the two divisions.

All along the irregular Confederate right, enemy skirmishers kept starting out menacingly, at first one place, then another. Although nothing came of the probings, the threats kept Law and McLaws on edge. Half their general officers were gone, the separated brigades were commanded by untried colonels and a major, and Law had been in temporary command of a division only since the day before.

Then the extreme right was unsettled by a reckless cavalry attack that Brigadier General Farnsworth was ordered to lead against the flank. The newly promoted brigadier had protested that the charge was "suicidal," and so it turned out for him. Law faced a brigade about to drive off the enemy troopers, and his line against the Federal infantry was thus stretched even thinner. Uneasy about his flank, he sent a courier to Lafayette McLaws to request a brigade in support.

The message had just reached the stocky Georgian when Longstreet's first order came. It was delivered by Longstreet's A.A.G., Colonel Sorrel, now in bad physical shape.

His left arm was partially paralyzed from the blow of a shell fragment the day before, and he had been shaken up during the afternoon when a shell burst under his favorite horse and he was heavily thrown to the ground.

When McLaws told Sorrel of Evander Law's request for a brigade, the staff officer said: "Never mind that now, general; General Longstreet directs that you retire to your position of yesterday. Retire at once, and I will carry the order to General Law to retire Hood's division."

Lafayette McLaws immediately protested against the order. He explained that his advanced ground had been won at great cost and, though Pickett had been defeated, there was no reason for him to retire where no enemy pursued.

Colonel Sorrel interrupted McLaws and said: "General, there is no discretion allowed. The order is for you to retire at once."

Having protested against Longstreet's orders three times the preceding day, General McLaws resignedly turned his attention to the withdrawing of his four brigades. They were no sooner posted in a new position back from the Emmitsburg road than McLaws saw the enemy advancing "clouds of skirmishers," with, he supposed, "their lines of battle behind." Apprehensively he sent a skirmish line back into the peach orchard. The enemy halted there on his front.

At the end of the Confederate right, McLaws's withdrawal had exposed the flank of Hood's division. The encroaching enemy immediately threatened on the front and both sides, and the fierce fighters of the Devil's Den and Little Round Top action had to run to get out of an envelopment. Colonel Sorrel had *not* taken the order of retirement to Evander Law.

In his shaky state, the chief of staff had been driven frantic by Longstreet. Sorrel was sent back by Longstreet to McLaws, whom he asked if it were possible to retake the position his division had just been ordered to abandon.

McLaws said that he "demurred most decidedly at the suggestion," and asked Sorrel why he inquired.

Colonel Sorrel said: "Because General Longstreet has forgotten that he ordered it, and now disapproves the withdrawal."

"But," McLaws replied, "recollect that you gave me the order."

"Yes, sir," the staff officer said, "and General Longstreet gave it to me."

They tacitly agreed to ignore the countermanding order. At the best, only loss of life would be accomplished by trying to retake the position. As it was, McLaws said, "the enemy made no attempt to advance against my part of the line after it had been re-established."

While sending orders that he forgot about and not going near the ground himself, Longstreet rushed about among Alexander's batteries on a job that the young cannoneer was doing quite well himself. Longstreet never remembered that the ammunition was low: Alexander did. In this final expression of his turmoil, Longstreet was acting like an excited field officer, with no communication with army headquarters and only sporadic and unsettling communication with his own command. At something that tickled his fancy, his laugh rang out immoderately over the somber field.

The personal behavior of the burly Dutchman revealed anything except the collaborative strategist of the memoirs. The fact that he was opposed to the attack—to all or any attacks—even before the army left Virginia cannot properly be cited in debating the question of his rightness on the third day. The third day occurred because of Ewell's failure on the first and Longstreet's on the second, within the pattern made necessary by Stuart's failure to provide reconnaissance. Longstreet had been opposed to the offensive even before anyone could have conceived of their cavalry leader's disappearance, and he held to it when Ewell's victory needed only to be grasped. Because the final attack did fail—with various assists from him along the way—he was able to make out a case for his opposition.

What antagonized brother officers was that he built a case for the superiority of his own rejected strategy by denigrating and misrepresenting Robert E. Lee. His ultimate ignobleness, as the Confederates saw it, was to claim that Lee's assumption of all blame for the third day was actually an admission that he alone was to blame. In using the commanding general's magnanimity to buttress his own position, Longstreet became a villain to all the supporters of Lee. And with the passing of years, as Confederates sought reasons for their failure, Longstreet became the accepted goat.

More recently, objective historians and Longstreet partisans have tried to re-evaluate him outside the text of controversy. This is almost impossible. All evaluation must largely depend on his demonstrably inaccurate and inventive defenses, and on judgments of his contemporaries which read like a prosecutor's plea for conviction. More than any other man on either side, Longstreet is inextricably involved with the happenings at Gettysburg in terms of the controversy of the following decades.

Yet, that Longstreet himself was disturbed about his part in the battle at the time is indicated by a letter of vindication which he wrote his uncle as soon as camp was established back in Virginia. And in the emergency at the end of the third day he certainly reverted to the role of a subordinate. He gave no thought to the commanding general, to decisions concerning the army's course, or to any consideration except the details of his immediate front. As this was accepted by everyone as natural, it seems evident that the drama of Longstreet's rejection as Lee's strategical adviser was played out largely in Longstreet's own mind. Because of this interior conflict, he lost control of himself and of his troops, and for two days was a poor corps commander. Many other men performed below their potential at Gettysburg, but only James Longstreet absolved himself by blaming Lee.

18

On the afternoon of the third day at Gettysburg, General Lee assumed that his most dependable subordinate was doing whatever was indicated on the right flank. In taking over the center himself, the commanding general adopted the role of personal field commander which he was to fill from that day onward.

His famous line "It's all my fault" has been attributed to Lee's magnanimity. He was magnanimous, and certainly he had no reason to blame his men or General Wilcox, but it was not merely the nobility of his character which was speaking. As a patriarch, he was acting very purposefully for the good of his clan.

Colonel David McIntosh, who commanded one of the gun battalions of A. P. Hill that opened the first day's action in support of Heth, was a thoughtful man, and he said this of Lee after the charge: "His greatest concern at the moment seemed to be to break the shock of the repulse, and its possible effects upon the troops, and probably it was this, coupled with his great magnanimity, that led him to say as reported, 'It is all my fault.' "

General Lee could not conceivably have believed that the failure of the three-day battle was *all* his fault. He had made mistakes in judgment, of which the most fundamental was to attempt Jacksonian tactics without Stonewall Jackson. At some time after the battle he recognized this. He never believed that the invasion as such was a mistake. As the army's ability to sustain that invasion had been tested, the failure demonstrably was in its command personnel, as, from perspective, Confederate participants pointed out. But as commander in chief, as Robert E. Lee, the patriarchal leader assumed responsibility for his people, and he was then most truly the "Uncle Robert" that his men called him.

When stricken soldiers paused around him, it was as their older kinsman that he soothed them. "All this will come out right in the end. We'll talk it over afterwards. In the meantime, all good men must rally. We want all good men just now. . . ."

He formed them personally—squads out of what had been companies, companies out of what had been regiments—and skirmish lines were stretched along the brow of the hill.

If the counterattack came, he planned a defensive line in the woods along the crest of the hill. Constantly his words were directed toward heartening the officers and men in the performance of the next duty. He was trying to remove from them the sense of cataclysm and quiet them into orderly competence.

Wilcox, shaken by his purposeless losses, came up with the brim of his straw hat flapping. He had just brought his brigade out, and, as he tried to make a report to Lee, his voice broke.

Lee took his hand. "Never mind, general, all this has been my fault. It is *I* that have lost this fight, and you must help me out of it the best way you can."

Wilcox's brigade, despite their losses of the past two days, represented one of the six unbroken units in the nearly two miles from McLaws's unsettled left to the two brigades from Rodes's division, Doles and Ramseur, deployed in Long Lane south from the town.

Of the other brigades in Anderson's division (omitting Perry's as a wreck) Wright's was also cut up, and one of the two unused brigades, Posey's, had revealed egregiously bad leadership on the second day. Dick Anderson's actions were

341

vague, as they had been all through the battle. Apparently his brigades that had started out late in support and then been recalled were returned by him to their original line of battle in readiness to receive attack. Wilcox reoccupied his position in support of Alexander's batteries.

Farther north along the ridge, Powell Hill seems to have left Anderson to his own discretion, or Longstreet's (as Longstreet had recalled Wright and Posey), and directed his attention to bringing order to his six fragmented brigades behind the line of the two unused brigades of Pender's division. Only one of these latter, Colonel Perrin's South Carolinians, had suffered heavily on the first day, and the men had been rested since and were ready. Along this stretch the enemy, having just seen what happened to Pickett, made no advance over the open country between the two ridges.

The position along Seminary Ridge as seen by the enemy assumed at least the appearance of order. What six brigades, three reduced in number, would have accomplished against a determined advance is problematical. Unquestionably, the corpses and the wounded littering the 1,400 open yards between the lines would have had a restraining effect on enemy troops who themselves had just been severely buffeted.

While the threatening advances were made against the Confederate right, a breakthrough at that end, or an overlapping of McLaws's left, could quickly swell the action over against the uncertain center. General Lee for all his outward calm, showed his apprehension of a counterattack by his ceaseless efforts to form lines from the fragments in cover on the hill.

He dispatched all the officers of his staff to the task of reforming those troops, entirely without field officers, and alone on his gray horse rode among the disorganized and slightly wounded along the brow of the hill. Many as they reached that point of safety simply threw themselves on the ground.

Lee was attracted to one fellow lying face down in a ditch, whose groans seemed a little loud and dramatic. After an inspection of the soldier, Uncle Robert personally hoisted him to his feet and sent him into a unit.

Many of the men had halted in the woods back of Alexander's guns, and Lee went among them quietly, saying: "Don't be discouraged. . . . It was my fault this time. . . . All good men must hold together now."

Indefatigable young Alexander had been sending his batteries to the rear singly to be refitted. As the sun lowered behind them, his guns were assembled in fair shape, and that corps artillery was definitely one unit commanded by a cool, undaunted officer. One of the cannoneers said to Colonel Fremantle: "We've not lost confidence in the Old Man. This day's work will do him no harm. Uncle Robert will get us into Washington yet; you bet he will."

This spirit became increasingly evident among all the soldiers. Suffering disappointment, grief over the death of comrades and the wreckage of famous units, the men had been spared a sense of calamity by the assurance spread by General Lee's physical presence. Where panic might have spread, an almost unnatural calm settled over the troops.

At sundown Lee left the advanced rows of guns, some of which were not supported by even a skirmish line, and rode among the reorganized groups waiting in line of battle in the woods on the crest. Most of the men looked very tired, and some seemed numbed, but they were resting quietly as they would have in camp after any other action. There was little talk, and that mostly about the officers and men who were gone.

At that time neither Lee nor the troops knew the fates of individual officers left on Cemetery Ridge. Many of the wounded—including old General Trimble, whose frustrating efforts to serve resulted in one hour of shattering action and

343

the loss of a leg—had been captured. They were treated in Federal hospitals and later exchanged.

After seven o'clock a silence began to descend on the whole field. Then, along the crest, the men could hear the cries and moans of the wounded below them. The Confederate medical corps were always understaffed, and, because medicines were shut off by the blockade, the doctors and medical volunteers always worked without proper drugs. In amputations without anesthesia, screams would be torn from even the most courageous men, and these agonized sounds scraped across the nerves of the soldiers more harshly than the whine of the largest shells.

The wounded on whom no such sudden agony was inflicted bore their suffering with casual stoicism. They awaited their turns at medical care patiently, each trying to avoid creating a disturbance that would unsettle the group. Scores and even hundreds of the soldiers who had not reformed in the battle line were helping friends from their own units. Many of the helpers had been themselves slightly wounded. When some of these first returned to their sanctuary, they showed as curiosities welts along ribs from bullets that had torn through clothes and grazed the skin, and darkening bruises from spent shell fragments that had knocked them down. When they saw the silent suffering of the men more seriously hurt, those who had enjoyed narrow escapes became gentle and solicitous of their wounded fellows.

The Army of Northern Virginia never seemed more of a family than in that July dusk on Seminary Ridge. They were not aware that their struggle for self-determination had passed the point of logical hope. They were not thinking of their cause at all, but rather of the immediate details of life in the army. Their confidence in General Lee was unshaken, and their thoughts were not burdened with apprehension.

Lee was the one who was worrying about the safety of the

men. During the afternoon hours as he rallied and formed the troops, he let slip one recorded remark that revealed his own feelings. To Colonel Fremantle, in suggesting that the British observer go to a less exposed position, he said: "This has been a sad day for us, colonel—a sad day." Quickly recovering himself, he added: "But we can't always expect to gain victories."

When the general was sure that the enemy would not attack that day, and that his men had restored order, he went to his headquarters tent. There the mask of statuesque composure began to fall away. His staff officers and visitors observed the sorrow settling over his features as he began the somber task of planning the details of a retreat.

19

Although Lee took no one into his confidence, the necessity of withdrawing his army must have been evident from the moment he watched the fragments of brigades retire in disorder from the point of their assault. To ensure the army's safe withdrawal, he had been forced first to restore its order and prepare against a counterattack. The success of Lee's first emergency measures was indicated by General Meade's later testimony that he observed "no demoralization" in the enemy forces following the repulse of the charge at his center.

But even while Lee was stabilizing his line and presenting a bold front, the decision to retreat had been formed. This decision did not entail a balancing of alternatives open to the army. With enough ammunition for only one action and food almost gone, his problems were reduced to the logistics of moving his men, his wounded, and his trains away from the front of a powerful enemy in a hostile country.

No would-be collaborators such as Longstreet sought to share these unheroic chores with him. In his headquarters tent, with his gloomy staff officers resting outside, the general worked alone over the same maps he had studied so diligently while waiting for word from Jeb Stuart only six days before on that Sunday at Chambersburg. Now he knew where the enemy was. Under the candlelight, he was tracing courses to where the enemy would not be.

First, routes were selected for the miles of canvas-topped, springless ambulances that would carry the thousands of wounded judged capable of making the trip. (The torture of those men riding over muddy roads became a prolonged ordeal that surpassed any action of the three days.) Hundreds of the more critically wounded, along with hundreds of the enemy's wounded, were left in houses and barns to be cared for by Federal doctors and sent to prisons.

The ambulances, intermingled with supply and ordnance wagons, were strung out on the side of the Chambersburg pike westward from Gettysburg almost to Cashtown, eight miles away. On the return trip, the ambulance train would not retrace the way through Chambersburg. Angling southwestward, the train would go through less hostile Hagerstown and on to the Potomac at Williamsport. The passes behind it would be guarded by Stuart. To guard the helpless men who were to make the trip, Lee selected Brigadier General John Imboden. His 2,000 troopers were the freshest of the cavalry—and the least dependable for regular work. General Lee dispatched a courier with orders for Imboden to come to his tent to receive *written* instructions.

Then Lee dictated *written* instructions to Longstreet for preparing to retire his corps the next day. After the divisions of Hood and McLaws were withdrawn to a line farther west of the enemy, the troops were to wait in line of battle, alert for enemy action, and move out in marching columns when ordered. First Corps ordnance and supply wagons would move with the troops. Possibly not trusting Longstreet to move out with celerity, Lee assigned him the middle place in the march, following A. P. Hill. Ewell, the farthest away, would form the rear guard with his wagons.

To spare Pickett's shattered brigades further fighting, Lee appointed the 1,000-odd survivors to walk as provost guard. In addition to enemy prisoners paroled at Gettysburg, there were some 5,000 captured Federals to be marched southward with the army. They would maintain a balance in later exchange for the Confederates captured at Gettysburg. Some of Pickett's men wrongly felt that Lee intended a slight in assigning them to a police patrol. When the commanding general heard of their complaints, he published an order of explanation and congratulations to the division.

The proud division was never the same. Gradually, the belated return of Corse's brigade and of recuperated wounded, exchanged prisoners, and conscripts filled its complement to about 5,000. This process was slow, and for months the units were scattered among Davis's defense projects in southeastern Virginia and North Carolina. When returned to the Army of Northern Virginia the following year, the division acted as a sort of detached reserve and was not again incorporated in a corps. The loss of the leaders of its regiments—really the basic unit in the Confederate army—had destroyed the potential material for field command, and there were no colonels of comparable quality to replace them.

Pickett himself never recovered. He married Sallie and found solace for his wounded spirit, but he remained haunted by the vision of his men breaking backward out of the smoke and down the hill.

All that was in the future when Lee thoughtfully assigned the survivors to provost guard for the retreat and sent a staff officer with the orders to Longstreet. It was now late in the night, and Lee gave no more work to his exhausted staff. He left his tent alone, mounted his saddled gray horse, and rode through the quiet bivouac to Powell Hill's headquarters.

347

Instead of giving written instructions to Hill, the commanding general traced on his maps the line of march for the Third Corps—a course parallel to the ambulance train's. They talked over the details until Lee, in a blur of fatigue, was convinced that General Hill was clear on every item.

Robert E. Lee was certainly too exhausted and saddened after the charge to have determined consciously that he must abandon his system of working through channels from a general headquarters. But there must have been in his reaction an unarticulated awareness that the old method of operating by suggestion and allowing discretion had failed. His assumption of immediate personal command from before four o'clock in the afternoon until after midnight was different from the nervous concentration on details with which any shocked person may busy himself. It was an unconscious admission that he no longer trusted the delegation of authority to others. Later he necessarily gave limited responsibility to subordinates, but on his last night at Gettysburg Lee revealed in actions—as he never did in words—a knowledge that he had been failed. In the task of saving his army, he trusted no one with any discretion at all.

A. P. Hill, relieved of the inner division caused by discretionary orders, on the way home performed his assignment with high competence. He showed again the initiative, aggression, and sound field control that had characterized his command of the old "Light Division." The Light Division, divided after Chancellorsville to make a division each for Pender and Heth, on the retreat from Gettysburg was remerged into one division under Harry Heth, then recovered from his first day's head wound. Later the division was reshuffled again. Pender's four fine brigades went to Cadmus Wilcox, upped to major general, and new brigades were added to fill out Heth's complement.

General Richard H. Anderson, who had not distinguished

348

himself with the Third Corps, the following year was promoted to lieutenant general and given the First Corps after Longstreet was wounded at the Wilderness. Not Lee's choice as corps commander, Anderson was given the assignment on personal consideration. Well liked by brother officers and men from his earlier association with the First Corps, he was their choice as Longstreet's successor. Like Ewell, who had been chosen as Jackson's successor for the same reasons, Anderson was promoted beyond his capacities. Never doing anything spectacularly wrong, by well-mannered and curiously listless performances he vindicated Lee's judgment of him.

In Hill's corps, Anderson's division went to Billy Mahone, the self-confident bantam who had for personal reasons refused to act on the second day at Gettysburg. He performed capably and aggressively, and became one of the stalwarts toward the end. With Mahone, Heth, and Wilcox, Hill's Third Corps retained more of its Gettysburg identity than the other two.

When General Lee completed the arrangements with Powell Hill, the time was nearing one o'clock in the morning. The night was now completely still, warm, and the moon was bright. He rode his spent horse at a walk among the clumps of sleeping figures and silent guns. Looking at what was to be the last bivouac of the invasion, the heartsick Old Man of the army must have been weighted with the knowledge that it was also the last invasion.

From the retreat, he would return to the defense of Virginia knowing that there was no more possibility of larger strategy. Never having believed that the Southern Confederacy could win its independence without defeating the armies of the states joined in union, Lee now looked into a future consisting of a long rear-guard action in which the Confederates could only hope for a weakening of the enemy's will to conquer. It was a wan hope, and the nature of the resistance was foreign to Lee's nature as a man and to his concepts of warfare. In his heart he must have known that the retreat home started him along a road that could have only one destination. With his training, no choice was left him save to do his duty to the end of that journey.

20

At his group of six headquarters tents, only two men were awake. The young staff officers had gone to sleep so tired that not even a sentry was posted. The two men watching Lee from the shadows of a tree, where they were lying on the grass, were General Imboden and an aide. Lee had asked the cavalryman to wait for him there to receive instructions for escorting the ambulance train.

Lee spoke to them and reined in his horse, which looked as "weary," Imboden said, as its rider. When the general started to dismount, Imboden feared that in his "physical exhaustion" he would not make it. The young cavalry leader impulsively hurried forward to help him to the ground. Before Imboden reached him, the older man stepped down from the stirrups, then threw his arm across the saddle and leaned there to rest. With eyes on the ground, Lee stood motionless against the motionless horse.

As Imboden saw the tableau, "The moon shone full upon his massive features and revealed an expression of sadness that I had never before seen upon his face. Awed by his appearance, I waited for him to speak, until the silence became embarrassing. . . . To break it and change the silent current of his thoughts, I ventured to speak, in a sympathetic tone, and in allusion to his great fatigue."

The cavalryman said: "General, this has been a hard day for you."

Lee raised his head and made no effort to disguise his grief.

"Yes, it has been a sad, sad day to us." He had also used the word "sad" to Fremantle.

The general remained silent for a while, his eyes glazed by inner images. Then one of the images excited him and suddenly he stood straight, "at his full height," and when he spoke it was one of the few times that anyone heard his voice choked with emotion.

"I never saw troops behave more magnificently than Pickett's division of Virginians did today in that grand charge upon the enemy. And if they had been supported as they were to have been—but, for some reason not yet explained to me, were not—we would have held the position and the day would have been ours."

Then the glory of the lost moment faded and he returned to the reality of preparing a retreat. "Too bad," he said in an anguished voice. *"Too bad!* Oh, too bad!"

Slowly the emotion passed, and he collected himself. With habitual courtesy he invited Imboden into his tent to examine the maps.

Lee said: "We must now return to Virginia."

A Note on Sources
and Selected Bibliography

As the late Dr. Douglas Southall Freeman pointed out, the richest single source of Confederate material for the Gettysburg campaign is scattered through the forty-nine volumes of the *Southern Historical Society Papers*. Started in January 1876 under the editorship of the Reverend J. William Jones (author of *Christ in Camp: Religion in Lee's Army*, and chaplain with A. P. Hill's corps), the gray-backed magazine opened its pages to any contributor who wanted to write on any conceivable aspect of the Confederacy and its armies. Nothing was too short or trivial, nothing too long or controversial. The war was fresh in the minds of the survivors, and hundreds of ex-Confederates were eager to carry on with the pen where they had left off with the armed forces.

Many wrote in nostalgia, some in a genuine desire to provide information on phases of the army, others to pay tribute to a fallen hero or to attack an enemy. Along with all the irrelevancies and the sentiments of another age—perhaps because of them—a total picture of the Confederate soldier emerges. Some fifty articles on Gettysburg, ranging from brief sketches to full studies, are included.

As the eyewitness accounts are subject to the fallibility of memory, and many of the articles suffer the distortion of advocacy or indictment, it would be unsafe to use any single article as a guide. Their value lies in the minutiae of personal observations, in the expression of reactions and opinions. Where there is a preponderance of agreement on a single phase of action, particularly when physical details coincide, a composite impression can reasonably serve as a guide.

The most useful source for comparing and cross-checking this material is the battle reports and correspondence in *Official Records*. Most of the reports and correspondence relating to Lee's army in the Gettysburg campaign are in Volume 27, parts 2 and 3, Volume 25, part 2, and Volume 51, part 2. (Federal reports are in part 1 of Volume 27.)

353

A Note on Sources and Selected Bibliography

While there is a tendency in some quarters to revere the *Official Records* as infallible, these reports also are by no means free of the distortions of self-vindication. There are reports written by opponents in one action which read as if the accounts referred to different battles. Frequently generals in reports and correspondence stated as facts what they believed to be the condition of the enemy. It was customary for both sides to exaggerate the numbers opposing them: it was, of course, more heroic to defeat a numerically superior foe and less blameworthy to lose to "overwhelming numbers." On the first two days at Gettysburg, when Federal forces were thrown into action piecemeal and were keenly aware that they lacked their usual numerical superiority at the point of contact, all Union officers overestimated the size of the forces opposing them.

As an illustration, Doubleday, whose troops fought magnificently against Heth in the morning action and stubbornly against Pender in the afternoon, was a vainglorious man. To explain the defeat of his fine regiments, he estimated Heth's and Pender's divisions as a force of 25,000, when half that figure would be more nearly accurate. He also stated that he captured 1,000 prisoners from Archer's brigade, which was only 50-odd less men than the brigade's complement at Gettysburg. In dramatizing the heroism of his men by overplaying the losses they inflicted in defeat, Doubleday doubtless estimated Archer's brigade at a normal Confederate complement of between 1,500 and 2,000 men at that period; he had no way of knowing that on July 1, 1863, Archer's brigade was dangerously below its normal strength. But, if Doubleday's report of the first day's action is accepted as accurate, one must be prepared to believe that on the third day Archer's brigade charged up Cemetery Ridge with 50 men.

On the other side of the same action, Heth, two of whose brigades were badly cut up and driven from the field in the first spontaneous contact, was equally inaccurate. Understandably reticent, he listed "60 or 70" of Archer's men as lost to "heavy masses" in his front and "overwhelming numbers" on both sides, and said: "The enemy had now been felt, and found to be in heavy force in and around Gettysburg." Although this statement is true, it gives no hint of the desperate action which he was unable to break off and which, in effect, brought on the Battle of Gettysburg.

Thus, the *Official Records* also must be cross-checked, for, however official, these papers were prepared by all too fallible humans. Yet these records are generally the most accurate available. They were prepared shortly after the battles and, except for small, isolated actions, the reports were cleared through the staffs of the commanding generals of the battles and had to agree both with what the staff knew had happened and with the reports of other generals in the battle.

The *Official Records,* however, contain nothing about Longstreet's behavior at Gettysburg or about the post-war controversy that illuminated his behavior on the second and third days. Almost the whole controversy, except where it was continued in book form, appeared in the *Southern Historical Society Papers.*

In Volume 23, pages 342–8, the Reverend J. William Jones traces the controversy from its beginning, when in Swinton's *Army of the Potomac,* published in 1866, Longstreet was quoted in derogation of Lee. Longstreet was not answered then. After Lee's death in 1870, he apparently permitted circulation of an 1863 letter to his uncle which claimed, Jones wrote, that "we lost Gettysburg because the Napoleonic genius of General James Longstreet could not overcome the obstinate stupidity of Robert Edward Lee."

The contents of this letter were referred to in the first public speeches made against Longstreet, first by Jubal Early and then by Pendleton, who after the war had returned to the rectorship of the church in Lexington where Lee worshipped in his last years. Longstreet's answer was to attack Lee more violently than before in various articles written for publication.

The Count of Paris had asked Jones to obtain answers from Confederate officers to some questions about "the causes of Lee's defeat at Gettysburg." More than a dozen officers answered the questions in considerable detail, and all listed Longstreet as prominent among the causes of defeat. Some devoted the bulk of their studies to a hostile treatment of Longstreet's failures, and a few revealed outrage and even hatred. Longstreet replied to his critics in the Philadelphia *Weekly Times,* and Jones reprinted the replies in the *SHSP.* Then Early, Wilcox, and Fitzhugh Lee replied to Longstreet with open vindictiveness, and the battle raged through twenty issues of the magazine, now in three bound volumes.

In Volume 4 of the *SHSP* are the papers of Early, Colonel Long, Fitzhugh Lee, Colonel William Allan, Alexander, Wilcox, Colonel Walter Taylor, Hood, and Heth. In Volume 5 are Longstreet's two papers from the *Weekly Times,* the bitter replies of Early and Fitzhugh Lee, and less personal studies by the Count of Paris, foreign observer with the Federal forces, and Major Scheibert, foreign observer with the

A Note on Sources and Selected Bibliography

Confederate forces. In Volume 6 are Wilcox's lengthy angry reply to Longstreet, and a vivid battle account by Colonel Oates, whose Alabama regiment in Law's brigade came the closest to capturing Little Round Top. Volume 7 contains a very full anti-Longstreet account by McLaws and a less controversial article by General B. D. Fry, who led Archer's brigade in the third day's assault.

Although passing references, usually in uncharitable language, were made to Longstreet's failure in other articles, the formal phase of the "Gettysburg Controversy" was concluded in Volume 7. Longstreet never accepted Jones's invitation to present his case in the magazine, but he continued to argue his side in print, and multiplied his self-contradictions in articles in *Battles and Leaders* and *Annals of the War*, and in his own book, *From Manassas to Appomattox*.

The controversy in the *SHSP* went far beyond an expression of former brother officers' bitter feelings about Longstreet and their contrasting devotion to Lee. The articles, as well as revealing much about the men writing them, provide a body of material on Gettysburg as Confederate officers view their lost opportunities and failures from the perspective of fourteen years. While, for reasons already stated, the individual accounts are not always accurate in detail, in bulk the articles are rich in information on the campaign as seen by general officers and staff officers of the commanding general and of other generals.

In other volumes accounts, uneven in quality, are left by privates, line officers, and field officers, to complete the presentation of the battle from all viewpoints. Without attempting to make an inclusive list of every item dealing with Gettysburg in the *SHSP*, I will list the articles that were most useful to me. As all of them relate to Gettysburg, I omit titles except where information regarding the battle was found in articles not specifically on that subject.

VOLUME 9. Pages 29–35: Major General Isaac Trimble.

VOLUME 10. Pages 170–4: Colonel William Allan, in a review of Doubleday's book on the battle, is concerned largely, in disproving Doubleday's high estimates, with arriving at an accurate figure for Confederate troops. His total—64,159 infantry and artillery as of the time the army moved northwest from the Rapidan—is the same as my composite of all records. (Volume 10 is, for some reason known to collectors, a rare item, though it contains nothing of special value except a dozen Gettysburg battle reports from the *Official Records*. Reports from *OR* are scattered through several volumes of *SHSP*.)

VOLUME 11. Pages 98–113: Alexander, the most literate of all South-

356

ern soldiers, mentions Gettysburg in "Confederate Artillery Service." Pages 320–7: G. W. Beale, in a running letter to his mother, gives a vivid description of Stuart's ride as seen by a young soldier. Pages 283–6: An editorial, with published letters, refutes Doubleday's representation of Armistead's dying words.

Doubleday wrote that Armistead, "dying in the effort to extend the area of slavery over the free states, . . . saw, with a clearer vision, that he had been engaged in an unholy cause, and said to one of our officers, who leaned over him, 'Tell Hancock that I have wronged him and wronged my country.'" W. H. Moore, a soldier with the 97th New York, was lying wounded beside Armistead when the Confederate general died, and he denied that Armistead had made the statement, which Doubleday claimed had reached him secondhand. Moore said that all who saw Armistead were impressed by his "intense, all-consuming desire for the Confederates to win the battle . . . [and] . . . to die like a soldier."

A number of Confederates wrote indignantly about Doubleday's statement and about the harshness of spirit that attributed to Armistead, a regular-army man of a regular-army family, a purpose "to extend the area of slavery over the free states." In his post-war references to "rebels" (he never called his former enemies anything else), Doubleday aroused lasting resentment by a vicious piety that ignored the avowed purpose of the war—preserving the Union. In praising the charge of a cavalry colonel, Doubleday said that he "saved the army and the country from the unutterable degradation of the establishment of slavery in the Northern states."

As Doubleday was not so big a fool as to believe any such outlandish statement, which charge would include Confederates who had once been his brother officers in the U.S. Army, his post-war hate-mongering against a beaten foe made him seem contemptible in contrast to the majority of old-army Federal officers, many of whom resumed former friendships with Southerners.

Volume 20. Pages 370–95: General James A. Walker, in a long sketch on Hill, includes the battle under the title "Oration on the Unveiling of A. P. Hill's Statue."

Volume 23. Pages 205–29: Colonel Charles Marshall. Pages 229–37: Captain Martin Hazlewood. Pages 253–59: Captain Leslie J. Perry, of the Federal War Office. Pages 238–47 and 348–53: Colonel John S. Mosby.

Volume 26. Pages 116–28: Trimble. Pages 12, 13: References to

A Note on Sources and Selected Bibliography

the battle in "War Diary" of Captain Robert Emory Park, 12th Alabama.

VOLUME 31. Pages 228–36: Captain Robert A. Bright—a vivid account of the third day by one of Pickett's staff officers.

VOLUME 32. Pages 33–8: Charles T. Loehr, of Kemper's brigade. Pages 183–9: Colonel Rawley Martin—a personal description by an officer who reached the stone wall with Armistead and fell, wounded, near his leader. Pages 189–95: Captain John Holmes Smith, who went up the hill with Kemper, was wounded near the wall, and made it back to the Confederate lines. The narratives of both Colonel Martin and Captain Smith are literate, detailed, informative, and among the best.

VOLUME 33. Pages 26–31: Colonel Winfield Peters. Pages 118–34: Judge James F. Crocker. Pages 135–60: Captain James Power Smith— an interesting and valuable record by Jackson's former staff officer who, en route to staff service with Ewell, rode with Lee. Smith, a thoughtful young man, was later a minister and secretary of the SHSP.

VOLUME 34. Pages 327–35: Colonel Joseph C. Mayo, of the 3rd Virginia—his account is rich in details in individuals in the charge, and he has a sharp eye for horses.

VOLUME 37. Pages 21–37: Colonel T. M. R. Talcott, sometime staff officer of Lee. Pages 74–143, Colonel David G. McIntosh—a full and reflective study by Hill's fine cannoneer, with an adverse though temperate criticism of Longstreet. Pages 144–51: the Reverend James E. Poindexter, formerly captain in the 38th Virginia, with Kemper. Pages 210–31: Dr. Randolph Harrison McKim, first lieutenant and A.A.G. with a fellow Marylander, Brigadier General Steuart, and later chaplain.

VOLUME 38. Pages 184–96: Mosby in private controversy with Talcott. Talcott counterattacks on pages 197–210. Pages 253–300: McKim, very full and scholarly, with a warm defense of Lee and a strong, though brief, indictment of Longstreet.

VOLUME 41. Pages 37–48: Talcott shifts his attack from Mosby to Longstreet, with a well-documented study of the third day.

VOLUME 44. Pages 233–40: Under the title "The Heth Papers" there are letters from Longstreet and Early which reveal the continuing controversy between former comrades, and a touching 1877 letter addressing Heth as "Dear Friend" from the Federal hero of Little Round Top, General G. K. Warren.

There are no military references beyond Volume 44; the last issues

A Note on Sources and Selected Bibliography

are devoted to reprints of the sessions of the Confederate Congress, which were not published in the newspapers of the time.

All through the first forty-four volumes are scattered little items of personal detail, such as a description of a Confederate soldier making his camp and a description of Lee's horse, Traveler, which have not been cited because they did not deal specifically with Gettysburg and the line has to be drawn somewhere in mentioning references. An illustrative exception is a newspaper editorial, reprinted in Volume 41, pages 82–7, on the death of Colonel Walter Taylor, Lee's personable young A.A.G., who wrote so informatively and modestly of his wartime association with the commanding general and is himself a source for any study of the Confederate army at Gettysburg.

Other comparative articles by participants appear in Volume 3 of *Battles and Leaders.* Representing the Confederates are two articles by Longstreet, a single article by Mosby and General Beverly H. Robertson, superb pieces by Law, Kershaw, and Alexander, another of the "replies" to Longstreet by Colonel William Allan, and a fine account on Lee's retreat by General John D. Imboden, the late-arriving leader of the cavalry raiders, who showed himself a far better writer than a soldier.

The Federals, while outnumbering the Confederates, are less loquacious. They offer a number of brief sketches by Major Halstead, H. M. M. Richards, General Gibbon, H. S. Melcher, General Grindlay, Captain Jones and General Greene, J. B. Smith, Captain Parsons, General Walker, John L. Collins, excerpts from official reports, a vivid account of the third-day assault by Brevet Lieutenant Colonel Rice, and fragments of private controversies between Major General Henry J. Hunt and General Francis A. Walker and between General Meade and General Sickles. Three long accounts, one of each day, by General Hunt, chief of artillery, are among the best available records of the battle. He was highly observant, with a fine eye for the detail of terrain, thoughtful, and generous.

Among other sources in collected volumes, the *Photographic History* contains some splendid scenes of the ground and the men, very helpful on physical details. *The Confederate Veteran*, published in Nashville, is somewhat similar to the *SHSP* but not so well done; it is larded with trivia, and the lack of an index would make a life's work of sorting through the literally countless short items. Mr. Ray D. Smith, of Chicago, is performing this herculean service, and generously provided me with nearly three hundred references to Pickett and Gettysburg; but no specific article was used, though the body of reading contributed to the general impression.

The *Dictionary of American Biography* and Clement Evan's twelve-volume *Confederate Military History* were used for biographical sketches of general officers. The publications do not always agree and errors can be pointed out in each, but they are far and away the best sources for statistical details of the lives of the leaders.

The maps used were a non-military map of the terrain prepared on the authority of Secretary of War Elihu Root, made under the direction of the Gettysburg National Park Commission, from an original survey made by General Warren in 1868 and 1869 (reprinted in the Atlas of *OR*); and the more famous maps of John D. Bachelder, published in 1876, which place the positions of the opposing forces on this terrain. These maps (32" by 47") were placed at my disposal through the courtesy of Dr. Frederick Tilberg, historian of the battlefield, who also gave unstintingly of his time and knowledge in walking the fields, explaining the ground from the large contour map in his office, and in suffering long harangues gallantly in person and in correspondence. Although many other maps were examined, I found nothing significant that was not included in these basic maps. Having studied the big maps, however, it is interesting to follow the progressive maps in the third volume of *Battles and Leaders* and in the second volume of Matthew Forney Steele's *American Campaigns*.

Concerning maps, a note must be entered. Presumptuous though it may seem, I do not feel that the position of Pickett's division during the cannonade is properly placed on the Bachelder map, and I have not followed the map in the movements of Kemper, Garnett, and Armistead into action. There are three reasons why I think the position of the troops is placed inaccurately on the open ground running north and south from the Spangler house and farm buildings.

(1) All of Pickett's officers and men who described the terrain where they endured the cannonade placed themselves either on a wooded ridge or in an open field extending south from the woods on Seminary Ridge. Garnett and Armistead were placed in the woods, and Kemper in the field. There were no woods in the swale. Specific witnesses are: with Armistead, Colonel Rawley Martin (cited in *SHSP*), Captain James Poindexter (pamphlet cited); with Kemper, Charles Loehr (cited in *SHSP* and book), David E. Johnston (book cited), Captain John Dooley (book cited); with Garnett, Colonel Eppa Hunton (book cited), Captain H. T. Owens (in Hoke, cited

with books, reprinted from *Weekly Times*), W. H. Swallow (also in Hoke, in reprint from *Times*); Major Walter Harrison, inspector general of the division (book cited); Wm. W. Chamberlaine, of Hill's corps (book cited). M. Jacobs (book cited), a native whose observations are not disputed, wrote that "the division was seen to emerge from the crest of Seminary Ridge. . . ." Mrs. Pickett (book cited) quotes the general: "Wilcox's brigade was lying about 200 yards in front of our line. . . . The troops which were to make the attack were screened from view by the ridge. . . ."

(2) All agreed that the men did not see the ground over which they were to attack until they moved out from the wooded ridge; if they had left Seminary Ridge to form near the Spangler farm buildings, they would have viewed the ground on their way down from the ridge.

(3) Alexander's batteries were posted along the Emmitsburg road east of the Spangler buildings. In that vicinity, where the road bent sharply to the northeast, the gun placements curved west from the road. Without question, Wilcox's brigade was placed in immediate support of the guns. But it would be contrary to both military logic and ordinary intelligence to place the troops composing the spearhead of an assault in close proximity to guns engaged in a tremendous artillery duel.

Only Wilcox, writing twelve years after the war in an article manifestly intended to derogate Longstreet, stated that Pickett did not come "out of any woods"; but his account is full of errors that reveal a hazy memory. To refute Wilcox, observant young Alexander specifically stated that he went *back* to find Pickett in the woods, where his troops were waiting. And Walter Harrison, who with Garnett and others was having lunch with Wilcox in the Spangler yard, wrote at "the signal, I told Gen. Garnett that we had better be getting *back* to our line. . . ."

A final point: Bachelder placed Archer's brigade on the wooded ridge, where all agree it formed. Colonel Fry, then commanding Archer's troops, and Harrison both placed Garnett immediately to the right of Fry and adjoining his troops. Garnett was so close to Fry that Armistead was forced to form in the rear—in the woods on the western side of Seminary Ridge where the ridge slopes southward. In support of them, Chamberlaine, with Hill, wrote: "I passed on down the line and soon came to Pickett's Division, also lying under the crest of the hill."

361

A Note on Sources and Selected Bibliography

As Garnett and several officers from his staff joined Wilcox for lunch in the Spangler yard, it can reasonably be assumed that over the years Wilcox confused the presence of Garnett with the nearness of his brigade. His faulty memory is indicated by his statement that Garnett was the center brigade, with Armistead on his left; actually, Armistead remained in reserve from the formation of the lines until the regiments converged at the stone wall. There was no center brigade.

Frequently, in reports, troops were mentioned as being on the field when only their commanders were present. Pickett personally arrived on the field late on the afternoon of July 2, and even the historians who prepared the markers on the Gettysburg battlefield (still there) give the 2nd as the time of his division's arrival. They came up between 7:00 and 9:00 on the morning of the 3rd.

In fine, it does not seem reasonable that all of Pickett's officers and men who recorded the event could be wrong as to the locale in which they formed and waited; it does not seem militarily reasonable that assaulting troops would wait where Bachelder placed them; and, in consulting participants, Bachelder did not interview any of the general officers with Pickett's division.

In placing Pickett's brigades, I am deeply indebted again to Dr. Tilberg for his generous efforts in reworking the ground personally and in the study he made toward properly locating the troops.

I do not suppose that this explanation for the deviation from Bachelder's long-accepted map will come under the head of what some academicians are pleased to call "original research." However, it should indicate the nature of the research necessary in effecting a resolution from the conflicting testimony on the Gettysburg campaign. David Donald recently wrote that nothing significant can be achieved by adding new oddments of data; the need is to interpret the existing material. At Gettysburg this includes the field, which cannot yield any new research material, but only a ground to walk over with maps and brood upon.

The only unpublished material actually *used* was the moving letters of General Pender to his wife, to which Dr. Freeman gave me access some years ago; a letter of Charles Pickett, younger brother and aide, a copy of which was given me by Major Pickett's grandson; and the letters recently deposited in the Virginia Historical Society from Pickett's staff officers. Although these letters are largely devoted to refuting the canard that Pickett huddled in the Spangler barn

362

(which, in any case, had been burned), they give very sharp impressions of the activity around General Pickett on the field.

In all truth, I did consult, as does everyone, other "unpublished material"—chiefly packets of old letters, which are as commonplace around Richmond as Confederate money—only to discover why it remains unpublished. A long letter to Dr. McKim recounted a wonderful first-day episode of some troopers of Lige White's cavalry with Ewell, but it simply did not fit into the plan of the chapter. I have in my possession the diary of a great-uncle who, a chemist, was transferred from Richmond's Company "F" with Jackson to the field medical corps and served at Gettysburg. But he was obsessed with working out a formula of meat juice to serve as a meat substitute for the wounded and ill, and, try as I might, I could not justify the inclusion of Uncle Ira's findings in a narrative of the invasion.

Also, as is probably true of everyone trying essentially to interpret, I have received impressions from readings and long since forgotten the volume in which some fragment, some passing reference, made a lasting impression. There is a small book of letters by a South Carolina army doctor from which I used one sentence: I borrowed the book from the State Library, had it around for several weeks, and can neither remember the title nor find it listed anywhere. In another way, a pamphlet published by Emory University on *The War Letters of Jeb Stuart to His Wife* was extremely illuminating on the man. Someone stole my copy, no other was obtainable, and I cannot remember whether or not any of the letters were written from Gettysburg.

Growing up in an era when Confederate veterans retained their full faculties and clear memories, I absorbed through listening innumerable impressions of army life and some of Gettysburg. At Gettysburg I had, in addition to the medical-corps great-uncle, three great-uncles in the infantry (one was killed there and one who was wounded later recovered), another great-uncle in the field-quartermaster corps, one grandfather in the Emmett Guard of Richmond, which became incorporated in the 1st Virginia Regiment of Kemper's brigade, and the other grandfather in Cabell's artillery battalion, the most advanced guns on the third day; wounded there, he recovered enough to serve again, but never fully regained his health.

I have never used any of their anecdotes, having been taught to distrust the lies of "old veterans," but two of their tales I have seen authenticated in print. Uncle Robert, the quartermaster, described the fighting with the wagoneers when, on the retreat, the wagons of the wounded were attacked by Union cavalry at the Williamsport crossing; they formed the wagons as pioneers did in Indian fights and fired between the spokes. It turned out that his account of a neglected action of minor heroics was completely true.

Uncle Walter, asked about Pickett at Gettysburg, said the only time he personally saw the general in action was on the retreat toward Appomattox, when Pickett was bent over his horse's neck and hurrying to the rear. At the time I suspected that Uncle Walter, a banker and a realist, was enjoying reversing the romantics on which Southern children were raised. Other witnesses to Pickett's flight, after his heart was no longer in the fighting, have described it in print.

Because of these confirmations I trust the spirit and detail of the impressions made on me by these long-dead Confederate gentlemen, and, though I can not cite them as authorities, I wish to make my acknowledgments to them for their contributions to this book.

I also wish to express my appreciation to Mr. Samuel Neal, of Chatham, Virginia, for the gleanings from his great personal library on the Army of Northern Virginia, for his knowledgeable support in examining the battlefield, and for his continuing interest in puzzling over obscure points and new findings; to Dr. Louis Rubin, of Hollins College, Roanoke, Virginia, for lengthy consultations on Longstreet and on the second day's fighting, and for invaluable suggestions on the presentation of both; to Mr. Richard Harwell, now of Chicago, Illinois, for long consultations on the personnel of the army and for advice deriving from his long scholarship on the Confederacy; to Mr. Monroe Cockrell, of Evanston, Illinois, for tireless and generous consultation by correspondence, and for particularly painstaking work in helping to locate the precise positions of Pickett's brigades; to the Reverend Joseph Heistand, Dr. Beverly Randolph Wellford, and Mr. McDonald Wellford, all of Richmond, redoubtable field companions of many campaigns in the "reconnaissance car" of Mr. Wellford; and for consultation on medical matters, particularly Lee's health at Gettysburg, Dr. Harry Warthen, Dr. David Markham, Dr. DuPont Guerry III, and Dr. St. George Tucker, all of Richmond.

I also wish to thank Mr. Stuart Rose, ex-U.S. Cavalry, of Cheyney, Pennsylvania, for advice given across the years on the use of firepower, on the study of terrain, and on the proper function of mounted troops—specifically as relating to Jeb Stuart; and posthumously to the late Colonel John W. Thomason, Jr., for advice concerning Jeb Stuart given long ago, and for his stress on (what comes somewhat portentously under the heading of "logistics") the vital importance of the miles of cumbersome wagon trains in considering any military movement—especially as relating to the strategy Longstreet allegedly offered on the third day.

For the list of general books consulted, some of which are extremely hard to come by, I am deeply indebted, as in all my work, to the staff of the Virginia Historical Society, and particularly to its director, Mr. John Jennings; to the staff of the Virginia State Library, and particularly to Mr. Milton C. Russell, Miss Eudora Elizabeth Thomas, Mrs. Pinkney Smith, Mrs. Lewis Causbey; to Miss India Thomas, the regent of the Confederate Museum; and to her assistant, Miss Eleanor Brockenbrough. The Confederate Museum, in the former White House of the Confederacy, contains unpublished material that would make volumes. In some of the Heth papers there, I found an item of significant information in a letter by Colonel Robert C. Mayo, 47th Virginia, of Brockenbrough's brigade, a copy of which was generously supplied me by the thoughtfulness of Miss Eleanor Brockenbrough.

In listing these books, the same process has been followed as in culling the *SHSP*, with the difference that some books must be listed which do not specifically deal with Gettysburg. These add to an understanding of the army, the soldiers and leaders, in that period. General books on the war which make no direct contribution to an understanding of Lee's army or Gettysburg have been omitted.

In reviewing books on the war, I have too often seen bibliographies swelled to impressive lengths by a listing of "authorities consulted" when I knew that certain of the books could not possibly have contributed anything specifically on the subject. If a bibliography is intended to serve as a guide to readers interested in the subject, in all fairness such books should be listed as "Consulted Without Profit," and this seems a pointless device for all concerned.

For those who might wish to check the background from which the specific material was drawn, a listing of general books consulted appears in *The Land They Fought For*, by Clifford Dowdey (Garden City, 1955). The background for references to the Confederacy in general, to President Davis, War Secretary Seddon, the war office, and Davis's relations with Lee is in *The Land They Fought For* and in *Experiment in Rebellion*, by Clifford Dowdey (Garden City, 1946). The recently published diary of the Head of the Bureau of War, Robert Garlick Hill Kean, edited by Edward Younger, while containing nothing at all about the Gettysburg campaign, is extremely

A Note on Sources and Selected Bibliography

valuable for the operation of the Confederate war office and appraisals of Jefferson Davis based on firsthand impressions.

The listing of other books will follow the usual alphabetical order after mentioning first, in order of its importance, the work of Dr. Freeman. For the organization and presentation of the awesome quantity of material which he distilled, for the helpful guide of his footnotes and bibliographies, his *R. E. Lee* and *Lee's Lieutenants* are the fountainhead for all students of the Army of Northern Virginia. While it is difficult to lift his chapters on the Gettysburg campaign out of context, there is a straight sequence in the third volume of *R. E. Lee*, pages 1–161, and in the third volume of *Lee's Lieutenants*, pages 20–189, which also contains an appendix by Dr. Tilberg and Dr. Walter Coleman, superintendent of Gettysburg National Military Park, pages 775–6, and an appendix prepared with the assistance of Dr. Tilberg, Dr. Coleman, and the Messrs. Runyon Colie and Harry W. Howerter, Jr., pages 757–60. In Volume 2, pages 683–714, there is a study of the reorganization of the army in preparation for the invasion.

Alexander, E. P.: *Military Memoirs of a Confederate* (New York, 1907). Nothing better, in general and for the third day.

Annals of the War. Written by Leading Participants North and South (Philadelphia, 1879). Worth the culling.

Beale, G. W.: *A Lieutenant of Cavalry in Lee's Army* (Boston, 1918). Personalized reminiscences by Colonel R. L. T. Beale's son.

Beale, R. L. T.: *History of 9th Virginia Cavalry* (Richmond, 1899). A standard source and collector's item, by the colonel of the regiment, with fine details of Stuart's ride.

Blackford, Susan Leigh, compiler: *Letters from Lee's Army* (New York, 1947).

Blackford, William Willis: *War Years with Jeb Stuart* (New York, 1945). Valuable episodes and impressions of Stuart's ride by a staff officer.

Borcke, Heros von: *Memoirs of the Confederate War for Independence.* 2 vols. New edition (New York, 1938). Stuart's Prussian volunteer aide, the herculean baron, had been wounded out before Gettysburg, but his ebullient, if highly colored, description is indispensable for an understanding of Lee's mounted force, and very pleasant reading.

A Note on Sources and Selected Bibliography

Bushong, Millard Kessler: *Old Jube: A Biography of General Jubal A. Early* (Boyce, Va., 1955).

Caldwell, J. F. F.: *The History of a Brigade of South Carolinians.* New edition (Marietta, Ga., 1951). One of the best books on life in Lee's army, with a detailed description of the first day's fighting at Gettysburg with Pender.

Casler, John O.: *Four Years in the Stonewall Brigade.* New edition (Marietta, Ga., 1951). One of the most realistic revelations of soldiers' life in the Army of Northern Virginia. With Ewell at Gettysburg.

Catton, Bruce.: *Glory Road* (Garden City, 1952). A graphic and stirring narrative of the three days as seen from the Federal viewpoint. Mr. Catton tends to accept Union estimates of Confederate forces.

Chamberlaine, William W.: *Memoirs of the Civil War* (Washington, 1912). One of the more moving accounts of the third day by a highly intelligent soldier in Hill's corps.

Chamberlayne, C. G., editor: *Ham Chamberlayne—Virginian* (Richmond, 1933). Extremely illuminating letters by a young Richmond lawyer who served as lieutenant with Hill's corps artillery. Chamberlayne and four of his men were captured outside Chambersburg while foraging for horses for their battery, but his letters are valuable, as well as interesting, for a picture of Lee's artillery and for details of the campaign up to Chambersburg.

Cockrell, Monroe F.: *Where Was Pickett at Gettysburg?* Privately printed pamphlet placed at my disposal by the courtesy of Mr. Cockrell. Cites more sources for its length probably than any other publication on the battle, and all of them specifically to the point.

——, editor: *Gunner with Stonewall: Reminiscences of William Thomas Poague* (Jackson, Tenn., 1957). The first publication of the informative memoirs of the good gunner who commanded a battalion of A. P. Hill's artillery on Seminary Ridge.

Cooke, John Esten: *Robert E. Lee* (New York, 1871). This cousin of Jeb Stuart's wife, an ante-bellum professional writer, had a novelist's eye for detail, and he is one of the two sources for A. P. Hill's appearance of illness on the first day (Fremantle is the other).

——: *Wearing of the Gray* (New York, 1867).

A Note on Sources and Selected Bibliography

Daniel, Frederick S.: *Richmond Howitzers during the War* (Richmond, 1891).

Dawson, Francis W.: *Reminiscences of Confederate Service* (Charleston, 1882). A frank appraisal by a British volunteer staff officer with Longstreet at Gettysburg.

Dickert, D. Augustus: *History of Kershaw's Brigade* (Newberry, S.C., 1899). Another of the standard brigade histories.

Douglas, Henry Kyd: *I Rode with Stonewall* (Chapel Hill, 1940). Personalized details by Jackson's former staff officer, who served with Major General Edward "Allegheny" Johnson in the Gettysburg campaign and was one of the witnesses of Ewell's breakdown in the Blocher house arbor on the first day.

Dunaway, Wayland F.: *Reminiscences of a Rebel* (New York, 1913). A captain with the brigade, Brockenbrough-Mayo, of Heth's division that broke on the left flank during the third-day assault. He admits it tacitly, without lingering on the details.

Durkin, Joseph T., S. J., editor: *John Dooley, Confederate Soldier* (Georgetown University Press, 1945). Brief, graphic, though not wholly accurate personal impressions of a captain with Kemper.

Early, Jubal A.: *Autobiographical Sketch and Narrative of the War between the States* (Philadelphia, 1912). Largely a compilation of his articles in *SHSP*.

Eckenrode, H. J., and Conrad, Bryan: *James Longstreet: Lee's Warhorse* (Chapel Hill, 1936).

Eggleston, George Cary: *A Rebel's Recollections* (New York, 1875). With nothing on Gettysburg or any battle, this curiously neglected book by one of the best and most engaging of Southern writers on the war is invaluable for the impression it gives of the formation, personnel, and character of Lee's army. The sketches of Stuart and Ewell are particularly sharp.

Fletcher, W. A.: *A Rebel Private, Front and Rear*. New edition (Austin, Texas, 1954). Another realistic account of soldier life, by a member of Hood's Texas Brigade. Contains a good description of the Gettysburg campaign, particularly the second day.

Fremantle, Arthur James Lyon: *The Fremantle Diary*. New edition, edited by Walter Lord (Boston, 1954). This much quoted standard by a

A Note on Sources and Selected Bibliography

visiting colonel of Her Majesty's Coldstream Guards is extremely valuable for observations of personalities in the campaign, particularly of Longstreet, with whose entourage the sharp-eyed Britisher rode.

Gordon, John B.: *Reminiscences of the Civil War* (New York, 1903). Not much on Gettysburg, but a helpful book.

Hamlin, Percy Gatling: *Old Baldhead: General R. S. Ewell* (Strasburg, Va., 1940). The fullest portrait of the strange personality, done tenderly, with fine episodes.

Harrison, Walter: *Pickett's Men* (New York, 1870). This division history by its inspector general contains useful details of the personnel and of the campaign, particularly helpful on the forming of the troops and the wait before the charge.

Hay, Thomas Robson, *see* Sanger, Donald Bridgman.

Henderson, George F. R.: *Stonewall Jackson and the American Civil War*. American one-volume edition (New York, 1936). The standard work on the lost leader whose absence at Gettysburg was a determining factor in the campaign; valuable for Colonel Henderson's study of warfare and the manner in which it was waged by the Confederate forces during Jackson's brief span of war life. Probably more than any other single book it shows by implication the hopelessness of Lee's attempt to apply the techniques he had used with Jackson.

Hoke, Jacob: *The Great Invasion of 1863* (Dayton, Ohio, 1877). Graphic impressions of the Confederate army by a citizen of Chambersburg. Its violently anti-Confederate bias might be partially explained by the merchant's losses to Ewell's confiscations.

Hood, John B.: *Advance and Retreat* (New Orleans, 1880). Its brief account of Gettysburg is a source for Longstreet's actions on the Confederate right on the second day, especially for Longstreet's insistence on a literal obedience of Lee's order to attack across the Emmitsburg road. (Hood is corroborated in detail by Law in *Battles and Leaders*, III, 321–2.)

Howard, McHenry: *Recollections of a Maryland Soldier and Staff Officer* (Baltimore, 1914). An old reliable as a source on the Second Corps.

Hunton, Eppa: *Autobiography* (Privately printed, Richmond, 1933). A colonel in and later commander of Garnett's brigade who was wounded in the charge. Contains an informative account of the brigade's forma-

369

tion by a thoughtful observer who, with dispassionate flatness, charges Longstreet with responsibility for the failure of the second and third days.

Irby, Richard: *Historical Sketch of the Nottoway Grays.* A soldier who went up the hill with Garnett.

Jacobs, M.: *Notes on the Invasion . . . and Battle of Gettysburg* (Philadelphia, 1863). Another anti-Rebel account by a Pennsylvania native with well-developed powers of observation.

Johnston, David E.: *The Story of a Confederate Boy in the Civil War* (Portland, Ore., 1914). Among the best accounts of Pickett's men, by a young sergeant major with Kemper who, severely wounded during the cannonade, lived to become a judge.

Jones, Rev. J. William: *Personal Reminiscences of General Robert E. Lee* (New York, 1875). This old-fashioned anecdotal collection was written by the *SHSP* secretary, a personal friend of Lee and intimately associated with him when Jones was chaplain at Washington College and the general was its president. With nothing specific on Gettysburg, the book is useful for its firsthand impressions of Lee and for revealing the attitude of his contemporaries to him.

Lee, Robert E., Jr.: *Recollections and Letters of General Robert E. Lee* (New York, 1905). Quoted.

(Lewis, John H.: *Recollections from 1860–1865.* This is said to be an accurate account of the charge by a lieutenant with Armistead, but I was unable to obtain a copy of the book.)

Loehr, Charles T.: *History of the 1st Virginia Regiment* (Richmond, 1884). A standard for Kemper's brigade. Brief but graphic on the third day.

Macon, T. J.: *Reminiscences of the 1st Company of Richmond Howitzers* (Richmond).

Marshall, Charles: *An Aide-de-Camp of Lee. . . .* Edited by Major General Sir Frederick Maurice (Boston, 1927). A thoughtful book, very helpful on Lee and, though incomplete, on Gettysburg.

McCarthy, Carlton A.: *Detailed Minutiae of Soldier Life in the Army of Northern Virginia* (Richmond, 1882). Nothing specific on Gettysburg but indispensable for physical details of life in Lee's army.

A Note on Sources and Selected Bibliography

McClellan, H. B.: *Life and Campaigns of Major-General J. E. B. Stuart* (Richmond, 1885). To Stuart what Henderson is to Jackson.

McKim, Randolph H.: *A Soldier's Recollections* (New York, 1910). The aforementioned Dr. McKim is, in his book, a source on the Confederate action at Culp's Hill.

Meade, George Gordon: *Life and Letters of George Gordon Meade* (New York, 1913). Indispensable. As generous in spirit as he was crotchety in manner.

Moore, Edward A.: *The Story of a Cannoneer under Stonewall Jackson* (New York, 1907). Another private's-eye view, and a good one, by a gunner with the Rockbridge Battery. With Ewell at Gettysburg.

Morgan, W. H.: *Personal Reminiscences of the War, 1861–65* (Lynchburg, Va., 1911). With Kemper at Gettysburg.

Oates, William C.: *The War between the Union and the Confederacy* (New York and Washington, 1905). Among the best and fullest accounts of the second day, and a thoughtful survey of the entire action on the Confederate right. Colonel Oates was one of the few to place the blame on Longstreet specifically for the nature of his failures in the battle. Not diverted by the generalities in the controversy, Oates, on page 223, develops his charge that Longstreet "was responsible and at fault for the negligent and bungling manner in which it [the attack] was done." With Law, Hood, Kershaw (all cited), and to some extent McLaws, Oates served as the basis for the stress, in the "Lee's Warhorse" chapter, on Longstreet's specific failures in command as opposed to the more familiar pros and cons over his alleged strategy.

Owen, William M.: *In Camp and Battle with the Washington Artillery of New Orleans* (Boston, 1885). An artillery standard by a member of the battalion that fired the signal gun for the charge.

Pickett, George E.: *Soldier of the South . . . Pickett's War Letters to His Wife* (Boston, 1928). These letters have evidently been doctored for publication. It can only be assumed that Mrs. Pickett included in her version of her husband's letters material which he had told her, as some of the questionable passages (and the spurious Lincoln letter of 1842) equate with the known facts.

Pickett, LaSalle Corbell: *Pickett and His Men* (Atlanta, 1899). Highly sentimentalized narrative by the widow, who typified the Victorian age in romanticizing her "hero." To my knowledge, there is no biography of Pickett and very scant material. The numerous members of the present Pickett clan are curiously un-Virginian in their apathy toward antiquarianism, and no effort has been made to organize the material of the prominent nineteenth-century Pickett family in relation to its member who is best known outside the state. However, I wish to acknowledge that I have received every personal courtesy from Mr. George E. Pickett III, of Winston-Salem, North Carolina, and Mr. Charles Pickett, of Fairfax, Virginia, the grandson of Major Pickett, the general's aide and younger brother.

As for his contemporaries, it must be stressed that Pickett was to them only another division commander, though a colorful personality. Gettysburg did not loom as a decisive battle to Confederates until years after the war when the states of the Union made so much of it. At the time, the moment by which history knows Pickett was, in a general failure, a personal defeat the first time he took his division into action. Although it is doubtful that any major general in either army could have done better in the conditions at Gettysburg, Pickett's post-Gettysburg war record was indifferent, he made some articulate enemies, and the more the historical view tended to glorify him as the leader of "Pickett's charge," the more some ex-Confederates tended to derogate his part in the third day.

McLaws was correct, if embittered, in describing the assault as "what is known as Pickett's charge." Several officers of the division were careful in post-war writings to refer to their part as "the charge of Pickett's division."

Yet, his men, uninvolved in the sharing of historic glory, felt very sentimentally about him, and, with all the superior leadership the division enjoyed at brigade and regimental level, no division could have performed with such efficiency and morale without capable leadership at the top. Trying to strike a balance would be another case of factualists fighting a losing battle against legend. Nothing will stop people from calling the third-day assault "Pickett's charge." Even the battlefield authorities are baffled over a proper designation to replace the inaccurate title.

A sound biographer would be working against an American myth, and no more welcomed than the biographer who, by proving the egotistical blundering of Custer at Little Big Horn, made lies of the memories of a generation whose lasting impressions were formed by the lithograph of "Custer's Last Stand" which decorated the walls of turn-of-the-century saloons, ice-cream parlors, and general stores.

372

A Note on Sources and Selected Bibliography

Poindexter, James E.: *Address on the Life and Services of General Lewis A. Armistead* (Richmond). The best of the slim material on this greatly loved soldier.

Polley, J. B.: *Hood's Texas Brigade* (New York, 1908). Including first-hand accounts of the Gettysburg campaign by other members of Hood's Texas (Robertson's) Brigade, this book contains the most detailed and informative material on Devil's Den and Little Round Top.

Ross, Fitzgerald: *A Visit to the Camps and Cities of the Confederate States* (Edinburgh and London, 1865). Contains a chapter on Gettysburg sidelights by (despite his name) an Austrian military observer attached to Longstreet's entourage.

Sanger, Donald Bridgman: *James Longstreet: Soldier,* and Hay, Thomas Robson: *James Longstreet: Politician, Office-holder, Writer* (Baton Rouge, 1952).

Sorrel, Moxley G.: *Recollections of a Confederate Staff Officer* (New York, 1917). Excellent narrative by Longstreet's chief of staff and very valuable on Gettysburg.

Stewart, William H.: *A Pair of Blankets* (New York, 1911). Some useful observations on Gettysburg by a lieutenant colonel of Mahone's brigade of Anderson's division.

Tankersley, Allen P.: *John B. Gordon* (Atlanta, 1955). Little on Gettysburg but several illuminating personal details about the impressive Georgian during the battle.

Taylor, Walter H.: *Four Years with General Lee* (New York, 1877). Intelligent and informative on personal observations and on general appraisals during the whole war and at Gettysburg.

Thomas, Henry W.: *History of the Doles-Cooke Brigade* (Atlanta, 1903). Fine account of Rodes's division in the first day's fighting.

Thomason, John W., Jr.: *Jeb Stuart* (New York, 1930). This colorfully written biography contains what amounts to an apologia of Stuart in the Gettysburg campaign. The cavalry leader was a hero to the late marine colonel.

Wellman, Manly Wade: *Rebel Boast* (New York, 1956). A narrative based upon and using the war letters of a group of North Carolinians who fought with Junius Daniel in Rodes's division on the first and third days. Informative detail of march and fighting, and of Confederate personnel of that period.

A Note on Sources and Selected Bibliography

West, John C.: *A Texan in Search of a Fight* (Waco, Texas, 1901). More on Hood's (Robertson's) brigade on the second day. The brigade was still called "Hood's" after the Texan by adoption was an army general in the west—indeed, after he was in his grave.

Wood, William Nathaniel: *Reminiscences of Big I.* New edition edited by Bell Irvin Wiley (Jackson, Tenn., 1956). This sprightly narrative in the unheroic tradition, by an unsentimental lieutenant in Garnett's brigade, was so long a collector's item that its contributions have been somewhat overrated. A few pages are valuable for placing Pickett's men and describing their sensations in the hours immediately preceding the attack. Revealing sidelights on the army and the attitude of the men are scattered throughout.

Worsham, John F.: *One of Jackson's Foot Cavalry* (New York, 1912). On the invasion, depleted Company "F" halted at Winchester to guard prisoners taken by Ewell and did not get to Gettysburg. Despite its omission of the battle, Private Worsham's book is one of the really indispensables in a study of Lee's army, and is especially interesting for its depiction of the effects of war on a *corps d'élite* from Richmond.

Appendix

Organization of the Army of Northern Virginia as of the Gettysburg campaign, after the chart compiled by General Jubal A. Early. The dates are the dates of rank.

FIRST CORPS
Lieut. Gen. James Longstreet (Oct. 9, 1862)

McLAWS' DIVISION
Maj. Gen. Lafayette McLaws (May 23, 1862)

Kershaw's Brigade:
Brig. Gen. Joseph B. Kershaw
(Feb. 13, 1862)
2nd South Carolina Regiment
3rd South Carolina Regiment
8th South Carolina Regiment
15th South Carolina Regiment
3rd South Carolina Battalion

Semmes' Brigade:
Brig. Gen. Paul J. Semmes*
(March 11, 1862)
10th Georgia Regiment
50th Georgia Regiment
51st Georgia Regiment
53rd Georgia Regiment
*Mortally wounded July 2, 1863.

Barksdale's Brigade:
Brig. Gen. William Barksdale*
(Aug. 12, 1862)
13th Mississippi Regiment
17th Mississippi Regiment
18th Mississippi Regiment
21st Mississippi Regiment
*Killed July 2, 1863.

Wofford's Brigade:
Brig. Gen. W. T. Wofford
(Jan. 17, 1862)
16th Georgia Regiment
18th Georgia Regiment
24th Georgia Regiment
Phillips's Georgia Legion
Cobb's Georgia Legion

DIVISION ARTILLERY BATTALION
Col. Henry C. Cabell: four batteries

PICKETT'S DIVISION
Maj. Gen. George E. Pickett (Oct. 10, 1862)

Garnett's Brigade:
Brig. Gen. Richard B. Garnett*
(Nov. 14, 1861)
8th Virginia Regiment
*Killed July 3, 1863.

Armistead's Brigade:
Brig. Gen. Lewis A. Armistead*
(April 1, 1862)
9th Virginia Regiment
*Mortally wounded July 3, 1863.

375

Appendix

18th Virginia Regiment
19th Virginia Regiment
28th Virginia Regiment
56th Virginia Regiment

Kemper's Brigade:
Brig. Gen. James L. Kemper*
(June 2, 1862)
1st Virginia Regiment
3rd Virginia Regiment
7th Virginia Regiment
11th Virginia Regiment
24th Virginia Regiment
*Wounded out of active duty July
    3, 1863.

Jenkins's Brigade:*
Brig. Gen. Micah Jenkins
(July 22, 1862)
1st South Carolina Regiment
5th South Carolina Regiment
6th South Carolina Regiment
2nd South Carolina Rifles
Hampton's Legion
*Not at Gettysburg; retained by
    order of President Davis in
    North Carolina. Never rejoined
    division: was transferred to
    Hood's Division.

14th Virginia Regiment
38th Virginia Regiment
53rd Virginia Regiment
57th Virginia Regiment

Corse's Brigade:*
Brig. Gen. M. D. Corse
(Nov. 1, 1862)
15th Virginia Regiment
17th Virginia Regiment
29th Virginia Regiment
30th Virginia Regiment
32nd Virginia Regiment
*Not at Gettysburg; retained by or-
    der of President Davis at Han-
    over Junction.

DIVISION ARTILLERY BATTALION
Major James Dearing: four batteries

HOOD'S DIVISION
Maj. Gen. John B. Hood (Oct. 10, 1862)

(Hood was wounded July 2, 1863. On recovery, went with division to campaign with the Army of Tennessee; later corps commander in the West, then
army commander. Never returned to the Army of Northern Virginia.)

Law's Brigade:
Brig. Gen. Evander M. Law
(Oct. 3, 1862)
4th Alabama Regiment
15th Alabama Regiment
44th Alabama Regiment
47th Alabama Regiment
48th Alabama Regiment

Robertson's (formerly Hood's)
    Brigade:
Brig. Gen. J. B. Robertson*
(Nov. 1, 1862)
1st Texas Regiment
4th Texas Regiment
5th Texas Regiment
3rd Arkansas
*Wounded July 2, 1863.

376

Anderson's Brigade:
Brig. Gen. G. T. Anderson
(Nov. 1, 1862)
7th Georgia Regiment
8th Georgia Regiment
9th Georgia Regiment
59th Georgia Regiment
11th Georgia Battalion

Benning's Brigade:
Brig. Gen. H. L. Benning
(Jan. 17, 1862)
2nd Georgia Regiment
15th Georgia Regiment
17th Georgia Regiment
20th Georgia Regiment

DIVISION ARTILLERY BATTALION
Maj. M. W. Henry: four batteries

CORPS RESERVE ARTILLERY
Col. J. B. Walton, corps artillery commander

(Although he was officially in command at Gettysburg, the guns were in fact commanded by Col. E. Porter Alexander)

Alexander's Battalion: six batteries

WASHINGTON ARTILLERY BATTALION
Maj. B. F. Eshleman: four batteries

With rare and temporary exceptions, four guns were the standard number for Confederate batteries; six guns were the standard number for Union batteries.

SECOND CORPS
Lieut. Gen. Richard S. Ewell (May 22, 1863)

EARLY'S DIVISION (formerly Ewell's)
Maj. Gen. Jubal A. Early (Jan. 17, 1863)

Hays's Brigade:
Brig. Gen. Harry T. Hays
(July 25, 1862)
5th Louisiana Regiment
6th Louisiana Regiment
7th Louisiana Regiment
8th Louisiana Regiment
9th Louisiana Regiment

Hoke's Brigade:
Brig. Gen. Robert F. Hoke°
(Jan. 17, 1863)
6th North Carolina Regiment
21st North Carolina Regiment
54th North Carolina Regiment°°
57th North Carolina Regiment
1st North Carolina Battalion
°Out of action with a wound. Brigade commanded at Gettysburg by Col. Isaac Avery, who was mortally wounded July 2, 1863.
°°Not at Gettysburg: detached at Winchester to guard prisoners and captured supplies.

377

Appendix

Smith's Brigade:
Brig. Gen. William ("Extra Billy")
Smith* (Jan. 31, 1863)
13th Virginia Regiment**
31st Virginia Regiment
49th Virginia Regiment
52nd Virginia Regiment
58th Virginia Regiment**
*Replaced after Gettysburg by
Brig. Gen. John Pegram.
**Not at Gettysburg: detached at
Winchester.

Gordon's Brigade:
Brig. Gen. John B. Gordon
(May 7, 1863)
13th Georgia Regiment
26th Georgia Regiment
31st Georgia Regiment
38th Georgia Regiment
60th Georgia Regiment
61st Georgia Regiment

Division Artillery Battalion
Lieut. Col. H. P. Jones: four batteries

Johnson's Division

(originally formed by Stonewall Jackson as an all-Virginia unit, the division suffered high mortality in its commanders, and Maj. Gen. Trimble, designated by Lee to assume command, was absent with illness when the army was reorganized)

Maj. Gen. Edward Johnson (Feb. 23, 1863)

Stonewall Brigade (the official
name of Jackson's first command):
Brig. Gen. J. A. Walker
(May 15, 1863)
2nd Virginia Regiment
4th Virginia Regiment
5th Virginia Regiment
27th Virginia Regiment
33rd Virginia Regiment*
*Parts of this unit were left at
Winchester.

Jones's Brigade:
Brig. Gen. J. M. Jones
(May 15, 1863)
21st Virginia Regiment
25th Virginia Regiment
42nd Virginia Regiment
44th Virginia Regiment
48th Virginia Regiment
50th Virginia Regiment

Steuart's Brigade:
Brig. Gen. George H. Steuart
(March 6, 1862)
10th Virginia Regiment
23rd Virginia Regiment
37th Virginia Regiment
1st North Carolina Regiment
3rd North Carolina Regiment
1st Maryland Battalion

Nichols's Brigade:
Brig. Gen. Francis T. Nichols*
(Oct. 14, 1862)
1st Louisiana Regiment
2nd Louisiana Regiment
10th Louisiana Regiment
14th Louisiana Regiment
15th Louisiana Regiment
*Not at Gettysburg; brigade commanded by Col. L. A. Stafford,
later its brigadier.

378

Appendix

DIVISION ARTILLERY BATTALION

Maj. J. W. Latimer (*mortally wounded July 2, 1863*): *four batteries*

RODES'S DIVISION (formerly D. H. HILL'S)

Maj. Gen. Robert E. Rodes (*May 2, 1863:* his promotion was antedated as of the Battle of Chancellorsville, when he commanded as a brigadier)

Daniel's Brigade:
Brig. Gen. Junius Daniel
(Sept. 1, 1862)
32nd North Carolina Regiment
43rd North Carolina Regiment
45th North Carolina Regiment
53rd North Carolina Regiment
2nd North Carolina Battalion

Doles's Brigade:
Brig. Gen. George G. Doles
(Nov. 1, 1862)
4th Georgia Regiment
12th Georgia Regiment
21st Georgia Regiment
44th Georgia Regiment

Ramseur's Brigade:
Brig. Gen. S. D. Ramseur
(Nov. 1, 1862)
2nd North Carolina Regiment
4th North Carolina Regiment
14th North Carolina Regiment
30th North Carolina Regiment

Iverson's Brigade:
Brig. Gen. Alfred Iverson*
(Nov. 1, 1862)
5th North Carolina Regiment
12th North Carolina Regiment
20th North Carolina Regiment
23rd North Carolina Regiment
*Replaced after Gettysburg by R. D. Johnson, who was later promoted to brigadier.

Rodes's Brigade:
Col. E. A. O'Neal*
3rd Alabama Regiment
5th Alabama Regiment
6th Alabama Regiment
12th Alabama Regiment
26th Alabama Regiment
*Replaced after Gettysburg by Colonel Cullen A. Battle, later promoted to brigadier.

DIVISION ARTILLERY BATTALION
Lieut. Col. Thomas H. Carter: four batteries

CORPS ARTILLERY RESERVE

Col. Stapleton Crutchfield (out with an amputated leg; at Gettysburg the corps artillery command devolved temporarily upon J. Thompson Brown):

Thompson's Battalion: five batteries

Nelson's Battalion: three batteries

Appendix

THIRD CORPS
Lieut. Gen. Ambrose Powell Hill (May 24, 1863)

HETH'S DIVISION

(newly created, containing two brigades from A. P. Hill's old "Light Division")

Maj. Gen. Henry Heth (May 24, 1863)

(wounded July 1, 1863, did not command during the remainder of the battle)

Pettigrew's Brigade:
Brig. Gen. Johnston Pettigrew*
(Feb. 26, 1862)
11th North Carolina Regiment
26th North Carolina Regiment
42nd North Carolina Regiment
47th North Carolina Regiment
52nd North Carolina Regiment
*Assumed command on Heth's incapacity; killed on the retreat to Virginia.

Davis's Brigade:
Brig. Gen. Joseph R. Davis
(Sept. 15, 1862)
2nd Mississippi Regiment
11th Mississippi Regiment
26th Mississippi Regiment
42nd Mississippi Regiment
50th North Carolina Regiment
1st Confederate Battalion*
*According to Gen. Early's chart, but nowhere else listed; probably not at Gettysburg.

Cooke's Brigade: *
Brig. Gen. John R. Cooke
(Nov. 1, 1862)
15th North Carolina Regiment
27th North Carolina Regiment
46th North Carolina Regiment
48th North Carolina Regiment
*Not at Gettysburg; retained south of Richmond by order of President Davis.

Archer's Brigade:
Brig. Gen. James J. Archer*
(June 3, 1862)
1st Tennessee Regiment
7th Tennessee Regiment
14th Tennessee Regiment
13th Alabama Regiment
5th Alabama Battalion
*Captured July 1, 1863; died after release from prison. Succeeded by Col. B. D. Fry, who was wounded July 3, 1863.

Heth's Brigade:
(actually the brigade of Brig. Gen. Charles W. Field, long out with wounds):
Col. J. M. Brockenbrough*
46th Virginia Regiment
47th Virginia Regiment
55th Virginia Regiment
22nd Virginia Battalion
*There is evidence that he was succeeded on the third day by Col. Robert Mayo of the 47th Virginia; after Gettysburg Col. H. H. Walker was promoted to brigadier and assumed command.

Appendix

DIVISION ARTILLERY BATTALION
Lieut. Col. John J. Garnett: four batteries

PENDER'S DIVISION
(four brigades from Hill's old "Light Division")

Maj. Gen. W. Dorsey Pender (May 28, 1863)
(mortally wounded July 2, 1863)

Lane's Brigade:
Brig. Gen. James H. Lane*
(Nov. 1, 1862)
7th North Carolina Regiment
18th North Carolina Regiment
28th North Carolina Regiment
33rd North Carolina Regiment
37th North Carolina Regiment
*Temporarily assumed division command after Pender was wounded; superceded on July 3 by Maj. Gen. Isaac R. Trimble, who was wounded and captured; after Gettysburg, Cadmus Wilcox was promoted to major general and assumed command of the division.

Thomas's Brigade:
Brig. Gen. E. L. Thomas
(Nov. 1, 1862)
14th Georgia Regiment
35th Georgia Regiment
45th Georgia Regiment
49th Georgia Regiment

Scales's Brigade:
Brig. Gen. A. M. Scales
(June 13, 1862)
13th North Carolina Regiment
16th North Carolina Regiment
22nd North Carolina Regiment
34th North Carolina Regiment
38th North Carolina Regiment

McGowan-Gregg Brigade:
formed by Maxcy Gregg, who was killed at Fredericksburg; his successor, Brig. Gen. Samuel McGowan (Jan. 17, 1863), was out wounded during the Gettysburg campaign, and the brigade was commanded by Col. Abner Perrin.

1st South Carolina Regiment (Provisional)
12th South Carolina Regiment
13th South Carolina Regiment
14th South Carolina Regiment
1st South Carolina Rifles

381

Appendix

DIVISION ARTILLERY BATTALION
Maj. William T. Poague: four batteries

ANDERSON'S DIVISION
(transferred from Longstreet's corps)

Maj. Gen. Richard H. Anderson (July 14, 1862)

Wilcox's Brigade:
Brig. Gen. C. M. Wilcox*
(Oct. 21, 1861)
8th Alabama Regiment
9th Alabama Regiment
10th Alabama Regiment
11th Alabama Regiment
14th Alabama Regiment
*After Gettysburg, when Wilcox assumed command of Pender's division, he was succeeded by Col. Abner Perrin, who handled McGowan's brigade so well on the first day.

Wright's Brigade:
Brig. Gen. A. R. Wright
(June 3, 1862)
3rd Georgia Regiment
22nd Georgia Regiment
48th Georgia Regiment
2nd Georgia Battalion

Posey's Brigade:
Brig. Gen. Carnot Posey
12th Mississippi Regiment
16th Mississippi Regiment
19th Mississippi Regiment
48th Mississippi Regiment

Mahone's Brigade:
Brig. Gen. Wm. Mahone
(Nov. 16, 1861)
6th Virginia Regiment
12th Virginia Regiment
16th Virginia Regiment
41st Virginia Regiment
61st Virginia Regiment

Perry's Brigade:
Brig. Gen. E. A. Perry
(Aug. 26, 1862)—commanded at Gettysburg by Col. David Lang
2nd Florida Regiment
5th Florida Regiment
8th Florida Regiment

DIVISION ARTILLERY BATTALION
Maj. John Lane: three batteries

CORPS RESERVE ARTILLERY
Col. R. Lindsay Walker, corps artillery commander

MCINTOSH'S BATTALION
Maj. David G. McIntosh: four batteries

PEGRAM'S BATTALION
Maj. William J. Pegram: five batteries

382

STUART'S CAVALRY DIVISION
Maj. Gen. James Ewell Brown Stuart

With Stuart on the ride that brought the cavalry to Gettysburg on July 2:

Fitzhugh Lee's Brigade:
1st Virginia Regiment
2nd Virginia Regiment
3rd Virginia Regiment
4th Virginia Regiment
5th Virginia Regiment

W. F. H. ("Rooney") Lee's Brigade, commanded by John Chambliss:
2nd North Carolina Regiment
9th Virginia Regiment
10th Virginia Regiment
13th Virginia Regiment

Wade Hampton's Brigade:
1st North Carolina Regiment
1st South Carolina Regiment
2nd South Carolina Regiment
Cobb's Legion
Jeff Davis Legion
Phillips's Legion

The brigades that waited in the Shenandoah passes and arrived July 3:

Beverly Robertson's Brigade:
4th North Carolina Regiment
5th North Carolina Regiment

Wm. E. ("Grumble") Jones's Brigade:
6th Virginia Regiment
7th Virginia Regiment
11th Virginia Regiment
34th Virginia Battalion

HORSE ARTILLERY
Maj. R. F. Beckham: six batteries

Only six guns accompanied Stuart on the ride.

The cavalry commands of Imboden and Jenkins were not a part of the Army of Northern Virginia

Index

Index

Index

iv

Index

A Note on the Author

THE STUDY of the Civil War has occupied Clifford Dowdey for nearly thirty years. It has produced several novels and a number of notable works of history, including *Experiment in Rebellion, The Land They Fought For,* and *Death of a Nation.* The author, who lives and works in Richmond, Virginia, has made an intensive study of the official and private records of the Gettysburg campaign and has walked the battlefield many times. He has had the co-operation and assistance of the Battlefield Historian in these researches. It is his intention to continue the story of the Army of Northern Virginia in future volumes.